REFUGE

Refuge

How the State Shapes Human Potential

Heba Gowayed

PRINCETON UNIVERSITY PRESS
PRINCETON AND OXFORD

Published by Princeton University Press
41 William Street, Princeton, New Jersey 08540
99 Banbury Road, Oxford OX2 6JX

press.princeton.edu

Library of Congress Control Number 2021950466
ISBN 978-0-691-20395-9
ISBN (pbk.) 978-0-691-20384-3
ISBN (e-book) 978-0-691-23512-7

British Library Cataloging-in-Publication Data is available

Editorial: Meagan Levinson and Jacqueline Delaney
Production Editorial: Jill Harris
Cover Design: Felix Summ
Production: Erin Suydam
Publicity: Kate Hensley and Charlotte Coyne
Copyeditor: Michele Rosen

Cover photo by Sean Gallup / Getty Images

This book has been composed in Adobe Text and Gotham

10 9 8 7 6 5 4 3 2 1

For Yasser, my Baba, an immigrant,
and for Nick, my refuge

CONTENTS

REFUGE

1

Finding Refuge

The vacuum kept shocking Amjad[1] as he pushed it across the factory floor. He tried to explain to his supervisor what was happening, using hand gestures to relay that static buildup was raising the hair on his arms and making his janitorial work unnecessarily uncomfortable. But she couldn't understand what he was saying. Amjad had only been in the United States for five months and only had a grasp of the most rudimentary English phrases. The translation app on his phone was not much help because, semi-literate in his native Arabic, he wasn't sure what to type into the program. Amjad smiled and walked away from his supervisor. Despite their failure to communicate with each other, Amjad did not want his supervisor to think that he was someone who complained. He couldn't afford to lose this job. "I felt sorry for myself," Amjad told me.

Six years earlier, in his native Homs, Syria, Amjad was a tile contractor. He had his own workshop and owned a company van. He employed workers. On a visit to the Yale University Art Gallery, Amjad waved me over. On the wall before us was a fragment of a mosaic floor from 540 CE, a part of an exhibit of ancient art excavated from Gerasa, Jordan. "I used to make things like this," he told me, as we admired the small square tiles, some the color of natural stone and others dyed olive green and pink that formed an abstract flower pattern. Most of Amjad's work, he clarified, was tiling businesses, but every now and then he worked on more complicated projects. He was doing so well that in 2011, after seven years of saving, he had enough money to buy land on which he planned to build a bigger workshop and a home for his wife Rima and their two children.

As Amjad spent his life savings investing in the foundations for their new home, three thousand miles away a street vendor named Mohamed Bouazizi was slapped across the face by a police officer who confiscated his wares. He set himself on fire in protest, an act which was the catalyst for civil disobedience across Tunisia. Inspired by these protests, dissidents in Egypt and then Qatar and Bahrain took to the streets, protesting their own despotic rulers.[2]

As Syrians too demanded *isqat el nizam,* the "downfall of the regime," those with knowledge of the country's history and politics held their collective breath. Hafez al-Assad, former president of Syria, had massacred his people in response to their calls for change decades prior.[3] Bashar al-Assad, who took over after his father's death, is a British-educated optometrist whose wife, Asma, was once profiled in a spread in *Vogue.* Early in his presidency there was hope that he would be a political and economic reformer. The world watched, however, as Bashar followed in his father's footsteps, responding to civilian uprisings with live ammunition and plunging his country into one of the bloodiest civil wars the modern world has ever seen.[4]

Homs, deemed the "Capital of the Revolution," was an early and exceptionally deadly site of regime violence. Rima, Amjad, and their two toddler sons, escaped to Damascus after the fatal shootings of Amjad's father and his eleven-year-old sister two weeks apart. They thought that their departure was temporary and that they would soon return to enjoy the home that they had just begun to build. Instead, following a car bomb explosion during a funeral procession that propelled Amjad's infant son from his arms and claimed the lives of sixty people walking alongside him, the family knew they had to move further away. They left Syria for Jordan. There, in July 2012, uncertain if they'd ever see home again, they registered as refugees.

Their story is not unique. The United Nations reports that in 2021, there were over twenty-six million refugees[5] registered globally, the most since World War II.[6] Syria is the country that has contributed the most, with over six million who have fled. The vast majority remain in nearby countries of immediate refuge including Jordan, Turkey, and Lebanon—which despite having a population of six million people hosted one million Syrians. Life in these countries can be precarious—refugees lack documentation and a right to work, their children attend overcrowded schools, and millions are relegated to indefinite stays in camps where their mobility is restricted.[7]

For those in these situations of protracted displacement, there are two legal options that promise a reprieve from a life of precarity, and a chance at a new beginning as legal residents of a new country—resettlement and asylum.[8] Resettlement refers to a third country selecting registered refugees with humanitarian needs from United Nations rosters and offering them an opportunity to travel as recognized refugees. Asylum is when someone travels to a new country, often making difficult journeys over land or sea, and applies for legal recognition as a refugee.

After two years in Jordan, Rima and Amjad received a call from the United Nations Higher Council for Refugees—they had been selected for resettlement to the United States provided they passed the vetting requirements. They were overjoyed, and they dreamed of a future in "America" that was even brighter than their Syrian past. But as they underwent the extensive security process over the following two years—five interviews, fingerprinting, health screenings, and behind-the-scenes review by thirteen security agencies—their anxiety built. They were wracked with worry about what this move would mean for them. Amjad and Rima, who carried the traumas of war and displacement, had little to their name and knew that their language, religion, and ethnicity marked them as stigmatized minorities in the "West." What lives would they be able to build?

This book follows the journeys of Rima and Amjad and other Syrians who sought refuge in the United States and Canada, world leaders in resettlement, and Germany, which, in response to the men, women, and children who boarded rafts across the Mediterranean, offered asylum to more than half a million Syrians. Arriving in all three countries are people who come from similar backgrounds as Amjad and Rima, members of a broadly construed middle class who had stable lives in Syria, but who lacked formal education, credentials, and proficiency in English and German. Through resettlement and asylum, they come face-to-face with national systems shaped by inequalities foreign to them that determine their access to resources as they rebuild their lives and imagine their futures. Their experiences reveal that these destination countries, while offering legal solutions to displacement, do not guarantee bright futures—they can deny newcomers' potential by failing to recognize their abilities and invest in the tools they need to prosper.

Rima and Amjad were selected for resettlement in the United States because of their humanitarian need as displaced parents of young children. As they crossed the Atlantic, however, they transitioned in the eyes of the United States government from humanitarian cases to workers—people who were expected to quickly become self-reliant. As refugees, they were held responsible for the cost of their flight, and so they arrived USD 4,000 in debt. They received limited federal resettlement assistance—only ninety days of funding that barely covered rent and basic expenses. The only other assistance available to them was Temporary Assistance for Needy Families (TANF), or welfare, which for a family of four provided USD 701 a month, while their rent was USD 1,000.

Rima and Amjad were ensnared, like other low-income Americans, in the United States' threadbare social safety net. At the core of the 1980 Refugee Act is the goal of *self-sufficiency* or non-reliance on government assistance,[9] which is also the goal of TANF.[10] This is not a coincidence, as both the resettlement program and TANF are products of the limited social welfare system in the United States, a feature of the country's neoliberal economy. This system treats poverty as an individual failure, an approach inextricably linked to the disenfranchisement of Black Americans who are disproportionately impoverished by it.[11]

The new arrivals, facing this dearth of support, needed to earn an income *now*. "How?" Amjad asked the caseworker when she told him that he and Rima needed to find work immediately. He did not know anyone, and though he had been attending English classes, three months was too short a time to learn a new language. Amjad asked a question that I would hear repeated by almost everyone resettled in the United States: "Why did they bring us here if they were not going to help us?"

Amjad saw himself as the breadwinner of his family, so it was his responsibility to seek out employment. Without time to learn English or support for translating his skills, the only jobs available to him were those on the bottom rungs of the United States' stratified post-industrial labor market, characterized by long hours and isolation from other workers. These conditions, which describe his janitorial job, thwarted any possibility for building economic capital or learning English—two of the primary tools for a US immigrant's upward mobility.[12] Using his skills as a tile contractor to derive a middle-class income was a distant memory.

As the family's caretaker, Rima stayed home to look after their sons. When they went to school, she was able to attend English classes with other Syrian women, reaching an intermediate level. Some of the other Syrian women, responding to the dire need for additional income, also reimagined their existing skills for economic profit by selling their cooking and handcrafts to combat family poverty. However, women's language learning and economic enterprise was thwarted by the absence of progressive family policy: along with Rima, many eventually dropped out of English classes due to a lack of childcare options. And, five years after their arrival, while the women knew more English than the men, neither had strong enough language proficiency to sit for the United States citizenship exam.

The United States' incorporation policy not only shaped Rima and Amjad's immediate circumstances, but also the ways they could use and develop the skills through which they earn economic returns—or their *human capital*. We typically understand human capital as a testament to individual merit and hard work.[13] Immigrant human capital is often measured as credentials earned, years of education, or employment in a given field.[14] But what did Amjad's decades of work as a contractor, his skill in putting together mosaic tiles, really mean in the United States? And was Rima "unskilled" simply because she had an elementary school education and hadn't been formally employed before?

Human capital, as Amjad and Rima demonstrate, is not a static account of merit, but a dynamic product of the immigration process.[15] In this book, I advance a theory of *state-structured human capital*, arguing that human capital is augmented, transformed, or destroyed by national incorporation policies through two mechanisms. The first is *investment* in newcomers, or whether the state allocates or denies resources and opportunities that enable them to use their existing skills or gain new ones. The second is *recognition*, or whether the state sees or ignores immigrants' histories as economically viable skills. Because, as we saw in the case of Amjad and Rima, this process is shaped by gender stratification within state institutions and households, as well as by racism, human capital formation is gendered and racialized.

To understand this process, we need to compare the lives of Syrians in the United States to those who sought refuge elsewhere—what of their human capital? Omar, Yasmine, and their three children live five hundred miles northwest of Amjad and Rima, in Toronto. Like Amjad, Omar was an artisan; he was a blacksmith in Syria. Like Rima, Yasmine was a stay-at-home mom. But because of Canada's policy of *integration*, which focuses on language learning as a vehicle to "multicultural" inclusion, the government *invests* in refugee arrivals.[16] This draws on the broader, more generous Canadian approach to social welfare, albeit one that exists in the context of the country's restrictive and selective immigration policy.[17]

Omar and Yasmine received a substantial start-up sum, as well as a stipend that covered their expenses in full for their first year. After twelve months, they had access to a generous welfare system. From the time of their arrival, they could attend free English classes and classes for skill development—including forklift operating and food safety or learning to run a kitchen up to health codes. There was publicly funded childcare support for English language learners. Both Omar and Yasmine were able to attend English classes. After a year, Omar found work as a blacksmith and, after his bad back gave out, he was able to switch occupations. And, Yasmine, through a contact in her English class, began to work part-time at a restaurant, using her culinary skills in new ways. Both Omar and Yasmine were able, through the state's *investment*, to express and build their human capital—to use their existing skills, and gain new ones, within the Canadian system.

Even further away, across the Atlantic, in Stuttgart, Germany, Nermine, her brother Ali, and their mother, who goes by Om Ali, sought asylum. There, yet another incorporation system revealed why, on its own, *investing* does not ensure the expression of human capital. Germany's generous social service system offered newcomers the most financial support of all three countries; but the system also featured a heavily regulated labor market.[18] While the newly arrived family would have all their needs covered by the German Jobcenter, the same agency that supports unemployed people in Germany, Nermine's family would not be allowed to enter the German labor market unless they learned German and then earned the credentials required of other working Germans.

This German system of *credentialization* did not *recognize* Syrians' existing skills. This had different effects on Nermine, Ali, and Om Ali, who were all skilled cosmetologists. Om Ali, like others (often men) with long-established careers in Syria, experienced the credentialization as an erasure of her human capital. Young people, by contrast, including her two children, and women who never had careers, saw the system as creating a pathway to gain new skills. Still, both young and old felt that an assumption that led to the rigidity of the system, "a German system for Germans," as one put it, was that not only their skills, but they themselves, were less-than and needed to prove their worth.

In this book, I follow men and women[19] from similar economic and social backgrounds (some of whom are related), who arrived within a similar time frame to the United States, Canada, and Germany. I argue that each of these states, through their incorporation systems, differentially *invest* in and *recognize* refugee skills and abilities. Through the quasi-experimental vantage offered by the men and women's simultaneous experiences in these three countries, we can see how state policies structure human capital. Because incorporation systems derive from social welfare systems that are patterned by racial and gender inequalities, the processes of human capital formation become racialized and gendered.

By considering human capital as a dynamic product of national systems, rather than a static attribute of individuals, we gain new insight into immigrant lives. It is true that, as immigration scholars have long shown, human capital matters for economic trajectories.[20] This shapes the lives of refugees in these countries' capitalist systems and, through remittances and family reunification, the lives of their loved ones elsewhere.[21] And, it matters for political rights—citizenship exams in all three countries require language proficiency. But there's even more at stake. The loss of recognition of one's abilities and the denial of resources needed to explore one's possibilities is traumatic. How would any of us feel if our years of education or work experience were suddenly denied, discounted, and dismissed due to an unwillingness to invest in us or to recognize our potential?

But, what's more, by focusing on human capital production, we reexamine how states structure human potential more broadly. The national incorporation systems that shape the human capital formation of refugees are the *same systems* that low-income people have navigated in these three countries for decades, well before this cohort of Syrian refugees arrived. The experiences of these newest arrivals, and the ways in which they are minoritized across these countries, reflect what refuge means for these men and women. But their cases also make the familiar strange, shining new light on how countries shape the lives of the disadvantaged within their borders, regardless of immigration status.

Determining Displacement

To understand the men and women's journeys to refuge is to begin with their displacement. Who becomes a refugee is determined by global inequalities.[22] People who have been persecuted and subjected to violence for who they are—such as being gay, a political dissident, or Bahai—or due to widespread violence of war, or genocide, petition to be recognized as refugees according to the 1967 definition in the United Nations' Protocol Relating to the Status of Refugees as someone who,

> owing to well-founded fear of being persecuted for reasons of race, religion, nationality, membership of a particular social group or political opinion, is outside the country of his nationality and is unable or, owing to such fear, is unwilling to avail himself of the protection of that country.[23]

While those seeking refuge are asking for safety from local violence, that brutality is often a product of states weakened by struggles over decolonization and the continued meddling of global hegemons.[24] In the case of Syria, French colonizers used a divide-and-conquer strategy to impose control. They selected Alawites, a Shiite minority, to join their army and to quell anti-colonial uprisings from the majority Sunni populace. The militarization of this minority was the precursor for the postcolonial 1966 ascendancy of the Ba'ath party under Alawite leadership.[25]

Over the coming decades, the Ba'ath party would go to great lengths to protect their fragile authority. The Syrian government denied Kurds their citizenship rights and the right to teach their language in schools or to use it to name their businesses, and painted them as "foreigners."[26] Across the country, dissent was forbidden, and the faces of deceased president Hafez al-Assad and later his son, President Bashar al-Assad, were posted in every shop to show allegiance to the regime. People lived in constant fear that "the walls have ears"—or that anything they said, even in private, could land them inside a Syrian prison.[27] What's more, in 1982, Hama was leveled during a massacre targeting a Muslim Brotherhood uprising in the city. People who had seen their fathers executed by the Hafez al-Assad regime in the 1980s were themselves executed by his son thirty years later.[28]

The Syrian crisis is also a product of contemporary meddling. Two Iraq wars, the second a unilateral effort by the United States, resulted in the formation of Da'esh, the so-called Islamic State, in a United States prison in Iraq.[29] Its rule would extend deep into Syrian territory. The Assad regime, included in President George W. Bush's "axis of evil," is an ally to the Soviet Union and Russia, and it supports Hezbollah, Iran, and Palestinian sovereignty. For all these reasons, the Syrian leadership was cast as an enemy to the United States, which made recognizing the refugees fleeing from Syria and from Da'esh politically palatable to the US government and its allies. This, coupled with the visibility of the Syrian men, women, and children crowding onto dinghies for the dangerous journey across the Mediterranean and then into train stations across Europe, brought the Syrian refugee movement to the global center stage.

Upon arriving in Germany or flying into airports in the United States and Canada as resettled refugees, the men and women's experiences of displacement do not end. Implicit in the notion that refuge and asylum are *solutions*, as they are termed by the United Nations and imagined by those of us watching the humanitarian crisis unfold and praying for safe endings to the difficult journeys on our television screens, is that life in these countries will be a good life. And, to a certain extent, refuge in countries of resettlement or asylum *is* an end to the legal limbo and to the long years spent in refugee camps.[30]

But, the experiences of displacement are not resolved upon arrival, and receiving countries are not saviors. Refugees arrive to the very countries whose foreign policies have subjugated either them or people like them, and whose domestic policies are patterned by the same racisms that facilitated those foreign policies. As W.E.B. DuBois once put it, in reaction to Egypt's 1919 revolution against British colonizers,

> We are all one—we the Despised and Oppressed, the 'n———' of England and America . . . our hearts pray that Right may triumph and Justice and Pity over brute Force of the Organised Theft and Race Prejudice, from San Francisco to Calcutta and from Cairo to New York.[31]

Viewed through this DuBoisian lens, we can see that the systems that receive and incorporate refugees and immigrants, and that have structured inequalities in these countries long before their arrival, are not altogether independent of those that shaped their displacement. The upholding of White supremacy at the expense of non-White lives and livelihoods animates both systems—though in different ways across these three countries.

Systems of Refuge

Throughout this book, I center policies of incorporation, but before refugees are incorporated, they must be admitted. Immigration laws structure who can enter, with what status, and what kinds of resources they will have when they do.[32] Across all three countries, the Syrians in this study were recognized as refugees, a privileged legal status that puts them on the pathway to residency and citizenship.[33]

In Germany, Chancellor Angela Merkel's suspension of the European Union's Dublin Regulation, which required asylum seekers to register at their first port of entry, far from inland Europe, allowed the country to shift away from its previously limited history of admitting refugees for permanent stays, to admit an estimated half million Syrian asylum seekers between 2015 and 2016.[34] In the United States, Syrians were admitted through the resettlement program established by the 1980 Refugee Act; this program stood for thirty-seven years as the largest in the world, until the Trump Administration slashed its numbers in 2017.[35] In Canada, Syrians entered through an expedited process, the result of Prime Minister Justin Trudeau's desire to "make up for" the conservative government that preceded him, which took in a very limited number of Syrian refugees, presenting their admission as a national security risk.[36] With these residency rights, the newly arrived Syrians in this study avoided what so many asylum seekers from places like El Salvador and Haiti face—a protracted liminal legality between temporary protections and no protections at all.[37]

Their legal status as refugees gave the Syrian new arrivals unique access to state incorporation systems. In the United States, a country that does not have an incorporation system for most immigrants, refugees are the exception.[38] Whether due to the United Nations' Refugee Convention's stipulation that refugees *should* have access to social services, or due to the nature of the 1980 Refugee Act, which identifies refugees as a unique category of immigrant, refugees were the exception to the ban on immigrants receiving state welfare introduced in the 1996 reforms under Bill Clinton. While Canada and Germany have more generous social service systems that are available to a larger group of immigrants, not all immigrants are eligible. Refugees are able to access a full year of financial assistance in Canada and multiple years in Germany.

Despite refugees' privileged position vis-a-vis immigration policies and thus incorporation systems, their legal status does not ensure a feeling of security.[39] They traversed the United States, Canada, and Germany while navigating xenophobia and racism targeted against them specifically as Syrian refugees.[40] They were *racialized*, or categorized in this specific historical moment, as Arabs and Muslims in a post 9/11, post-ISIS world.[41] Importantly, national histories determine different racialization processes.

In Germany, the generosity of the welfare state stems from the fact that it is imagined and constructed as a German system for Germans. Even though Germany has long been an immigrant destination, particularly for Turkish immigrants, its formal policy, through the 1990s, was that it was *not* a country of immigration.[42] Until 2000, immigrants were denied citizenship through the principle of *jus sanguinis*, which restricted citizenship to those with German blood.[43] This fuels an image of Germany, which continues to animate policy and politics, as a homogenous country with a leading culture, or *leitkultur*, that adheres to social norms that Turkish and Syrian immigrants, as Muslims, are seen to both lack and threaten.[44]

In the United States, by contrast, Syrians not only grapple with the poverty that results from the demolition of the safety net predicated on systemic anti-Black racism in social welfare policy, but they also deal with Muslim bans and with Trump calling their children terrorists, disturbing their sense of belonging.[45] While Syrians are legally "White,"[46] this does little to protect against racist policies and interactions in the backdrop of the United States' "war on terror."[47] And while in Canada, where Syrians are recognized as "visible minorities," and the policy of multiculturalism creates access to meaningful resources both as individuals and as members of an ethnic group—the system is not devoid of anti-Muslim racism. Harper's administration, which preceded Trudeau's, denied Syrian refugee arrivals on this basis, and questioned their ability to assimilate. The notion of multiculturalism obscures this and other racism within the Canadian system, including its incredibly restrictive immigration policy for unauthorized immigrants.[48]

Finally, to write about the racialization and racism experienced by Arab and Muslim people, whether in countries of origin or destination, is to write against the Orientalist assumption that took root in the colonial era that, as opposed to the progressive "West" that calls for human rights, the so-called Muslim world and Middle East are places where women are oppressed.[49] By travelling to the "West," the assumption goes, women escape the jaws of patriarchy. But belying this (racist) assumption are the realities of diversity among the world's three billion Muslims and five million Arabs, and of inequalities embedded in the institutions of destination countries that often fail to protect women's labor and time.[50]

As scholars of intersectionality like Kimberlé Crenshaw and Patricia Hill Collins clarify, gender, race, class, and legal status are inequalities that are experienced *simultaneously*.[51] Syrian refugee women will undoubtedly have opportunities open up for them through immigration, as do all immigrants, but they will also have new constraints. For those who are Muslims or Arabs, they experience being minorities for the first time. For those who are Muslim and who wear the *hijab*, they'll experience it as a marker of their membership into a stigmatized category. These identities can make them targets of physical and rhetorical violence and result in denial of employment and training opportunities. They are also experiencing being recent arrivals and poor in countries where there is either little social support or stringent labor-market entry systems. It is here, at the intersections of these various inequalities, that those seeking refuge enter new systems that structure their human capital.

State-Structured Human Capital

What is human capital? Economists who coined the term see it as our skills and capacities that reap economic returns: a measurable "value in a person," as Adam Smith first wrote in the *Wealth of Nations*.[52] However, this conceptualization is imprecise. There is nothing static or objective in how our human capital is formed, nor in how it's evaluated.

First, the formation of human capital is contingent on the resources at our disposal—our access to educational opportunities and jobs that provide us with skills is determined by inequalities of race, gender, and class. Second, our ability to use our skills and abilities is contingent on how we are perceived. As Devah Pager shows in the United States, the same skills held by a Black man result in lesser returns than if they're held by a White man, even if the White man was formerly incarcerated.[53]

In other words, human capital is less a measure of the "value in a person" than a measure of *who* is valued. Who is valued determines who receives *investment*—who is afforded the opportunities to build skills and credentials. And who is valued matters for who is *recognized*—whose skills and credentials are seen as economically viable and deemed worthy of pay. Human capital, rather than an individual attribute measured at a given moment in time, is better understood as a dynamic *product* of relationships that reflect other inequalities—within families, with employers, and most importantly, with the state.

In the context of immigration, policy analysts and academics have measured human capital as the credentials and skills that immigrants report on arrival, which are seen as informing their economic mobility.[54] And there is value to this approach. If someone arrives in the United States speaking English, they are likely to get a better job than Amjad, who does not speak the language. It's also true that someone trained as a physician is in many ways better equipped to navigate a foreign labor market than someone who barely finished elementary school.

But just because someone was a physician in Syria, or India, or anywhere else, does not necessarily mean that they will be able to work as a physician in the United States, or Canada, or Germany. The trope of the overqualified immigrant taxi driver who was once a Cairene architect or an Accran engineer is based in reality.[55] Economists have described this phenomenon as the "imperfect transferability" of human capital.[56] Regardless of the skillset, skills developed in one place don't always result in economic returns in another.

While there is agreement that immigrant skills aren't always transferable, it is unclear how this nontransferability happens. The passivity of the term "transferability" serves to obscure the actor. One explanation is that immigrant skills, developed in a subpar economy, are just subpar.[57] But this explanation is refuted by "signaling theorists" who argue that immigrants may have the right skills, but they lack the certifications employers recognize or the ability to "signal" their skills in ways employers will understand.[58] These explanations, however, look at the immigrant as a puzzle piece and the labor market as a puzzle, without considering the games' designer and key player: the state that regulates the labor market and decides who from outside its borders enters and how.

By determining *who* is admitted, with what legal status, and with what kinds of support, states structure immigrant human capital. First, regarding *investment*, states can provide refugees with resources during the early, intense years of transition to a new country, in the form of cash support, childcare services, and language training or other educational resources that support their ability to use their skills or build new ones. Studies find that post-migration education can outweigh the benefits of pre-migration education and amplify the returns of skills gained by the immigrant in their country of origin.[59] In our comparison, the United States lags Canada and Germany in terms of investment. Second, regarding *recognition,* states can shape whether employers understand immigrant skills. Germany, with its regimented labor market, only values those skills gained in and certified by the German system, limiting the recognition of immigrant's labor market histories.

Examining human capital as state-structured clarifies that it is also gendered and racialized. In Syria, men and women had their own expectations for their labor in the context of formal laws and informal familial expectations.[60] When they arrive in destination countries, they come face-to-face with incorporation policies that feature gender inequalities and expectations for family life different from their own.[61] What's more, these systems of incorporation, which are rooted in historical racial inequality, are traversed by new arrivals who are themselves experiencing being ethnic, racial, and, in most cases, religious minorities for the first time. *Refuge* captures how their experiences of discrimination and stigma across contexts can diminish participation in public life in ways that detract from human capital development and feelings of belonging.

Importantly, and as elaborated in the book's conclusion, this book contributes to what I'm calling a *human-centric* approach to immigration research, which eschews a focus on long-term outcomes—or on how or whether these new arrivals are net contributors to a notion of a national whole—for a focus on how they experience the destination country. While the concept of human capital derives from a capitalist framework that reduces people to their monetary contributions, through this reorientation, I ask how recognition of and investment in a new arrival shapes their potential and possibilities to be who they want to be, and with it their economic, social, and emotional well-being.

Conducting the Research

I did not set out to study refuge. In the summer of 2015, I found myself in New Haven, Connecticut, where my husband was in graduate school. I had just been unceremoniously pushed out of my field site in my native Cairo. My removal from my field site was the consequence of dictatorial retrenchment after the "Arab Spring" protests succeeded in removing Egypt's authoritarian President Hosni Mubarak but not the military, which supported the authoritarian system.

Over that summer, I watched as Syrian nationals, people whose fellow citizens, like my own in Egypt, had demanded better for themselves and for their children, were forced to make the very dangerous decision to cross the Aegean

Sea on inflatable rafts. I learned that the United States government, through its longstanding resettlement program, had begun to admit Syrian refugees. The local resettlement agency, IRIS, a national leader due to its innovative programming, was receiving a large number of them.

I contacted the agency and introduced myself as a researcher. As a native Arabic language speaker, I was invited to interpret for families through the agency. Upon meeting with families, I also introduced myself as a researcher and sought their consent to participate in this ethnographic project. Within the first months, however, I stopped interpreting on behalf of the agency, to make it clear to the families that I was not affiliated with the organization that was providing them with necessary services. At this point, those who had arrived had my number, and they could call me as they could any other member of the local Arab community. This decision to stop interpreting for the agency, and to have families contact me on their own terms, facilitated consent, which in an ethnographic relationship, as I describe more fully in the methodological appendix, is predicated on mutual respect.

This book reflects the experiences of eighteen families in New Haven. Over three years, I interpreted for them in meetings with the resettlement agency staff, with the department of social services, in negotiations with off-the-books employers, and as they surreptitiously tried to send money home via Western Union. I developed close relationships, attending birthday parties, childbirth celebrations, and funerals, and I enjoyed countless Arabic coffees and dinners. I received unprompted contributions to my "book" and would later conduct recorded interviews with the families after Trump instituted and reiterated the travel ban.

As I watched these families adjust to the United States and to its incorporation system, I recognized how crucial the country's approach to welfare was to their stories. The US resettlement program is not uniform. Welfare is funded differently from state to state, which means that in some states, where TANF amounts are lower than Refugee Cash Assistance (RCA, a shorter duration program that offers similar amounts of money), refugees receive RCA instead. Other state agencies offer the Match Program—an assistance program funded through federal money and agency fundraising that offers higher amounts of financial support for shorter periods of time.[62] But regardless of the specific form of cash assistance, across the country cash assistance is low, the self-sufficiency policy is upheld, and refugees early in their resettlement are thrust into poverty. This raised the question: what was going on in other countries?

Just then, Prime Minister Trudeau, who ran on a platform of resettling twenty-five thousand refugees to Canada, won the premiership and was making good on his promise. I got to Toronto in February 2016, just in time to see thousands of people crammed into hotels and motels and government offices, trying to find apartments in the brutally cold Canadian winter. I found the initial families in my Toronto study through snowball sampling—through a cousin and a friend of Syrians in my US study.

Overall, resettled refugees in Toronto are comparable to those in the United States because they were selected through a similar vulnerability assessment from the same United Nations rosters in a similar time frame. Importantly, Canada has two systems for sponsoring refugees: government and private. The families included in this book are government-sponsored refugees. However, two are also supported by a private sponsoring group through a policy called the Blended Visa Program. This sampling allows us to observe what the addition of private sponsorship does for a similarly selected refugee, without losing the comparability between cases that government-selection promises.

In spring of 2016, I spent a month in Toronto. After that visit, and for the next two years, I visited biannually for two weeks each time to keep up with five families, using WhatsApp and Facebook to keep in touch during our time apart.[63] Like the United States, Canada has a federal system, where each province offers different kinds of support. However, across Canada, the goal of "integration" is central, and refugee cash assistance is offered across provinces.

Finally, I included the case of Germany due to the sheer number of refugees admitted and because of its distinct political economic approach to welfare. On my first trip, I conducted five interviews—with families and individuals connected to others elsewhere in my study—who lived in Cologne, Stuttgart, and Berlin. Because this part of the research would not be longitudinal, in that I did not follow the experiences of families over time as I did in the United States or Canada, I returned to Germany in the summer of 2018 to conduct an additional fifteen interviews in Regensberg, Bavaria, with a sample of participants in the University of Konstanz' national survey on refugees, which was just being launched. Germany is a country that has a federalist system where different regions, particularly those in the former East and West Germany, have drastically different histories and approaches to assistance. Experiences of racism also differ widely across regions. However, the *credentialization* system that I report on is federal.

What is different about Germany, as opposed to the other cases, is selection. Unlike resettled refugees, who were picked from UN rosters based on their humanitarian needs, the backgrounds of those who arrive in Germany vary. Some were quite like the Syrians who ended up in the United States and Canada. But others had higher educational achievements and credentials—they were lawyers or Arabic teachers, people who were able to self-finance their journeys. Still, they experienced the German system of credentialization acutely, as "regulated occupations" like law or teaching required even more training than "unregulated occupations" like being a hairdresser, a driver, or a plumber, which as the case of Nermine demonstrated, also requires training.

Finally, it is important to note that my own human capital, and particularly my native Arabic, was invaluable for writing this book and conducting the ethnographic work it entailed, as I explain more fully in the "On Methods" appendix to this book. But the most meaningful determinant of this study is that the men and women opened their homes to me as a researcher, out of generosity, and because they wanted their experiences to be shared in the hopes of improving systems for those who came after them.

———

The chapters of the book take us deeper into the lives of Amjad and Rima, Omar and Yasmine, Nermine and Ali, and the others who arrived in these countries along with them. In the next chapter, "Becoming a Refugee," I explore how these men and women became refugees. How their lives in Syria, as middle-class men and women, were disrupted. And, how they lost their loved ones, their livelihoods, their legal status, and their sense of belonging, as they got further and further away from home, becoming resettled refugees and asylum seekers in new places. The men and women in this study do not start as stateless victims, but as people leading full lives that were disrupted by war.

Chapter 3, "American Self-Sufficiency," follows the experiences of new arrivals, including Amjad and Rima, as the lack of investment in them by the country's incorporation system left them to the quicksand of American poverty. While men saw their labor-market histories erased and their ability to form new skills truncated by immediate entry into the labor market, women, driven by family poverty, began to reimagine their skills as economic assets. However, they were limited by a lack of support for caregivers in the United States. Even with these re-imaginations, attempts to resist family poverty were futile. In other words, the experience of refugee resettlement in the United States is one of integration into American poverty which, by design, is populated by people of color and marked by stagnation.

Chapter 4, "Canadian Integration," demonstrates how a generous approach to social welfare and a policy of "multiculturalism" together mean investment in newcomers. Refugees arriving in Canada were more able than those arriving in the United States to learn the language and find opportunities to build new skills; they were also more insulated from the threat of dire poverty. However, the recognition of skills in Canada was imperfect. To understand the Canadian approach to refugees and the dual system of private and government sponsorship, it is important to situate refugee resettlement within the broader scope of Canada's restrictive immigration policy.

Chapter 5, "German Credentialization," shows that in contrast to the United States' system of self-sufficiency, Germany invests heavily in newly arrived refugees like Nermine and Ali. But it also requires them to acquire credentials equivalent to those held by native Germans to enter the labor market, and therefore fails to *recognize* their skills and abilities. For some, this pathway felt arduous and insurmountable—particularly for men who had employment experience. For others, this pathway bolsters their employment prospects— particularly for new entrants into the labor market. This chapter also shows how Syrians experience their position as stigmatized minorities, and how it impacted both their sense of security and their human capital formation.

Chapter 6, "Here and There," places state production of refugees' human capital in a broader context. It describes how state structuring of the human capital of those who sought refuge in the United States, Canada, and Germany impacts their families who remain in situations of protracted displacement in Syria or in nearby countries like Turkey, Jordan, and Lebanon. Syrians who are in countries of resettlement and asylum are a lifeline to their families, and the resources at their disposal determine the remittances they can send, and the possibilities for reunification they can offer, to loved ones left behind.

In Chapter 7, "Refuge," I conclude by placing the findings of this book within the broader sociological conversation on immigration, suggesting that the discipline is moving towards a *human-centric* study of immigration that centers how contexts work in the lives of immigrants, rather than how immigrants fit into notions of the "mainstream." This chapter also suggests that to move towards humane refuge, we need to invest in people, not borders.

Finally, the book's afterword is given over to the men and women whose stories animate its pages. Rajaa from the United States, Israa from Canada, and Mustafa from Germany reflect on their own pathways, in their own words, five years into their refuge. In "On Methods," I reflect on who I am, how I approached researching and writing this book, and how I translated what I learned from the men and women who generously allowed me, and by extension you, the reader, into their lives.

2

Becoming a Refugee

The majority of the men and women in this book came from Homs. Before the war, it was Syria's third largest city, after Aleppo to its north and Damascus to its south. At the center of Homs' old city is the Souk Maskuf or Covered Market. The market's Ablaq architecture, typical of the Ummayad dynasty, alternates light-colored limestone and black basalt in its arches, in the same style of the Grand Ummayad mosque of Damascus and the Great Mosque of Cordoba, Spain. The Covered Market complex, which got its name from its domed roof of stone and metal, is comprised of alleyways lined with shops, each framed by an arched metal grate.

During the day shopkeepers' wares—hair bows and children's toys, coats and dresses, garlic and dried spices—hang from the grates above the shops and spill out onto tables out front. The complex connects several specialized markets, such as *Souk al-Mansoojat* (textiles) or *Souk al-Atareen* (scented oils), making it a one-stop shop for Homs' residents. Adjacent to the market is the al-Nuri Mosque, which was converted from the Church of John the Baptist in the seventh century AD. Before that it was a temple to the Sun God, Elagabal. A house of worship and a market had stood on this plot of land for at least two millennia, making it a subject of interest for several medieval Arab historians and geographers, including al-Maqdisi in 985, al-Idrisi in 1099, and Ibn Jubair in 1185.[1]

The market and al-Nuri Mosque both linked Homs' residents to the place's ancient and complex history, while simultaneously serving as a mundane site of day-to-day commerce and worship. Like *Souk al-Hamidiyah* in Damascus and the covered market in Aleppo, this market was populated during the day by shoppers perusing the stalls. Photos from before the war showed groups of mostly women shopping, some wearing *niqabs* and *hijabs*, and others with hair exposed, capturing the town's diversity.[2] Homs had a Sunni majority but was also home to Alawites and Christians. At night, particularly around feast days, the market would be decorated with strings of lights. The men would gather at the coffee shops on its periphery over the gurgle of a hookah and the rat-a-tat of backgammon dice. Families would go in search of pistachio-covered *booza* ice cream.

Then, in 2012, the war began. For the following two years, the Syrian military besieged Homs' old city, fighting the rebels who hid within it.[3] The fate of the covered market is captured in a series of photographs by Associated Press photographer Joseph Eid. In a photo taken in 2014, an old man in a driving cap stands at the center of one of the market's wide thoroughfares. The corrugated roof above him is riddled with bullet holes, and whole sections are missing. The light that streamed through revealed the metal roller shutters that once kept the vendor's products safe at night, twisted and buckled by heat.

Another photo shows a woman clad in black pushing a baby stroller through one of the market's alleyways. To her left in an intersecting alley just beyond her view, a store is engulfed in bright orange flames reaching to the trusses that once upheld the market's eponymous cover. Eid's photos also capture the city around the market. Nearby, concrete buildings sagged under collapsed roofs. Air conditioners hung from the wreckage, reminding the onlooker of the once comfortable residents who built their lives within its walls. Rugs draped from bombed-out windows, airing out in the post-siege quiet, evidence of the people trying to live in that wreckage.

Deemed the "capital of the revolution," Homs saw an inordinate amount of early violence in what became the Syrian war.[4] For this reason, it is not surprising that the majority of the men and women in this study came from this city. The diffusion of protest from Daraa to Homs in March 2011 was seen by the Assad regime to be particularly threatening, as it meant that the protest movement was taking over the country as it had Tunisia and Egypt.

One year later, as the protests became a full-fledged war, the Assad regime brutally attacked the Sunni neighborhood of Baba Amr, around three kilometers southwest of the market, killing an estimated seven hundred people. The ongoing violence in Homs peaked again in February 2014, when the Syrian military bombarded the old city that housed the market and the mosque to take it back from the rebels.

Meanwhile, around the country, rival factions multiplied, including Da'esh, the so-called Islamic State of Iraq and Syria (ISIS). The destruction of Homs' market is one instantiation of the destruction seen across the country. It is impossible to know how many have died in Syria, or how many have been forcibly disappeared. Estimates put the number dead around half a million people, and the number disappeared at one hundred thousand.

In the midst of this violence across the country, twelve million Syrians made their choice to leave their homes. In doing so, they became internally displaced persons (IDPs). In total, an estimated six million of those IDPs would eventually leave Syria altogether. Importantly, to become *dis*placed is to be violently pushed out from the physical cities and streets where one had long and proud histories. It is to begin what Rawan Arar and David Fitzgerald have described as a "continuum of compulsion." Syrian refugees' decisions to move were not made after calm deliberation but while running an obstacle course structured by state violence.[5] They had to flee the danger posed by the Assad regime's brutal war while simultaneously navigating other nations' borders, which often became more rigid in the face of humanitarian need. Their decisions, made with limited control and incomplete information, resulted in unintended consequences.

The choice to temporarily leave one's home to go to the countryside for a few days often meant the permanent loss of one's physical home and the things that made up that home: things like family heirlooms or saved baby teeth or wedding albums. Those who made the choice to leave the country often thought of that move as temporary and that they would be able to return in a few weeks or months once some order was restored. But as the months turned into years, those who left Syria would become "refugees"—people fleeing persecution who could *not* return home.

To follow their journeys, this chapter begins with the Syrians families who are part of this study as they are *in* place before the war, when they navigated the streets and alleys they knew without knowing that these places would soon be preserved only in their memories. By the time these men and women become "refugees" in the legal sense, these histories are obscured behind the narrative of war and displacement, as though they were always stateless victims rather than people who led full lives disrupted by violence.

This chapter begins with the lives they built in Syria, the occupations they had, and the skills and abilities structured by the system there. It then follows their stories of protest, of war, and of making the difficult decision to leave the people and places they loved and valued behind. It captures journeys into refuge—shaped by local violence, impermeable national borders, and international law. As they got further away from home, the Syrians seeking refuge would get further from the people they loved, and from those with whom they shared the familiarity of language or culture. The safer they got, the stranger they felt.

Life as an Endless Tea Party

"Life in Syria was an endless tea party," Najlaa, a mother of four in her late thirties, declared with a laugh. "I really don't know what we did all day other than drink tea." A resident of Homs and the neighborhood of Baba Amr, Najlaa lived with and near an extended family network, a common setup for people she knew. She performed many of her household chores with family members: the time-consuming work of stuffing grape leaves or shaping *kibbeh* was a social affair that involved sitting around a circle full of joking and gossip. Little did she know that years later she would use her ability to make perfect teardrop *kibbeh* to earn money.

Once the household chores were over, the chatter would continue over tea. "We were *mabsooteen*," Najlaa's husband Nabil would later tell me. This Arabic word literally translates to "happy," but also refers to being financially comfortable. Nabil's day-to-day life in Syria was centered in close physical proximity to their apartment, which they owned. They shared the building with Nabil's brothers, their families, and his parents. His family had lived on the block for generations. Nearby was Nabil's workshop. A carpenter—a trade learned from generations of carpenters—he did not need to keep regular hours. People knew where to find him if they needed work done—calling up to the house or asking someone on the block to get in touch with him. At night, he would hang out with his friends on the same block.

Najlaa and Nabil's day-to-day lives were accented by days of leisure. And they were not alone in these experiences. Majid and Rajaa, too, remembered going on *siyaran*—weekend outings to the nearby lake. They recalled being in a line of cars, each packed to the brim with relatives, as well as with *safiha* and *kofta* to grill. Indeed, it is likely that these trips to the lake had also been a leisurely pursuit for their parents and grandparents, given that the same medieval scholars who write of the market also write of this fresh water source.

These memories of Syria *are* reflections of individual realities. The men and women in this book were middle class people who had the financial resources to leave Syria in the early days of the war. The majority owned their own homes and ran their own businesses. They lived near other family. They had hopes for their children to either take over these businesses, or if they were smart enough, to continue on to college.

But memories are also social tools.[6] We remember things with others who share our experiences—within families or clubs or nations—and in specific social moments. Memories of comfort in Syria not only reflect the individual experiences of those seeking refuge, but they also served as markers of self-worth—reminders that, while they are facing various indignities now, they weren't always *laji'een*, refugees, in other people's countries.

Men and women recalled these memories through the fog of war and violent displacement while sitting in rented apartments, often in low-income neighborhoods. They were recalled to me, a relatively comfortable Arab woman who was interested in their stories, perhaps to signal that just a few years prior, they would have hosted me in their owned family homes, that it would have been them helping *me* navigate a space that they knew, rather than the other way around. They were also recalled to each other as status markers of the life they had.

When I watched people introduce themselves to one another after their arrival, the first question they asked to get to know each other was what town are you from? And, if they knew that town, what neighborhood and which family? The men asked each other what occupations they held and identified themselves as "plumbers" or "electricians" or "carpenters"—jobs they may have not worked for the last four or five years. Like all of us, their identities are tied up in these various markers, which are now relegated to the realm of memory—shared only with others who were there.

But life in Syria was not without its difficulties. First, prospects for economic mobility within Syria were limited. While identifying a clear cause for the protests that were precursors to the war is impossible, economic inequalities in Syria were increasing. Droughts, a manifestation of the climate crisis, hurt the country's agricultural sector. Increasing inequalities were also caused by the Assad regime's privatization of once public assets, liberalization of the financial sector, and reduction of state subsidies, particularly for agriculture.[7] This fits with a pattern observed in other postcolonial contexts. Though eighty percent of Syria's economy was reliant on small businesses, these small businesses no longer had the kinds of returns that they once had, which pushed people towards migrant labor.[8]

Though Majid and Rajaa owned their own home, it was because Majid, a chef, worked in restaurants in Saudi Arabia and sent remittances home. More and more Syrians were moving outside of the country to work in the Gulf due to a lack of opportunities back home. According to the World Bank, remittances shot up in the last decade before the war from USD 180 million in 2000 to USD 1.62 billion in 2010, which constituted 2.4 percent of GDP.[9] This meant that workers not only had to leave home for months at a time, but they also had to navigate the oppressive Saudi system of sponsorship, where their presence in Saudi Arabia was at the behest of a Saudi patron who could rescind their stay for whatever reason.

Second, women had unique grievances. Though the women's remembrances most often echoed the good times that Najlaa recounted, at times there were also laments about their position within Syrian society. Sarah, a thirty-year-old mother of three, one time explained that in Syria she felt like she was expected to be a sort of completion of her husband. "Women are the dot that made the one a ten," she explained, referring to the Indian numerals with which Arabs write numbers, where a straight line is a "1" and a dot is a zero, which together comprise the number "10." It was not her relationship with her husband or even her father that made her feel like a nonentity on her own, she explained, but the wider social system that she felt denied her an opportunity to pursue her own interests.

Gender inequalities motivated the protests against the regime. Feminist participants in the 2011 protests saw their fight as one against local patriarchies.[10] As Samar Yazbek, a prominent Syrian feminist, explains,

> The war became extremely violent, and women's rights became a secondary issue. But despite the horrifying intensity of the war, there are still women activists working to create life and maintain a civil society, both within the heart of war and as refugees.

While the Assad regime presented itself as a liberal alternative to Islamists, particularly with the rise of ISIS, anti-regime feminists continued to point to the ways in which the Syrian legal system has long legally disadvantaged women, given the lack of protections against gender discrimination and a family code that limited women's financial rights if they worked outside of the home without their husband's consent. These kinds of institutions culminated in meaningful gender inequalities. A 2011 report by the United Nations Population Fund on Syria showed a low use of contraceptives, high rates of child marriage (thirteen percent), high rates of young childbearing for women and girls (forty-seven percent of births occurring under the age of twenty-four), and high rates of girls dropping out of school.[11]

Finally, Syrians were living in a country of diminished opportunities due to state violence, corruption, and oppression. Political opposition, whether by ethnic or religious factions or by pro-democracy advocates, was not tolerated. The Syrian regime was far more oppressive than those of Egypt or Tunisia, where the protests against authoritarian Arab leaders began. A visitor to Syria prior to the war would have seen images of Assad plastered on all of the city's streets and in each store. And, though talked about in hushed tones, the Syrians knew what happened to those who protested. In 1982, protests in Hama, Syria in support of the Muslim Brotherhood were met with a twenty-seven-day siege of the town that killed somewhere between twenty and forty thousand people.[12]

Worse off than the Sunni majority were the Kurdish minority. Zaid, a twenty-five-year-old who now lives in Germany, grew up stateless despite being born in Syria. A Kurd, he was considered a "foreigner" even though he and his parents, and their parents, were born in al-Hasakah, a Syrian city with a large Kurdish population. While he could attend schools and university, he was unable to get a government job or leave the country, as he could not apply for a passport. In 2003, his family joined seven other families who tried to flee the country by taking a boat from the seaside town of Latakia to Europe, with the goal of going to Germany, but the attempt was thwarted when the Syrian police stopped them at a checkpoint, and they were forced to return home. He and his family only received Syrian identification cards in 2011, when the government, attempting to appease the Kurds, regularized their status "so that we would not take up arms against them," he explained. This also meant that the Syrians could draft Kurdish men into the military.

In this way, Syria was a place of both joy and discontent. In March 2011, Majid was in Syria on two weeks' vacation from his job in Saudi Arabia. Ten days into his trip, there was a small, local protest in his neighborhood. The protest was in support of those who were protesting in Daraa, but it was also against the governor of Homs, who had been demanding bribes from shop owners. Majid went to the protests with a close friend. They had not even begun chanting when bullets began whizzing around them from the air and ground. Bodies dropped beside them, and a bullet grazed Majid's ear. He and his friend ran back home. Still, even after this terrifying experience, they thought that the protests would soon be over.

As a child, Majid had heard whispers of what had happened in Hama decades before, that the town had been completely flattened and everyone there killed by Hafez al-Assad, Bashar's father. Rumor had it that Hafez had callously said that he was clearing the land to make room for sweet potatoes. Everyone thought that Bashar al-Assad, a London-educated ophthalmologist, would be different from his father, that he would be less violent and take a sensible approach, and that things would settle soon.

"At Least I Know Where They're Buried"

Of course, things did not settle. And over the coming years, the men and women in this study would leave their homes behind for good. In November 2015, I sat with Rima and Amjad in their two-bedroom apartment on the top floor of what used to be a single-family home in Connecticut. They were resettled there by the United States government as Syrian refugees earlier that summer. Their four-year-old son, Boudi, lay on the rug in front of us, playing quietly with toy cars and action figures given to him by a neighbor. As we shared cardamom coffee and *ma'moul* cookies that Rima had made, the conversation turned to their departure from Syria. Rima asked to borrow my phone, leaning across the black metal of their secondhand Ikea futon couch to take it from my hand. The family had one cell phone and had already used up their month's data allowance. After trying a few different search terms, Rima finally found the video that she was looking for.

The video began with a woman journalist speaking into a camera. The camera's unsteadiness highlighted the amateur production. A second shot showed an older woman dressed in black, sitting on a low bench and sobbing. She said, between breaths, "she was only eleven years old; she was so young." The video then panned to a photograph in a floral frame of a young girl in a powder blue *hijab*, followed by an image of four men carrying a wooden casket. Amjad reached over and pointed at himself in the video, one of the two men at the front of the casket. The older woman in the video was Amjad's mother. She had lost her husband just a few months earlier to a sniper when he was caught outside during curfew. Now she had also lost her young daughter, who was killed when she went up onto the roof of the family's house to get some air.

The day after Amjad's sister's funeral, Rima and Amjad decided to leave Homs with his siblings and mother. They took refuge in Zamalka, a suburb of Damascus where they had relatives. But this reprieve from war was interrupted when a car bomb exploded during a funeral procession in Zamalka on June 30, 2012. Another YouTube video captured a procession of men walking with a casket, then darkness, and then bodies on the ground. Amjad was in the procession, as were people he knew who did not survive. In the mayhem, Amjad lost track of his son Boudi. Although he was later found with Amjad's brother, Amjad was left with an unshakable certainty that he would lose his children if he stayed in Syria. He felt that he had three choices: kill, die, or leave. As he put it,

> All of the time, people lost family and would go out and join the free army. I didn't. I will not kill anyone. What do they want me to do? Shoot an *Allawi* in the street? What if he has nothing to do with anything? What if he's better than me [in the eyes of god]? Then I have committed a sin. That's what made me not join them [. . .] As for my father and sister, at least I know where they are buried.

With the help of the Free Syrian Army, Amjad and Rima's family left the country. "We went to Jordan carrying this one, his brother, and two pieces of luggage," he said, pointing to their three-year-old son Boudi, who had moved up onto the foldout couch next to me, action figures in hand. They left with the equivalent of USD 100 in their possession.

Others chose to fight. I met Amina, a distant cousin of Rajaa, in her apartment in western Germany. She and her husband, Imad, a tall man with broad shoulders and dark features, had moved there in 2015. During our conversation, their three-year-old daughter moved in and out of the living room, parroting her father's words. The living room itself was set up Arab-style with upholstered benches. Amina prepared a hookah, offering it to me before setting it down in front of her husband. Occasionally, she would lean over to take a drag.

Imad was a public bus driver in Syria prior to the war. Originally from the outskirts of Idlib, he lived and worked in Damascus at Syria's National Transportation Authority. The biggest conflicts he had faced at his job prior to the war was whether someone wanted to get off between stops. Because they could drive large vehicles, bus drivers were recruited to Assad's military effort after the war began.

In the ensuing nine months, Imad would drive people and military equipment across the country. Imad recalls seeing women being raped and guns being put in children's mouths by Assad regime soldiers. Coming from a family that had long been sympathetic to the Muslim Brotherhood, and seeing what he had seen, he decided to change allegiances and to take an active effort in the Free Syrian Army. Although he had to surrender his phone at the beginning of each shift, he used the fact that he was moving between cities to help coordinate the Free Syrian military effort and inform dissidents about where regime trucks were headed. Imad, in short, became a spy for the Free Syrian Army.

This was brought to an abrupt end one morning when he went to work and his boss, Mr. Hanna, a Christian man, told Imad that the police had come by looking for him. He felt his knees go weak. "What did you do?" Mr. Hanna asked Imad. "Nothing, I did nothing," he responded. Mr. Hanna went with Imad to the police station, to show that Imad had his support. During the interrogation, the officers showed Imad television footage from Al Jazeera of him at a protest. They also suspected him of leaking information to the Free Syrian Army. Again, he vehemently denied the allegations. After ten days of torture, he was released. He believes that the only reason for his release was Mr. Hanna's intervention. At this point, Amina interrupted her husband and said, "show her your burns." I declined to see them.

Imad knew that he could not stay in Damascus. So, he and his brother devised a plan. His brother needed hemorrhoid surgery but could not be admitted to the hospital under his own name because he had been drafted into the Syrian military and was evading his draft notice. Instead, he checked into the hospital using Imad's identification. Imad then used the discharge papers from the hospital to get a stamped letter that allowed him to take two weeks off work. With this documentation, he was able to leave Damascus to go to Idlib. From there, getting out of Syria to Turkey was simple. The road to Turkey was under the authority of the Free Syrian Army. "We just drove our car over," Imad recalled. While Amina lived in Idlib with the children, Imad went back and forth across the border, transporting items to local rebels fighting the regime forces in Idlib. "I couldn't just sit there, like a woman," he explained. Although Imad continued to make trips between Idlib and Turkey, his family effectively stopped living in Syria in 2012. Government forces continued to shell Idlib, and while Imad was willing to take the risk, he did not want to subject his wife and children to it.

While the journey out was already precarious, the families of Amjad and Imad left early in the war, when paths out were relatively simple. Those who waited too long, however, found themselves with a much more perilous journey out of Syria. Abo Mahmoud, a man in his forties and a father of seven children, did not leave Homs until February 2013. A farmer who owned his own home as well as land and a tractor, he had a lot to lose by leaving. He and his family experienced the full assault on their neighborhood in Homs in 2012 and struggled to survive in their leveled city. As Lyse Doucet[13], a journalist who went into the city with a UN escort, wrote of Homs at the time,

> Sprawling neighborhoods stand deserted, desolate, destroyed in a haunting monument to months of brutal conflict. On some streets, you walk on a carpet of glass. Every window in every building is shattered. Gunfire rings out night and day, with occasional bursts of shelling. There is no ceasefire here and there will not be for some time. Homs, a lively Syrian city once regarded as a place of peaceful co-existence, has borne the brunt of violence in Syria's fourteen-month long uprising. The neighborhood of Baba Amr was its biggest target in a city activists now call the "capital of the revolution." Not a single building seems to have escaped the government's ferocious assault. Structures still standing are peppered with shrapnel, blackened by fire, fingers of concrete. Indiscriminate bombing ripped away entire floors of large residential blocks.

During the assault on Baba Amr, Abo Mahmoud's home was destroyed. He rented a second house, but that too was gone within the year. "Our family has seen violence that we cannot describe," he said between drags of a cigarette as we sat on a sheet on the floor of his Toronto apartment, where I'd joined him, his wife, and their seven children for lunch. He estimated that the war claimed the lives of at least sixty people in the city each day.

Abo Mahmoud and his family fled Homs on foot, carrying none of their belongings, taking advantage of a break in the crossfire and the Free Syrian Army's ability to create a pathway for civilians to leave the city. His family spent the next twenty-six days walking through the desert, taking circuitous routes to avoid military checkpoints, some days walking ten kilometers, and other days only a few hundred meters. Along the way they saw the corpses of people who had died of thirst and malnourishment. A 2013 *New York Times* report estimated that five thousand Syrians were fleeing the war each day at the time when Abo Mahmoud's family made their journey.[14]

The family arrived in Jordan with nothing and was placed in the Zaatari camp where they would live for the next three and a half years. But they felt lucky. Two of Abo Mahmoud's brothers had not survived the war. The last he heard, one had been tortured to death in prison, while the second was last seen years ago in a prison in Damascus. Unlike Amjad, Abo Mahmoud does not know where his brothers are buried.

Countries of Immediate Refuge

With their departure from Syria, each of the families in this study found themselves in countries of immediate refuge. These are countries that share borders with countries where a conflict takes place, are willing to take in refugees, and are predominantly in the global south. They are the frontline humanitarian responders to crises of displacement. Importantly, not all of the region's countries were receptive to taking in refugees. Though Saudi Arabia does not share a border with Syria, it had many Syrian nationals working within its borders but created no pathway for their families to join them.

Majid had worked in Riyadh for years, but when he petitioned for Rajaa and his family to join him, his request was denied. Rajaa and the children were stuck in Syria until mid-2012, with two attempts at leaving thwarted at government checkpoints. Majid, losing hope, contemplated flying back into Syria. It was only after paying a hefty bribe to an official in the Damascus airport that his family was finally able to fly out to Amman. Today, the vast majority of the six million externally displaced Syrians remain in Jordan, Turkey, and Lebanon. These men and women were grateful to escape the war. As Imad put it, "if the Turks did not invite us in, we would have rotted at the border."

When the men and the women in this study arrived in countries of immediate refuge, they approached the United Nations Higher Council for Refugees (UNHCR) to register. The UNHCR is tasked with identifying whether those registering satisfy the United Nations definition of a refugee: someone seeking refuge because they have a well-founded fear of persecution due to race, religion, nationality, opinion, or membership in a political group. The UNHCR recognized the Syrians as having a credible claim to refugee status due to the war. But, the UNHCR also had to ensure that each refugee claim was compatible with the "civilian nature of asylum"—that they had not, during or before the war, been participants in violence.[15] If someone satisfies these criteria, the UNHCR offers them a refugee identification document, which they then use to access basic services: healthcare, education for their children, and other NGO assistance for things like clothing or food items.

However, despite the fact that the Syrians had escaped from the war and that there were systems in place to support them, life in these countries of refuge was difficult, particularly as more Syrians arrived. For instance, Lebanon, a country with just six million people, at one point hosted over a million Syrian refugees. Countries of immediate refuge responded to these new arrivals by building camps to accommodate them. Refugee camps exist as a place for refugees to live in the context of indefinite displacement, isolated from the communities that surround them and from their labor markets. According to the UNHCR, the average time that a refugee lives in a camp globally is seventeen years.[16]

Refugees' experiences of camps were varied. Imad and Amina had a positive experience in the Altınözü camp, which was a container camp that offered refugees a trailer to stay in that protected the families from the elements and provided a semblance of privacy. "We had a room to ourselves and everything we needed," Amina explained. However, others, including Abo Mahmoud and his family, arrived at tent camps—such as Zaatari in Jordan, which is the largest Syrian refugee camp in the world—that lacked these amenities. Regardless of the quality of the camp where those seeking refuge stayed, these camps were not constructed to be long-term solutions to displacement. People who had any resources attempted to avoid them, preferring to live in cities among locals.

Like escaping Syria, avoiding refugee camps got harder over time. Najlaa and her husband Nabil's departure from Syria was delayed because, like Imad, Nabil had been imprisoned. He resurfaced miraculously three weeks later, but he too still carries scars on his back and his stomach from the torture he endured. Due to his arrest and the care he needed afterward, they arrived with their two children in Jordan during the winter of 2012, as the Zaatari camp was becoming fully operational. The tent to which they were assigned was a ten-minute walk from the bathrooms, and there was a shortage of blankets to stave off the frigid desert nights.

Living in a tent exacerbated the sense of insecurity for the family, who until months prior had been living in a brick-and-mortar home that they had owned. Making matters worse, Najlaa was pregnant. The family had been so afraid to stay in Syria that they had made the journey to Jordan just three days before her due date. Their baby girl arrived promptly. When Najlaa's water broke, Najlaa and Nabil were forced to rely on strangers after living their whole lives near their wide family network. Unable to leave the children alone in the camp, Nabil stayed behind to take care of them. Strangers went to the hospital with Najlaa so she would not give birth in a foreign country entirely alone.

Not willing to accept an indefinite stay in the camp, Najlaa and Nabil decided to find a way out. Having arrived with modest savings, they could afford to try to move. One night, Nabil slipped out of the camp on his own and found an apartment for his family. To secure it, he paid the first month's rent, USD 500. While it was relatively easy for one man to slide in and out, it was much more difficult to get the family of five and their belongings out unnoticed. An old man with a truck offered to smuggle the family out of the camp for another USD 500. They packed their few belongings on his truck. Najlaa remembered holding her breath and feeling her heart pounding against her infant held tightly to her chest. But the man's truck stalled. The Jordanian camp guards came up to the windows with their flashlights and sent the family back, detaining the man. Perhaps, she wondered, the man had an agreement with the guards all along.

Having lost the USD 500 they paid the man for the failed escape and the USD 500 Nabil had paid for their rent in Amman that month, the family had spent a substantial portion of their savings. Najlaa became increasingly resigned to life in the camp. Just as this reality began to set in, a Jordanian man who did business in the camp offered to smuggle them out for only the cost of gas, around USD 100.

The camp was a hub of commercial activity, its main thoroughfare termed the Champs Elysees by residents. But while Jordanians could come and go, Syrians were confined to the space. Najlaa and Nabil did not believe that the man would show up on the appointed date, or that he would be successful in getting them out. However, they had little left to lose—a reality that motivated many of the agreements those on the move made with smugglers. The man showed up, and the guards did not notice the passing car. When she entered the apartment in Amman, Najlaa felt like it was a palace: "I could not believe that I was finally free of both the war and the camp."

Life outside of the camp, however, was also difficult. Majid, arriving in Jordan before the refugee camps were fully operational, was able to rent an apartment a few hours from Amman without incident. He also got a work permit, necessary for foreigners who worked in Jordan, with the help of his Jordanian landlord. However, as more Syrians arrived, the Jordanian authorities stopped issuing foreigners work permits. The police also began to heavily monitor restaurants and other establishments where Syrians worked off the books.

Majid was arrested twice. Each time, he was placed in handcuffs and dragged from the *shawarma* shop where he worked to the local police station. "I had never been in trouble with the authorities in my life," he explained, referring to how embarrassed he was to be arrested. While Majid's Jordanian contact was able to negotiate his release, Zafir, a butcher in his mid-thirties, lacked Majid's connections. At the police station, Zafir was told that he would only be released if his wife and children came to the station with their luggage and agreed to be taken to al-Azraq camp, one of the three largest in Jordan. Zafir, recognizing that his wife and children would soon run out of cash, made the phone call. The family spent the rest of their time in Jordan in that camp.

In addition to these economic constraints, the Syrians seeking refuge felt marginalized and lacking rights in other ways. Narjis, an eighteen-year-old mother, described being taunted by Turkish kids, who would yell "çöp," or trash, as she walked back to her apartment from the market with her two very young sons. Reports of this kind of xenophobic violence in Turkey were rampant, with Turkish residents attacking Syrian shops and Syrian children reporting bullying at school. Despite clear legal interdictions on sending people back to Syria, or *nonrefoulement*, some Syrians were allegedly repatriated to Syria from Turkey and Jordan.[17]

Despite sharing a religion and having proximate heritage to the Turks, and sharing the same ethnicity as the Jordanians, this kind of intragroup violence was not uncommon. While the Syrians would later feel nostalgic for countries of immediate refuge, Muslim countries where they could practice their faith and where there were co-ethnics present, they also had these memories of violence that felt hurtful because they were perpetrated by people whom they felt should be allies.

Within this context, girls and women were particularly vulnerable.[18] Syrian new arrivals across my sample told of stories of marriages of convenience, where young Syrian women, and sometimes girls, would be married to well-off residents in order to secure the family's position in the country of refuge. This practice was born out of the legal weakness of Syrians and their financial precarity. And, because of their diminished legal position, girls, women, and their families were unable to stave off unwanted advances. More than one of the families in this study had a young daughter who experienced sexual harassment and targeting from an older man, which they felt unable to stop. Two women dealt with sexual harassment at work. After finding a job cleaning the stairwells of buildings, a woman was abused by local men who knew that they could treat her with impunity due to her lack of legal recourse, the weakness of laws protecting victims of sexual assault, and her own embarrassment by the assault, for which she feared she'd be blamed had she reported it to police. Another woman was the target of unwanted sexual advances from a woman who tried to corner her at the daycare where they both worked. The predator knew she would be unable to get another job. Like other undocumented and disadvantaged women globally, the women were in a position where not only could they not report their abusers, they also couldn't extract themselves from the abuse.

In addition to these issues, there was a lack of basic services for those who were displaced. While UNHCR registration enabled those recognized as refugees to receive help from multiple organizations, there was more demand for humanitarian assistance than there was supply. Healthcare was available in theory, but in practice medication and access to medical professionals was not regularly accessible. Neither was mental health care, which was needed by both adults and children suffering from post-traumatic stress disorder.

Finally, access to quality education was limited. Some of the children—whether they were in Turkey, Lebanon, or Jordan—lost years of schooling. Others went to school in overcrowded classrooms that operated on shifts. Syrian students did not have access to textbooks in some cases. Secondary school systems emerged, created by former educators in Syria, that catered to their children, but they offered an education that was not validated by any government. The result was that these boys and girls became what practitioners call Students with Interrupted Formal Educations (SIFE).

Even with these difficulties, the idea of travelling further, of trying to seek out asylum or resettlement, was not enticing for everyone. Countries of immediate refuge were not only proximate to the homes that these men and women were forced out of, but their residents also shared cultural similarities with the Syrians. In Jordan, Lebanon, or Turkey, these majority Muslim refugees could go to Friday prayers and their children could have friends that shared their religion. Arabs, Muslim or not, could speak their mother tongue to other Arabs. Moving onward also meant that the families would have to move further away from their loved ones, who could get to these countries of immediate refuge but would not be able to join them in countries like the United States, Canada, or Germany.

The choice to move again was yet another displacement, structured by a labyrinth of paperwork, impermeable borders, and physical barriers of seas and land. Today, the vast majority of Syrians—at least eighty percent of all those externally displaced—remain in countries of immediate refuge. Those who *do* move onward towards legal refuge, whose experiences are captured in this book, do so either by agreeing to an invitation for resettlement or by travelling to a new country and seeking asylum.

Resettlement

When a displaced person arrives in a country of immediate refuge and registers with the UNHCR, they become a potential case for resettlement. Resettlement occurs when a refugee who has fled their country of origin is offered safe passage to, and permanent residency status in, a third country. Refugees cannot apply for resettlement and cannot specify a country they want to be resettled to. Instead, they have to wait to be selected, and then if they agree, they must undergo and pass the vetting process that the state requires of those it offers refuge. Resettlement is often the safest solution for displacement, but it is also a very rare solution. Only one percent of refugees will ever be resettled, and only thirty-seven countries globally have a resettlement program. Since the 1980s, the United States and Canada had been global leaders in refugee resettlement, an accolade which ended for the United States when the Trump administration slashed refugee admissions from an anticipated 110,000 in 2016 to just 45,000, then to 18,000 in 2020.

In considering families for resettlement, the UNHCR evaluates whether resettlement is the most appropriate solution for a given person, as opposed to local integration in the country of immediate refuge (which often does not have the capacity or a pathway for legal integration), or repatriation back to their country of origin. Where repatriation is not possible, as in the case of Syria due to the ongoing war, the UNHCR considers the level of adversity that the refugees face in countries of immediate refuge, and gives preference to survivors of torture or violence, people who have acute medical needs, girls and women who were under threats of violence, children at risk, and people who do not have other foreseeable solutions for their displacement. They also prioritize resettlement for people who had families who had previously been resettled, or those who were at risk of being deported back to the war.

Given how rare resettlement is, Majid was shocked when, in July 2014, his phone rang and a UNHCR official was on the line. The official asked if the family wanted to be considered for resettlement to the United States. Majid responded that yes, "who wouldn't want to go to the United States?"[19] The family had been selected because they were on the UNHCR rosters, and they fit the UNHCR resettlement criteria.

Unlike her husband, however, Rajaa was not necessarily excited to be vetted for travel to the United States. As the family was waiting, their then twelve-year-old son, Ahmed, came up with a chant: "We're going to America where they'll mend our broken hearts." While his parents at first laughed at the verse, as time passed, Rajaa would get annoyed by it, and Ahmed would sing it to tease her. Rajaa was terrified both of being accepted for travel and of being rejected. Acceptance meant leaving behind everything she had known for a country where she and her daughter, who both wore the *hijab*, would be conspicuous outsiders. How would they all manage in a non-Muslim country? How would they get along without speaking English? She was also terrified of being rejected, of staying where her husband could end up in jail again for working, where they could be sent to the camps indefinitely, where her children would never have the chance of a good education.

Through these fears, the family moved ahead with the process of vetting. Refugees are the most heavily vetted immigrants in the United States—the process takes on average between eighteen and twenty-four months. After receiving the phone call, Majid and Rajaa met with *El-Hijra*, the International Organization for Migration (IOM). The IOM was tasked, through coordination with the United States Refugee Admissions Program (USRAP), with running its Resettlement Support Centers (RSC).

The RSC creates the refugee's file. Refugees are photographed and fingerprinted, and the particulars of the refugees' cases are documented through two additional interviews, one for "case creation" and one for "prescreening." For instance, the caseworker would note who was part of the family unit, if one file was linked to another file, or if there was an aspiration for reunification with family members elsewhere in the world. These interviews also repeated the questions that the UNHCR had asked refugees, confirming the classification of the person as a refugee, as well as their specific vulnerabilities. Rajaa felt that the repeated asking of the same questions was meant to ensure that they were being truthful.

Finally, the family was interviewed by the United States Citizenship and Immigration Services (USCIS) and by a Department of Homeland Security officer. While Majid and Rajaa described all of the other interviews to this point as cordial and relaxed, this last interview felt like an interrogation. The officer sat behind a desk and asked rapid-fire questions that both Majid and Rajaa were expected to answer without hesitation.

Meanwhile, as the family was waiting for this final Homeland Security interview, their data was going through additional screenings. The RSC submitted all of the gathered information to other intelligence agencies: the US counterterrorism center, the Federal Bureau of Investigation, the US Department of Homeland Security, the US Department of Defense, and others in the international intelligence community. Refugee fingerprints are run through these agencies' databases, and reports suggest that Syrian refugees, and particularly men, undergo a second stage of screening at this point. This second, opaque screening process—which existed under the Obama administration—went through the Fraud Detection Unit at the National Security Directorate Office.[20] The issue of vetting would become a flashpoint in United States policy, with advocates of refugees pointing to this system to show that refugees are more thoroughly vetted than any other immigrants. However, underlying this defense of the system by these advocates is an assumption that it is necessary to vet people from Syria in this exhaustive way, which feeds into the notion that they are inherently dangerous.

Majid and Rajaa were told to come back to Amman ten days after their Homeland Security interview to find out the results of their vetting process. Up to this point, they were lucky, having gone through all of the interviews in only eight months. For most of the people they knew, this process had taken at least a year. Along with around fifty other applicants, they were led into a room and given sealed envelopes which held within them their fate. While there were a few acceptances in the room, and a few rejections, Majid, Rajaa, and forty others found out that they had "suspended" files. When they asked what it meant to have a suspended file, and how long the wait would entail, they were given no explanation, and were told simply that they would be informed when their file was no longer suspended. In the room there were signs that advised the refugees not to call the IOM to inquire and that warned them against paying bribes or trying to influence their process in any way.

Majid and Rajaa returned home dejected. They knew another family who had gone through the resettlement process before them and who, in part to defray the costs of going back and forth to the IOM office, began to sell the furniture and appliances that they could not take with them when they moved. But like Majid and Rajaa, the other family's file was also suspended. Without the resources to repurchase what they'd sold, and without clarity on when or if their file would be reinstated, the family lived without basic items—without a bed or couches—for an indefinite wait.

Due to this uncertainty, Majid and Rajaa did not get rid of their furniture, nor did they tell their landlord that they were moving. Six anxious months would pass with no news. Majid estimated that by this point he had spent at least two-and-a-half months' salary on the application process. This included all of the public transportation to get the family of five back and forth to their appointments. For many of those seeking it, the prospect of resettlement, rare as it was, was one they could barely afford given these expenses, not to mention the days off from already precarious jobs that it would entail.

Then, about a year and a half after they started the process, the family was surprised to receive another phone call from the RSC asking them to come in for medical checkups. They knew that this was the last stage of the process. Rajaa remembers her anxiety peaking. The children and Majid were excited, believing it was finally happening. The family went back to Amman to undergo medical tests to ensure that they did not have "communicable disease of public health significance," but also to assess medical needs that could be addressed before travel and those that should be followed-up upon after their arrival. After the medical testing, as they expected, they attended cultural orientation sessions meant to inform them about the laws and systems in the United States. The cover of the seventy-one-page booklet they were given is adorned with a US map in the colors of the American flag and the IOM logo. On the inside flap is the Statue of Liberty and a statement in Arabic:

> Welcome to the United States. This book was made to help you prepare for your new lives in the United States of America. Making the decision to move to the United States is a big decision, and there are many challenges ahead of you on your journey. If you understand some of these challenges and what they entail, and what you should do in relation to them, it will help you to navigate life in the United States.[21]

Comprised of fourteen sections, the booklet offered a brief history of the United States, what they could expect to go through before traveling to the United States, and descriptions of the assistance they would receive in the United States, with warnings that they would not be able to make ends meet on public assistance alone. There was a description of how to access housing, educational services, and health care, as well as a two-page list of laws stating that you cannot bribe police officers, you cannot have multiple wives or rape or harass people, and that you cannot throw trash anywhere other than in designated areas, but that you can drink alcohol.

As Majid and Rajaa were attending these cultural orientation sessions, they were also being assigned to a resettlement agency in the United States through a process that matched resettlement agency capacities with newly arrived refugees. Over the next week, they prepared for their travel date and hurriedly sold their furniture, having waited until two days before their trip to feel certain that they were leaving. They ended up just giving most of it away for free. In the airport they would learn that their destination was Connecticut, a name that they would fumble over for years to come.

Months after Majid and Rajaa arrived in the United States, Abo Mahmoud was sitting in the Zaatari camp when he received a similar phone call, but with the question of whether he would like to go to Canada. Like Majid, he responded that he would like to be considered. However, his experience of the process was radically different. While those in this study who arrived during the administration of conservative Canadian Prime Minister Stephen Harper were vetted over the course of a year (still shorter than the eighteen-to-twenty-four-month average in the United States), Abo Mahmoud's family, which arrived under Trudeau, only had to wait a few months.

His family was resettled as a direct consequence of Justin Trudeau's election as Canada's Prime Minister in 2015. Trudeau ran on a platform of admitting twenty-five thousand Syrian refugees, differentiating himself Harper, whose policies he blamed for the death of three-year-old Alan Kurdi. The body of Kurdi, a nephew of a Canadian citizen, had washed up that September on the shore of Bodrum, Turkey after the family's boat capsized. The family said that if channels of resettlement to Canada had been open, they wouldn't have gotten on the boat. Upon winning the Canadian premiership, Trudeau made good on his promise immediately, bringing in the twenty-five thousand refugees over a three-month period—including the family of Abo Mahmoud. This meant that the wait between receiving the call and resettlement for Abo Mahmoud's family was a short two months.

The Trudeau's administration's admission of large numbers of refugees with just a few months' vetting, is a direct challenge to the notion espoused in the United States, in Canada under the normal process, and elsewhere, that those seeking refuge are inherently threatening and that only a years' long process can deem them otherwise. Waits in countries of immediate refuge, as shown by Majid and Zafir, who were incarcerated, can be dangerous in-and-of-themselves. These drawn-out processes therefore are not only unfounded and expensive, but also inhumane, and have, by some reports, led to the deaths of those waiting.[22]

Asylum

Resettlement is not an option for most people in need of refuge. Imad and Amina, the couple who along with their young children had escaped from the war, traveling from Damascus to Idlib and then Turkey, never got a call from the United States, or Canada, or anywhere else. Meanwhile, in March 2015, Jabhit al-Nasra, an al-Qaeda–derived group, took over Idlib. When the Jabhit al-Nasra sympathizers began to infiltrate the camps in Turkey, and a friend of his was killed by them, Imad recognized that he had to leave Turkey altogether. "We could fight the regime, we fought off ISIS, but we could not stop Jabhit al-Nasra," he explained.

The best option was to move to Europe—the family knew there was a limited future for them in Turkey even outside of the camp. Indeed, almost a million Syrians would choose this option. Some would go, like Imad and Amina, after spending years on end in countries of immediate refuge, waiting, in vain, for the war to end, or for an offer of resettlement that never came. However, for others, the journey was direct—they left a war-torn Syria to head towards a European destination, often unsure which country they would end up in. The journey to Europe, dangerous as it was, felt to many like the only opportunity to live a life that had a semblance of dignity, where their children could be educated, where they could have employment, where they could have legal status. That is, if they survived the journey.

Like a million other Syrians, Imad and Amina decided that it was worth the risk—the best of a series of bad choices. However, the trip to Europe was expensive, and Imad and Amina had no money or assets. Their home in Damascus had been ransacked after they left it, and Imad had been out of work for multiple years. Imad's mother, worried about losing her son, offered to sell land that she had in their village. Imad resisted at first, but his mother reached out to his sister, who was married to a wealthy businessman and who agreed to buy the land and allow their mother to live on it until she passed. The land sold for USD 8,000, and his mother gave him all of the money.

Like many other migrants who set out for Europe, Imad and Amina faced a difficult decision: should Imad make the journey alone, or should they go together? Their only way out of Turkey was to take a boat from Izmir to Greece, a dangerous trip that had claimed the lives of thousands. Then they'd move farther inland to a wealthy country like Sweden or Germany. If Imad went alone and all went well, he could send for Amina and the children to join him once he had established domicile. But there was always the possibility that things would not go well. What if he didn't make it? What if the destination country did not approve their family reunification? How would his wife and children make ends meet? In the end, Imad and Amina decided that the family should move together. Imad's brother went with them as well.

The first leg of their trip was an overnight bus to Izmir, a beach town in midwestern Turkey where smugglers ran boats to Greece. When they got there, Imad explained, it was like al-Hashr or the crowding, evoking an image from Muslim jurisprudence of the day of judgment, where people will stand crammed together, naked, the hot sun beating down on their bodies. Tens of thousands of people were there, all crowding the same bus stations and the same beachfront, looking for a way across the water. The majority were Syrians, but others, including Afghanis and Iraqis, who had themselves been victims of persecution, joined this new pathway to refuge.

There was no need to pre-contract with a smuggler, Imad explained. The smugglers were already waiting for them at the bus station. The smuggler, easily identifying them as Syrian asylum seekers, asked whether they wanted to go to Greece. The price was the same everywhere: USD 1,000 for each adult and USD 500 for each child. They bought life vests from vendors on the shore.

Everyone described the *bilim*, or boat, in similar terms. Walaa, a thirty-two-year-old mother of two, a boy and a girl, pointed to a rubber bounce house where we were watching her children play.[23] "You see that?" she said, referring to the rubber material, "That is what the boat was made of, just like that. And they crammed us into it." She explained that a boat that looked as if it were built for twenty people regularly carried three times that number. The smugglers, the men and women recalled, asked if anyone on the boat knew how to sail. If one of the Syrians themselves sailed the boat, they would give them a discount. This, of course, terrified everyone on the boat, who now were traversing the dangerous Aegean without an expert sailor.

Boat journeys were systematically referred to as the "most terrifying moments" of these men and women's lives, as they held onto their children, trying to put them to sleep "so at least they'd be sleeping if we drowned." Walaa asked abruptly as she recounted this journey, "do you know what it is to go into debt to put your children in the arms of death?" Despite choppy seas, the men and women in this book made it across safely. The same cannot be said for 3,771 known others in 2015.[24]

Although the Red Cross and UNHCR would later build refugee reception centers in Greece, at the time of Amina and Imad's arrival in the summer of 2015 their options were to stay in a hotel or keep moving. Having already spent much of the money they had getting to Greece, they lacked the resources to stay in a hotel. They purchased a tent for EUR 40, where they would sleep for the next month as they made their slow way from Greece to Germany by ferry, on foot, and via public transport and private taxis. Imad had downloaded a map, so that he could navigate off-line. Communication was almost impossible because, as he put it, "when we could find electricity, we couldn't find internet. And where there was internet, we couldn't find plugs." Still, they went on. Leaving Athens on a bus headed north, Imad typed "Macedonia" into his phone.

European immigration law jeopardized Amina and Imad's ability to travel to Germany. The Dublin Regulation, a European Union agreement that was in full effect at the time of their arrival in the summer of 2015, stipulated that immigrants be fingerprinted at their first port of entry. Thereafter, the national authorities that fingerprinted them would oversee handling their asylum case and perhaps referring them to another country within the EU for resettlement. In the event that a refugee left that country, they would be returned to their first port of entry. As a result of the Dublin Regulation, each country Amina and Imad traversed posed a new threat to their ability to get to Germany. Much to their relief, the family had been among those Syrians who were not finger-printed in Greece because the country did not have the capacity to process the hundreds of thousands of people showing up on their shores.

As they moved north, news agencies, which the Syrians felt had ignored them throughout their war, focused their coverage on them. Globally, we began to tune into their plight. From Macedonia, Imad and Amina went to Serbia. There, strangers would stop to help them; a woman stopped to give Amina her boots after noticing that hers looked uncomfortable. A farmer allowed them to eat corn from his field, a welcome departure from the sardines, tuna, and cheap pizza that they had been eating.

But, as the crowd moved onwards, comprised of mostly young men, the family fell behind, as both the adults and their young children struggled to keep walking for days on end. Crossing from Serbia to Hungary, they found themselves alone in a dense forest, and they retreated to Serbia to spend the night. The following morning, looking at his GPS, Imad realized that Hungary was only two kilometers away, a walkable distance. His brother decided to walk across. But Imad, worried about his young children being able to walk across the border and about police scrutiny, preferred to take a taxi across the border—Hungary was notorious for having violent, racist police. After a fight with his brother, Imad, Amina, and their two children parted ways.

Imad and Amina paid a driver USD 500 to take them to Budapest, about a two-hour drive away. From there they planned to board a train to Vienna and then Munich. But, around twenty minutes into the drive, they heard sirens. The police ran up to the stopped car, banged on the doors with their batons, dragged Imad, Amina, and their children out of the car, and beat them. "We could not imagine," Amina said, "that police in a European country were hitting our children."

They were taken to a prison, where the facilities smelled of feces, the water was murky, and the food inedible. The police told them that if they wanted to get out, they had to be fingerprinted and placed in a Hungarian camp. "*Obsom tetla' ma tobsom, ma tetla'*" [fingerprint and get out, don't fingerprint, and you won't get out], the Arabic-speaking interpreter kept repeating. Amina and Imad put nail polish on their fingers to try to distort their fingerprints. Young men tried to burn theirs off. If they were fingerprinted in Hungary, their asylum would be tied to that country—which, with its xenophobia and weak economic standing, was not where these people seeking a new beginning wanted to end up. Several of the young men, Amina explained, had families in Jordan or Turkey whom they'd left behind with the aim of applying for family reunification, an impossible prospect if they were stuck in Hungary.

On the third day of their detention, Amina and Imad succumbed to the pressure to be fingerprinted. They were put on a bus and given a map to get to a Hungarian refugee camp. But, when they got to the bus stop, which was close to Budapest, they found themselves swarmed by people. *Ahlan Wasahlan* [welcome], they said in Arabic. They gave the travelers bananas, water, and warm food, juice for the kids, and some blankets. They were Jewish residents of Hungary who had come to support the Syrians on their journey. Imad and Amina were shocked. Given anti-Semitic messaging and the expulsion of Jews from Syria—tied to Syria's war with Israel over its occupation of Palestine— they had not previously met any Jews, nor did they expect people of that faith to come to their aid. They would learn later learn the history of Jews in Europe, who, having themselves experienced oppression and refugee status, were sympathetic to their plight. Someone in the crowd directed the refugees to the Budapest train station. Despite having been fingerprinted, Amina and Imad had gone too far in their journey to entertain the possibility that they would not make it further north. Amina could not fathom living in Hungary. She told me,

> The whole journey I've forgotten, but Hungary I have not, I have not forgotten. All of the walking, the days we walked sixteen hours, the hunger, that all I can forget. But Hungary and what we saw there I can never forget. It was worse than the war.

In Budapest, Amina and Imad, now travelling with another family from Aleppo, met a Palestinian man and his son in the train station. He told them where to go to find someone who would drive them to the German border. With only EUR 600 left, Imad and Amina could not afford the steep fees of the drivers, who were charging EUR 400 a person. But, as Imad put it, eventually "we ran into an *ibn halal* Lebanese smuggler who agreed to take us at a discounted rate." He charged them EUR 1,000. The other family they were travelling with at the time loaned Imad the remaining EUR 400, which reduced Imad to tears.

Five hours later, they approached the German border. The driver let them off at a service stop near the highway. Imad wanted to go to Berlin, where his brother had arrived, but it was too far away. Meanwhile, their phones had died. It was around five in the morning. Amina, Imad, and the children had no choice but to begin to walk deeper into Germany. They heard sirens behind them, and Amina's heart sank, the trauma of Hungary still fresh. "*Wilkommen,*" the police officer said, as she covered Amina with a blanket. She sobbed with relief.

A month after Amina and Imad arrived in Germany, Angela Merkel would suspend the Dublin Regulation, making it so that their fingerprinting in Hungary would not matter and allowing Amina and Imad to apply for asylum there. But this change in the Dublin Regulation is just one part of a fluctuating legal context that surrounded Syrians seeking asylum. While those who left Syria nearly six months earlier than Imad and Amina, before January 2015, could make the journey into Europe from Turkey over land, through Bulgaria, increasing arrests made this route undesirable and expensive. Those who left six months later, by contrast, would be prevented from traveling to Germany due to the reinstatement of the Dublin Regulation. And, after March 2016, they would also be caught in the web of the EU-Turkey immigration deal in which Turkey promised to curb emigration to Greece by accepting the return of irregular migrants who had left from its shores—causing the cost of smuggling to spike and pushing it underground, thereby making it more dangerous.

Starting Over

Regardless of when they traveled, the journeys of the men and women in this book to countries of resettlement and asylum were long and arduous. For those who arrived in the United States, Canada, and Germany in 2015, they were journeys that entailed at least four years of war and displacement. They were journeys forged in the violence of siege, so much so that many of their children could now differentiate between the sounds of different kinds of bombs. Journeys that left them with keys to homes that no longer stood, love for people they would not see again, and mental and physical scars from being locked into prisons and out of safety. These involuntary journeys were mostly contorted waits for humanitarian recognition and refuge, which most displaced people will never receive.

But refugees' arrivals in the United States, Canada, and Germany were both the end of one journey and the beginning of another. Months after their move to Connecticut, Majid and Rajaa sat in the basement of a First Baptist Church at their resettlement agency's annual holiday party. People from Eritrea, Cuba, Afghanistan, and other countries of persecution huddled over phones selecting their playlists as they waited for their turn to plug into the loudspeaker. When the Syrians turn came, Majid began to dance, holding paper napkins between his thumb and forefinger, while he shifted his weight between his feet. His now seven-year-old daughter rustled the pink crochet dress her mother had made her while trying to mimic her father's steps. Rajaa reeled in laughter at her daughter's serious face. As the room emptied, I offered to drive Majid and Rajaa home. Lacking a car, they accepted. Rajaa asked if we could stay a few minutes longer. "We no longer have fun like this," she said apologetically. As I watched Majid do the *dabke* with a group of Syrian and Iraqi men, bending and rising to the beat of the line dance, I wondered how many times he'd danced at loved ones' weddings, and how many more of these dances were in store for him. Would their hearts be mended as Ahmed's song had hoped?

3

American Self-Sufficiency

On a crisp mid-November afternoon, a man, woman, and young child emerged from the sliding side door of an International Organization for Migration (IOM) van. The woman, Faten, wore a dark green *manteau*, a modest, double-breasted trench coat fashionable in Syria, and a tightly wound *hijab*. Her husband, Ahmed, wore distressed jeans and a leather jacket, his hair slicked back. As Ahmed moved the family's luggage into the caseworker's car, the couple's five-year-old stared at the horse and jockey mural that advertised Sports Haven, a three-story cylindrical, off-track betting venue, in whose parking lot refugees would be met by representatives from IRIS, the agency tasked with their resettlement.

The couple had first heard the word "Connecticut" at JFK Airport that morning. In Jordan, they were told by the IOM that they were headed to Indiana, which would be their resettlement state. In the backseat of my car, they listened intently as I explained that they were rerouted because Mike Pence, then governor of Indiana, refused to admit them.[1] Along with thirty other governors, Pence had banned Syrians from his state for the "safety and security of all Hoosiers." This decision was prompted by the Bataclan terrorist attacks in Paris that left 137 people dead.[2] A Syrian passport found near the scene led to later-disproven speculation that a Syrian refugee was involved. Faten and Ahmed, busy packing up their lives and saying goodbye to loved ones, hadn't heard about the terrorist attack. Faten cursed whoever perpetrated the attack. Then she said, "but what does that have to do with us?"

On their first day in the United States, Faten and Ahmed learned what it took others months to realize: that their identities as Muslims and as Syrian refugees were stigmatized in the United States, and that this stigma would have repercussions for their lives. But, as other non-White people have for centuries, while managing this stigma, they would also have to craft new daily routines.

Most new arrivals had apartments pre-selected for them by the resettlement agency, but Faten and Ahmed's sudden arrival meant that they'd be able to pick out their own, learning in the process the American obsession with open concept layouts, which, in their minds, uncomfortably blurred public and private space. "Why doesn't the kitchen have a door?" Faten wondered, annoyed. They visited the mosque and the Middle Eastern food markets where they bought familiar staples like paper-thin Syrian pita, young cheese, grape leaves, and olives. They learned to use public transit, becoming the newest additions to a sea of predominantly brown and Black faces that line the bus stop at the edge of the New Haven Green.

As refugees, the couple arrived in the United States with certain privileges. They were on a pathway to citizenship. They could access social services unavailable to other immigrants. But they also arrived already in debt. Their flights from Jordan to the United States were purchased by the IOM through a travel loan. The IOM has five years to collect on this interest-free loan. For this family of three, the loan was more than USD 3,000 dollars. For larger families, it was more than USD 5,000. This reality was an introduction to the country's incorporation policy: one that was based in notions of individual responsibility rather than state support.

Over the next few months, Faten and Ahmed became further acquainted with the United States' social service system and its goal of "self-sufficiency." This goal, stipulated by the 1980 Refugee Act, aims for refugees to quickly enter the labor market in order to avoid relying on government assistance.[3] Refugees receive ninety days of federal assistance called "Welcome Money," which is transferred to the resettlement agency to be spent on the refugee's initial needs and first few months' rent. Besides this, the only other cash assistance available to refugees is welfare, which for a family of three was USD 597 a month. "Per person?" Ahmed asked hopefully. "Per family," the caseworker responded. Ahmed laughed uneasily. Their rent was USD 1,000 a month, which was both cheap for the area and almost twice their income from welfare. They needed to find work quickly—a task which fell to Ahmed who, as a man, was expected to enter the labor market on behalf of the family.

An employment officer from the agency visited their apartment to help them prepare their resumes.[4] Ahmed, once an owner and manager of his family's consignment store, was a skilled salesman and knew how to clean and organize clothing.[5] But, when it came to skills to list on his resume, Ahmed was uncertain what to write, knowing that he was not qualified for a managerial or a sales position because of his lack of English skills. The only skill he felt he *could* list was dry cleaning, but he'd already tried local cleaners with no luck. The employment officer asked if he could cook or clean. Ahmed's face tightened as he stressed that he'd like to work in something he had done before.

Ahmed was proud of his identity as a worker. When he and the other men introduced themselves to each other for the first time, they stated what city they were from, their family name—"I'm from *beit* El Jamil"—and their occupation. Their cities and family homes had long been destroyed by the war. Relinquishing additional parts of their identity felt traumatic. "I need more time," Ahmed said to the employment officer. "How am I supposed to find a job if I cannot even speak the language?"

But the US system does not allow new arrivals time, because it does not *invest* in newly arrived refugees. As we will see in subsequent chapters, other countries, including Canada and Germany, provide a full year of financial coverage of refugees' needs, but the United States offers a mere ninety days of help plus welfare, which is insufficient to cover even the cost of rent. Put together these meant that Ahmed would need to begin working before he had any grasp of English. The employment officer was sympathetic: "Finding a job in America is like climbing a steep mountain, even for the native-born English speaker." In Connecticut's postindustrial landscape, white-collar jobs were returning to cities, while low-skilled jobs were hard to come by.

Then, the employment officer turned to Faten. Did she want to prepare a resume? Ahmed responded immediately "no" on behalf of his wife. "I have a child," Faten explained, as a self-evident reason for why she was not searching for work. But, after a short pause, she continued, maybe, in the future, after she learned enough English, she'd be interested in finding work, *suitable work*, she stressed, a phrase that would develop meaning over the coming months.

Ahmed soon began work at a local pub as a dishwasher. He took this work on when the agency assistance ran out, earning USD 11 an hour, which was a little over a dollar above the USD 9.60 minimum wage. This fell far short of a living wage, which was estimated by MIT's living wage calculator to be USD 26.01 an hour for a two-parent household living in New Haven County with one parent working and one child, or USD 16.05 if both parents worked full time. Moreover, shift work made it difficult to attend English class regularly, so he stopped attending.[6]

After enrolling their son in kindergarten, however, Faten began English classes at which she excelled, having had some English classes at the high school she attended in Syria. Soon she too would begin to work, but only part-time, doing catering gigs or teaching cooking classes at a local nonprofit, and even interpreting for the dentist in her building. However, as the women attended English classes, and even as they began to earn an income, there was a clear ceiling. In the absence of family-focused policies, they had little childcare support. When Faten had another child, all of these endeavors stopped.

The Case of the United States

The Syrian refugees that I write about in this chapter arrived in the United States through the resettlement program between the summers of 2015 and 2016. Most of their flights touched down at JFK Airport during Donald

Trump's campaign. During his presidency, they were favorite targets of his racist rhetoric and policy.[7] Trump banned immigration from Muslim majority countries and reduced both the admissions of Syrian refugees and the overall United States refugee program, which declined from a projected 110,000 for 2016 by President Obama to just 18,000 for 2021. For the first time since 1980, the United States was no longer the global leader on resettlement admissions.[8]

But the system that confronted the refugees in this book, for the most part, predated Donald Trump's jingoism. Though legally White,[9] Arabs were lynched in the Jim Crow South, and Muslims specifically were targeted after 9/11 by national policies such as the FBI's Countering Violent Extremism education program and the Patriot Act, as well as by hate crimes.[10]

United States immigration policy has always cast immigrants as threats. Since the creation of the Department of Homeland Security in 2003, for instance, USD 333 billion has been spent on immigration enforcement.[11] Within this focus on security, refugees are the most vetted category of immigrant. The red scare and anti-Semitic rejection of Jewish refugees during World War II brought us this vetting system, which was described in 1955 by Edward Corsi, then special assistant to the State Department for Refugee Integration, as one "wholly dominated by the psychology of security" in which "refugees are investigated to death."[12]

Today, this vetting process enjoys bipartisan support. In a letter to then-President Barack Obama, former Secretaries of Homeland Security Janet Napolitano and Michael Chertoff argued that the Trump administration should not be worried about the risk refugees posed because, "so long as [the vetting process] is fully implemented and not diluted, it will allow us to safely admit the most vulnerable refugees while protecting the American."[13] The assumption that refugees are a threat requiring an undiluted vetting process goes unquestioned.

The no-expenses-spared approach to vetting and security contrasts sharply with the miserly approach to refugee assistance. As we saw in the case of Faten and Ahmed, refugees are expected to immediately become self-sufficient. This is not surprising to students of social welfare. The United States operates on the neoliberal premise that the state is not responsible for mitigating the impacts of the market.[14] Poverty is seen as an individual failure. The 1996 Welfare Reform Act, which initiated the Temporary Assistance for Needy Families (TANF) program from which Faten and Ahmed received their primary cash assistance, was launched on the premise that the poor need to be incentivized to work.[15] Scholars show that the depletion of social welfare, and of this program, is rooted in anti-Black racism and fictions of a welfare queen who benefits off the state and is unwilling to work.[16]

This system, which does not invest in those who need support, structures the human capital of refugees. Men were quickly thrust into an exploitative labor market that discredited their skills and abilities built through years of effort.

Women, by staying out of the labor market, could attend English class for longer than the men. And, in the face of household poverty, they reimagined the skills they had developed for care-work—cooking and crafting—as economic tools. But they too were thwarted in this effort by a lack of investment in family-focused policy. Families that had been selected based on chronic need and having multiple children had no support in managing these needs. Unable to thrive, facing poverty and racism—particularly harsh for women who wore the *hijab*—they also struggled.

The story of Syrian refugees in the United States is not one of empowerment. Instead, it is a story of resilience. Of how people develop creative strategies for survival at the intersections of poverty, depleted social assistance, and racism. It is a story not only of refugees, but of the American poor. And while those who sought refuge were managing this system, foreign to them, they were also dealing with pasts and presents of a war that continued to rage.

The Work of Resettlement

The United States resettlement program is a federal program with nongovernmental partnerships. Nine Voluntary Agencies (VolAgs) across the United States have agreements with the federal government to resettle refugees. VolAgs subcontract with a fluctuating number of approximately two hundred agencies across the country to resettle refugees. Refugees are allocated through a lottery system conducted in Washington DC, in which the agencies specify the number of arrivals each agency can handle and what kinds of humanitarian issues they can support.[17] Unless a refugee has a family member or a friend they want to join, they go where they are allocated. The agencies receive limited federal assistance to handle resettlement, which is meant to occur within the first ninety days after refugees' arrival, termed the "Resettlement and Placement" period (R&P). From the federal government, the agency receives, per refugee, USD 975 in overhead and an additional USD 975 in "Welcome Money" that must be spent on *that* refugee, as well as USD 200 in flex money to be spent on any refugee in need.

IRIS, the resettlement agency which received Faten and Ahmed, was located in the quiet neighborhood of East Rock in New Haven, where homes with pitched, wood-trimmed New England roofs are painted brilliant blues and whites. On the sidewalks, mostly White couples, often affiliated with Yale, pushed strollers or followed their dogs past overpriced Italian grocers. By contrast, the new families were placed at the periphery of the segregated city, in neighborhoods that were predominantly African American and Latinx where apartments were more affordable. While the houses in those neighborhoods had the same architecture as those in East Rock, there the pitched roofs sagged, their trim missing in places, and the paint had dingier hues.

The agency was on the second floor of a two-story building (it would later expand to the first floor as well). Its narrow lobby—really a wide corridor—was the site of most of the agency's day-to-day work. Its walls were plastered with flyers that were written in multiple languages including Arabic, French, Spanish, and Pashto that advertised resettlement agency events. On a given day, Syrian, Sudanese, Iraqi, Afghani, and Congolese clients crowded the lobby, sipping tea from a constantly bubbling electric kettle, chatting with their co-linguists.

Most were waiting for their caseworker to emerge from behind the locked door that led to the hallway of staff offices, so that she (almost all were women) could decipher a letter that they had received in the mail or help them figure out why their food stamps were reduced or what to do about a bill they had received from the hospital. Sometimes someone sitting in the hall would be able to interpret, but other times, if no one was there who spoke both their language and English, the caseworker would call an interpreter or the client would call a friend. In their first months, the refugees brought in piles of mail, with credit card advertisements on top of welfare renewal letters, unable to differentiate what could be thrown away from what was consequential for the continuation of their assistance.

English classes were also offered by the agency—beginner, intermediate, and advanced. The largest, the beginner class, was held in the multipurpose room, where walls featured posters of ABCs and a map of the United States, and where surfaces were always littered with pens and papers and bits of thread from sewing workshops held in the same space. A computer in the corner was often the only one that new arrivals had access to for filling out online forms or performing other tasks that couldn't be completed on their phones. An adjoining daycare that at times had a year-long waiting list was available to a select few of the English-language learners who applied for it and who had children between two and five years old. The multipurpose room was also the site of the cultural orientation session, a repeat of the session on the United States rules and norms that they had learned in Jordan or Turkey or in other countries of immediate refuge. It included reminders against domestic violence, polygamy, or leaving children unattended.

It was in this multipurpose room that Faten, Ahmed, and the other refugees would attend a "Protect your Rights" session led by the head of the agency the day after Faten and Ahmed's arrival. People from Somalia, Congo, Eritrea, Sudan, Guatemala, Iraq, Afghanistan, and Syria were all taught to deescalate, and to call the police and the agency if they were attacked in the street. However, while many were indeed attacked over the coming year, they did not call the police. Coming from authoritarian countries, they were distrustful of the police. But also, their interactions with American police were not positive. Many had already received traffic tickets, unfamiliar with the state's driving rules. After one family's home was overrun with dogs after a wellness check gone wrong, it was further confirmed that the police were something to be avoided.[18]

The bulk of the agency's work, particularly during the R&P period, happened outside its offices. During this time, the caseworker accompanies the family to the government offices that make them legible to the state and its services. This involves hours of waiting on curved plastic chairs bolted to the floors of various government buildings: the US Social Security Administration, the school board, the primary care clinic, and the state's Department of Social Services (DSS). There, the new arrivals were registered for Medicare, SNAP (Supplementary Nutrition Assistance Program), colloquially called food stamps, and importantly, TANF.

During their first visit to DSS, Fawaz and Wedad, a couple from Latakia, and their three children who were in the United States at the time (a fourth would join later) waited to register for benefits. As we sat in the waiting area, their son, Ibrahim, then twenty-three-years-old, was fidgety. He kept hitting his younger brother on the head, acting like it wasn't him when his brother protested. Wedad yelled at him to stop. Together they made a loud commotion in Arabic. "Why are we being stared at?" he asked me. I told him maybe it's because we're speaking loudly in Arabic. He replied, "So we're here because we are refugees, but why are all these other people here?" Around us, those in the room were predominantly non-White. I explained that these were people who needed help too. "So now we're grouped with them?" he retorted.

I was taken aback, responding that there was no shame in it. I was struck by the racism underlying his comment, as the DSS office was in a Black neighborhood and others in the room were mostly Black or non-White. Like many other immigrants, including Black immigrants to the United States, anti-African American racism is common.[19] It's learned even before arrival through movies and media, and after arrival through pervasive anti-Black messaging. Arabic communities themselves are not immune to colorism and racism—it is common for beauty to be synonymized to Whiteness. There are also slurs used in some households—referring to Black people as "*abeed*" or "slave." In that moment, it struck me that though new arrivals, including Ibrahim, were both non-White and poor, they had never before been oppressed for their racial identity. Many new arrivals would not learn to identify with others who were minoritized, nor would they identify their own position within the American racial hierarchy.

Living as a Math Problem

By refugees' third month in the country, the agency assistance runs out. In the first week of a refugees' arrival, they're informed of this fact using a budget sheet, illustrated with clip art to overcome the language barrier. Next to a house is the rent expenditure, a bulb for electricity, a stove for gas, a bus for the bus pass, and a flip phone for the family phone bill. The top row is labeled with the next four months, which the Syrians relabeled from "February" and

"March" to "second month" and "third month" as they are commonly referred to, or by their Arabic names of *Shubat* or *Athar*. Each box, corresponding to an expense and a month, listed the family's expenses.

The largest expense was rent, and the agency expected new arrivals to spend half of their TANF assistance on rent, with the agency covering the rest with Welcome Money. After three months, the Welcome Money ran out and the family was on their own. The agency, which was popular in the affluent area and benefited from proximity to Yale, had additional nongovernmental funds at their disposal; in fact, more than sixty percent of their budget came from donations. If a family struggled, the agency could bail them out. However, this wasn't advertised or promised, and the agency policy was to end financial assistance after the Welcome Money was depleted or shortly thereafter.

The new arrivals would need to secure an income, a task that fell initially on men, who were expected to be the family's breadwinners. As the case of Ahmed showed, however, the only jobs available to them with limited English-language skills was low-wage unskilled work. These were the kinds of jobs that Arne Kalleberg has termed "bad jobs," which do not pay a living wage, have limited benefits, and provide almost no prospects of upward mobility.[20] This reality posed the problem of making ends meet. As Zachareya, a father of two boys put it, "in my country, you work, and you live. Here living is a math problem."

The contours of the math problem surfaced when Nader, a Syrian-American white-collar professional, complained at a fundraising dinner about the cohort of refugees who arrived in the summer of 2015. "They don't want to work," he told attendees. On a WhatsApp group that included both Syrian Americans, or the "old guard," and the "newcomers," or refugee men, he explained that a factory owner had offered newcomers jobs. The newcomers' response was to ask, "is it full time?" and "what's the pay?" Nader felt that these were inappropriate questions to be asked by people who complained about a lack of available work. The potential employer responded that the pay would be USD 9.60 an hour, minimum wage in Connecticut at the time, and full time. "All check?" came another response, meaning was the work on the books? "Yes," the factory owner responded. The thread went dead after that. "They just want a handout," Nader said, shrugging.

But the story of *why* the men responded as they did is more complicated, illustrating the inadequacy of low-wage jobs to enable the recipient to secure a living wage. Minimum wage was less than half of the living wage required in New Haven, which the MIT calculator puts at USD 28.64 an hour for a family of four. The new arrivals needed to get creative. TANF benefits were limited to eighteen months, so they tried to keep TANF while having other sources of income. Meanwhile, the DSS monitored their accounts and assets. If they were paid on-the-books and exceeded the poverty line of USD 24,500 a year for a family of four, or a little more than USD 2,000 a month, their TANF assistance would be suspended. The pay rate of USD 9.60 an hour on-the-books would bring refugees dangerously close to this number. Though they wouldn't be making a living wage, if they were a dollar over the federal poverty line, they'd be considered non-poor and would lose the TANF top-off that kept them afloat.[21]

However, if new arrivals worked entirely off the books for "cash," they would not be eligible to receive "*el-Tax*," which was what they called the Earned Income Tax Credit (EITC), a cash subsidy allocated to all working low-income families in the United States. Often considered by low-income families to be a normal part of their tax return rather than state assistance, the lump-sum amount has been shown to be one of the most effective components of the United States' safety net in lifting low-income families over the poverty line, as well as being the one that reaches the most people.[22] Through the EITC, a family with two or three children that earned between USD 14,000 and USD 19,000 could receive up to USD 6,000, the largest sum of money that most of the new arrivals, and most of the American poor, would have at their disposal at any moment in time.

The policy goal of "self-sufficiency," or non-reliance on government assistance, pushes new arrivals into low-income jobs where they cannot secure a living wage. This has the unintended consequence of discouraging "self-sufficiency" definitionally—it encourages the reliance on government assistance, not because people don't want to work, but because they cannot make ends meet from work. EITC, by contrast, incentivizes on-the-books work. Like everyone who looks for a job, low-income people in the United States evaluate each opportunity within the context of their resources and constraints—childcare needs, chronic health issues, the conditions of the work itself. They also do complicated calculations in the face of layered yet inadequate state benefits.

Importantly, even as they managed this math problem, resettled refugees in the United States were a privileged case of both immigrant and poor. Among immigrants, they are the only ones to have access to TANF. And many citizens of the United States face barriers to accessing TANF due to lifetime limits that restrict receipt of this benefit to a maximum of five years and the arduous nature of the application, leading them to realize that "welfare is dead," as Kathryn Edin and Luke Shafer describe in their book *$2.00 a Day*.[23] What's more, in Connecticut, the amount provided by TANF far exceeded welfare payments in other parts of the United States, like the USD 309 per month offered in Idaho, regardless of family size, or the USD 225.96 average per family in Missouri. However, to live this privileged experience of American poverty was to be stuck in place with limited prospects of upward mobility. The case of Zafir demonstrates the reality of finding a job in a stratified labor market with a tattered safety net.

The Insufficiency of Self-Sufficiency

The first time Zafir ever drove a car was to take his 2005 Kia Sedona off the salesman's lot, a week after hurricane Jonas hit New Haven with a foot of snow. His driving lesson consisted of a lap around the parking lot watching Amjad's feet. Amjad and Zafir had known each other from Homs, having grown up in the same neighborhood. Whereas Amjad had worked in construction and had his own tile shop, thirty-five-year-old Zafir was a butcher and restaurant owner; he prepared and sold both raw and freshly grilled meat, a traditional combination in Syria.

Zafir purchased the car after he was fired from his first stable job in America. He'd found the job—a dishwasher at a craft butchery in Westport, Connecticut—through the agency's employment office. Zafir loved the USD 11.50 an hour pay rate, which was almost USD 2 more than the minimum wage. He bragged about how the employer seemed happy with his work and promised that if Zafir learned some English, he would promote him to butcher. It was extremely rare for refugees to secure work in their line of business, so Zafir was elated to be working at a place that resembled the business he had owned, where he could put his know-how and skills to good use. Even though the coworkers that Zafir interacted with most often in the back of the kitchen were all other immigrants, which made practicing English difficult, and even though he could not attend English class because of his work schedule, he saw a future in that promise.

However, the commute from New Haven to Westport by public transit required two buses and a train, taking an hour and a half door-to-door on a good day, compared to the forty minutes it would have taken by car. On a Sunday in January, the same January that superstorm Jonas hit, the bus was not running, and Zafir got caught in icy rain on his walk to New Haven's Union Station. Lacking a good coat, by the time he got there he was soaked and numb from the cold. And to top it off, the train was delayed.

He called to explain to his colleague, who spoke Arabic and a little more English than Zafir, that he was not going to be able to make it to work that day. Zafir wonders whether his explanation may have been lost in translation. The employer terminated him immediately. Zafir had missed work a few times before, once when his father-in-law died suddenly in Jordan at the age of sixty-five, and again when his eight-year-old daughter went into surgery for a chronic condition. Still, he did not expect this reaction from his employer. He thought he had been doing well and that he was well liked.

This all happened six months into Zafir's resettlement, meaning that the family had depleted its Welcome Money. Zafir had been working at this job full-time for three months, which took him off welfare, a fact of which he was very proud. He was the only one of the new arrivals not on welfare at the time.

His food stamps had also been reduced, proportional to the increase in his pay. The loss of work meant that Zafir needed to go back on welfare and full food stamps. However, this required his employer to issue a letter as to why he was terminated. As TANF was a benefit intended to incentivize work, if the DSS suspected that you had lost your job for being a bad worker, you no longer qualified for the benefit.

When Zafir went to apply to get his welfare reinstated, he learned that his employer had reported his reason for termination as negligence and consistent absence from work. As a result, DSS would not reinstate Zafir's welfare money. Meanwhile, Zafir's family had no income to pay rent, and his food stamps had not been reinstated. On a visit to his house, he swung open his fridge to show me its bare shelves. He turned to the resettlement agency to ask for help, but they were unsympathetic. Encapsulating their position is one agency employee's email on the matter:

> Did this guy, without English, know how incredibly lucky he was to have full time work, in his field no less!?
>
> The final straw, after multiple no-shows / no-calls, was his explaining through an interpreter that he couldn't go to work on their busiest day because "it was raining."
>
> We'll try to plug someone else into this job. But we have to explain as a united front that IRIS cannot offer employment assistance to people who are failing to meet minimum job requirements and hurting the chances of other refugees.[24]

The agency refused to provide any assistance to Zafir. They let it be known to him, and set an example for others, that losing a "good" job would not be tolerated. Zafir, who spoke no English, was on his own to prove that he could not attend work due to circumstances beyond his control and that his employer was wrong to terminate him. Cobbling together interpreters, he made trips to the hospital for his and his children's medical records, which showed that his hospital visits far outnumbered the days of work that he missed. Though he did not get his job back, DSS reinstated his welfare money, USD 908 for his family of six, which was USD 292 less than the rent check he had to pay, before utilities.

This loss of a job is what put Zafir behind the steering wheel of a car he could not drive. When Zafir heard of a Turkish mosque-goer who was looking for a delivery driver for his pizzeria, he jumped at the opportunity. The job, which was entirely off the books, would pay USD 9.50 an hour, ten cents below minimum wage. When the employer, through a translator, asked Zafir whether he had a car, Zafir lied and said that he did. New to the country and to having a social security number, he lacked the credit that would allow him to buy a car on installments. So, he had to find someone to borrow money from. Another mosque-goer, from the Syrian old guard, gave him a USD 2,000 loan. They agreed that Zafir would pay him back when he got *El Tax* in April.

Zafir found the car through another Arab contact who worked in used car sales. Amjad, who had also recently acquired a car from the same lot, drove him to pick it up. Though neither man had a valid license, Amjad taught Zafir how to move his feet on the pedals.[25] After a few laps, Zafir set his Waze app to "no highways" and drove off the lot and into his new job delivering pizzas. During the next year, he would get into two car accidents.

As the email from the resettlement agency employee highlights, without English Zafir had little chance of becoming a butcher himself. Though he was dishwasher at a butchery, both the agency, and he himself, thought this was the closest he'd get to his actual profession. He was also dealing with vulnerabilities produced by the resettlement process. His family qualified for resettlement precisely *because* his daughter needed surgery that she could not receive in Jordan. But when his daughter had surgery, he was penalized for being there with her. They were resettled not only because they were victims of a war, but also because they had been in a precarious position in countries of immediate refuge. Zafir, for instance, had for weeks been imprisoned and forced into the notorious al-Azraq camp after working without documents. However, when his father-in-law died of a heart attack due to a lack of adequate medical care in Jordan, and after watching his home in Homs get bombed in a YouTube video, Zafir was fired for not showing up at work.

What's more, as the families managed these burdens, they would also struggle with a social assistance system structured to err on the side of protecting the state against the misuse of funds rather than on the side of the poor against hunger. He had to *prove* his right to any social assistance, the minimal welfare and food stamps the country offered. And, after he got those reinstated, he'd have to balance that welfare income with income from work by committing what the state would likely call welfare fraud. He had to drive without a license due to the unavailability, at the time, of an Arabic exam. For refugees to survive in the United States, they needed to bend the laws. And, getting caught, even on a misdemeanor (which they could incur for driving without a license), could derail their application for citizenship.

Immersed in the simultaneity of this aggression, of this poverty, the men and women needed to figure out how to manage. Part of that involved shifting their labor, as women and men.

Shifting Labor

Amjad, who went with Zafir to pick up his car, was, like Zafir, working a menial job. Amjad, as you'll remember from the introduction of this book, was once was a contractor who made tiles in Syria, and now, in the United States, was working as a janitor at a fiber glass insulation factory. Though Amjad hoped that he would be able to work in a field similar to what he had done in Syria, the first months in the United States were a letdown. He had a few off-the-books odd jobs working to tile gas stations, but they weren't regular. And, when he did find a job on a construction site, he was told he needed OSHA certification—a complex process, particularly for a man who was also illiterate in Arabic. If he wanted to work without certification, he'd have to work off the books. Knowing the hazards of construction sites, this seemed like too risky a prospect. With all of this in mind, Amjad took the janitorial position, the first safe job he could find. But he was frustrated, explaining,

> I want to work. But I am new here. We just got here. We don't understand anything, but you want to push me, *tedfeshooni*, to work. So, we work whatever, *hayallah*. Most work in restaurants, doing whatever . . . Everyone is working against their will. No one is happy. In other countries, they allow us to study, to get assistance, they say you're not allowed to work so you can learn. Not here.

Amjad compared his resettlement to that of family in Canada who were supported financially by the government for their first year, with the prospect of enrolling in welfare thereafter. It's not that Amjad wanted to stay on welfare, he explained, but he felt that he hadn't been given time to reorient, to try to learn the language, to try to get the certifications he needed to do the job he'd been trained for. The self-sufficiency imperative pushed Amjad into a dead-end job. As he put it, "the factory that I'm working at, even if I worked the rest of my life there, I am not going anywhere." Amjad could not speak to his colleagues—none of whom spoke Arabic. And he was isolated for most of the day anyway, working on the floor alone. A year into working there, unsurprisingly, his English had not improved.

Amjad supplemented his income by working off the books fixing cars. The small parking area behind his building—which only had three apartments—was packed with cars owned by co-ethnics, which got him into trouble with his neighbors. Amjad hadn't known anything about cars before, but he had an interest in them and was good with his hands. He hoped he could make it a full-time business one day. But for that he would need to acquire enough money to rent a shop and to acquire equipment. Unlike the immigrants of an earlier time, or even those in dense co-ethnic neighborhoods, Amjad had few opportunities to build his own economic capital.

Meanwhile, Amjad's work meant that he had less time to do things like take his children to school in the case of an emergency or to their medical appointments. When he owned a shop in Syria, he could close it down or leave it open under the supervision of his brother or one of his workers. But now, without this flexibility, he could not do any of that. Unlike the other women in this study, Amjad's wife, Rima, had grown up in an exceptionally conservative family. When I asked her if she'd ever climbed Jabal Qaison, which sits in the center of Damascus, she confided that she'd never left her neighborhood in Homs before the war began. "I'd never gone out on my own at all," she laughed. Other Syrian women were as taken aback by this information as I was. But now there was an imperative for her to go out on her own. As Amjad put it, "what if something happens to the kids while I'm at work?"

With the help of an agency volunteer, Rima would learn to use the bus. And then she'd begin to attend English class at the agency. While the demands of the self-sufficiency imperative were met by their spouses, women, including Rima, were able to attend English class. Rima reached an intermediate level of English, as did several of the other women in this study. At this level she was able, with difficulty, to communicate with service providers like her son's teacher or the resettlement agency. These are tasks that her husband, without any English, was unable to do.

Her ability to communicate in basic English reduced her isolation in part by facilitating the mundane day-to-day tasks of buying groceries, getting on the bus, paying bills, and accessing service providers. It also gave her hope that five years later, when she became eligible to take the citizenship exam, which had to be taken in English, she would be able to understand the questions.

The English classes themselves also became a social event. The women shared tea during their breaks, and on Fridays when there was no class, they held get-togethers, preparing meals of yogurt and bread *fatta* or eggs and *falafel* to share alongside strong Arabic coffee and black tea. These were spaces to unwind and crack jokes while listening to the latest in Arabic pop music, as their youngest, preschool-aged children played in front of them. These Friday events rotated between their homes and sometimes turned into a party with dancing to celebrate a birth or family events such as siblings' marriages in Syria or in Jordan. It was here too that important information was exchanged: information about sales or how to use Electronic Benefit Transfer (EBT) cards, but also information about elections or experiences of racism. For instance, it was at one such event that the women would gather around Afaf, a fifty-four-year-old mother of twelve, when she got news that her daughter's resettlement was put on hold by the travel ban.

English was imagined, particularly in these early stages, as a pathway into a dream future of good jobs. Sarah, for instance, expressed a desire to secure her certificate of high school equivalency. She contemplated the possibility that she could go to college and secure a high-paying job one day. Narjis, a twenty-year-old mother of two, told her mother back in Syria that she wanted to "become a doctor," which led to an international game of telephone that ended in congratulations from her cousins, who thought she had already begun her training as a physician.

But, while the women dreamed of high-status jobs, they were faced with the harsh realities of household poverty, a dearth of resources to support them in their pursuit of this dream—particularly in terms of childcare services and the immediate need for additional household income. Even with all of the work the men were doing to stay afloat, income and welfare was not enough. To be poor in the United States is to worry about eviction, feeding children, keeping them warm. In the face of this poverty, the women took on income-earning labor that fell far short of their lofty dreams.

Even still, their presence in English class, and even this new use of their time for earning income, meant that while the men were experiencing the erasure of their histories and an inability to translate those histories in meaningful ways for the United States' labor market, the women, as the next section will further draw out, were able to use their abilities in new, economically profitable ways. In the context of family poverty, this was yet another creative strategy to keep their families afloat. However, and unfortunately, while the women did gain crucial language skills and were able to express their existing skills in new ways, these gains, including language learning, were not linear. The analogy of Sisyphus pushing the rock is one that has been overused in descriptions of working one's way out of American poverty, because it is apt. In the absence of state support, womens' progress would be thwarted, their aspirations unrealized.

"He Can't Do It on His Own"

Rajaa, dressed in her best taupe *manteau* and a brown *hijab*, stood at a table, smiling. In front of her lay baby items she had made, one a fishnet pattern in blue and navy thread, another with a pink pom-pom skirt and matching hat. She also made red flower pins that were selling for five dollars apiece. Next to Rajaa's table, at this fair that was put on by an NGO on 74th and Broadway in New York City, Sarah was selling her *ma'amoul* cookies, buttery, date-filled, and stamped into neat cylinders. The first time I had Sarah's *ma'amoul* was when she pulled them out of her luggage on her first night in the United States. Each was wrapped in folded wax paper, prepared for her potential visitors, of which I was one of the first.

A fair attendee perused Rajaa's items. "What size is this one?" she asked her, picking up the pom-pom skirt. "It's for a twenty-one-month-old baby," Rajaa replied. The woman asked about the price, and Rajaa again responded, "fifty dollars." Having attended English classes on and off during the past two years, she did not need my help translating. "I could understand everything they said," she would tell me on the ride home, "whereas in the beginning I would understand nothing."

Armed with some English, even a limited amount, Rajaa felt more capable. Later that day, when we'd escape to the basement of the building so that Sarah could breastfeed her daughter, Rajaa would turn to us and say, "this is my dream." "What is?" I asked her. "To be a businesswoman. To have my own business." Although she felt she'd sold the children's dresses too cheaply—only USD 50 apiece for what took a few days' work—she made USD 4 profit on each on the red flower pins. Those only took ten to fifteen minutes each. Rajaa would go home with over USD 450 dollars in profit, the most she'd ever made herself. She almost sold out. And Sarah did sell out, making USD 250 for one hundred *ma'amoul* cookies. As we drove home, the women were on a high, chattering and excited.

Importantly, Rajaa was not the only woman in her family to take on the role of entrepreneur after the war. For Rajaa, the moment of selling at the fair was a culmination of a lifelong journey. While there had never been an expectation that she would be a breadwinner for her household, her parents had nevertheless taught their daughters skills, in keeping with the adage "you never know what life will bring." Her sisters were taught to do hair, a skill they shared with their mother. And while Rajaa was selling at this fair in the United States because her husband's income had become insufficient, her mother and sisters in Syria had opened a salon. The war took away many of the local businesses, and prices were sky-high. Hairdressing, however, which relied on labor, remained lucrative. Across the globe, the sisters were confronting different kinds of family poverties.

Majid, Rajaa's husband, was a chef who worked in a Syrian restaurant in Saudi Arabia before the war. He made good money there and sent home remittances, which had enabled them to build their own home. For the kids, this meant keeping up with the latest fads and even owning a laptop computer. For Rajaa, it meant that she was solely responsible for all of the caregiving and managing of the household. As she put it, "In Syria I took care of the house, and he earned the money. Here I have to help him out. He can't do it on his own."

Like Rajaa, the other Syrian women, recognizing that they too needed to step into this role of helping to earn an income, drew on their histories. While the men's skills were being diminished due to the immediate push into the labor market to satisfy the goal of self-sufficiency, the women's skills were being reimagined. This often centered on food. Syrian techniques of rolling cabbage and rice *mahshi* cigarette-thin, or shaping *kibbeh* filled with ground beef and pine nuts into tea-drop dumplings, led to profitable catering parties. A local NGO hired some of the women to give cooking classes and host pay-by-the-plate dinners. Afaf, a mother of eight children, four of whom were in the United States, also prepared food that the resettlement agency purchased from her for arriving families.

But the story of women's work and their English learning includes three important limitations. First, there are the limitations imposed by the women and men's expectations for their own labor, which maintained definitions of what constituted men's and women's work. Second, the *hijabi* women feared racist violence, which sometimes hindered their comfort in being out in public. Finally, and most importantly, women faced structural obstacles to gaining and expressing their human capital due to the structure of assistance in the United States.

Within families, the lines between men's and women's labor were maintained and delineated—where any breadwinning labor performed by women, or caregiving labor performed by men, was framed as "helping" the other partner. In Faten's case, for instance, she had "left [Ahmed] behind," since she was earning college credits and working as an interpreter, while he was washing dishes. But, when Faten was annoyed with Ahmed, she wondered why she "helped" him come up with extra income, saying, "I should just let him fend for himself." And, when she was at work or at school and he was taking care of their son, he was "helping her."

Women drew the line strictly on the kind of work they would take. The Syrian women were already the targets of snide remarks. "How could you accept to cook for pay?" one Syrian-American woman who had been in the United States for over twenty years asked a group of Syrian women disdainfully at a dinner. And, while the women brushed off this remark (though they did not forget it), they had no intention of working like their husbands did. While the men were supporting their families, a noble task, it was unacceptable for women to do such lowbrow work. As Rajaa put it, "I'm not going to lie to you, I don't want to be in a situation where I'm out there the way he [Majid, her husband] is. I am not used to it."

And when the poverty was so intense that this rule needed to be broken, it was particularly emotional. Najlaa and Nabil, parents of five children, were faced with this reality. A few months after their arrival, Nabil was diagnosed with cancer. He was not able to work but did not qualify for social security because cancer isn't considered a chronic condition. The resettlement agency helped the family for a year, but then came Trump's victory and the subsequent travel ban. Because agencies receive federal funding per arriving refugee, with the decrease in the number of refugees arriving, agency funding fell and so did the ability to assist this family. "What do you want me to do?" Nabil asked the agency caseworker who relayed this news. "Your wife has to work," the caseworker responded. Najlaa retorted, "and who's going to take care of my sick husband and five kids?" In the end, Nabil worked part-time, helping out at a shop downtown when he felt up for it. Najlaa did too, but she avoided Arab businesses, saying, "I can't work outside like that, what will people say? You know how they are. They'll talk about me behind my back."

Another factor limiting the building and expression of women human capital is the increase in hate crimes and incidents against wearers of the *hijab*. As a result, the women got more and more wary about being in public. Narjis, for instance, prayed under her breath each time she went to the C-Town Supermarket, right across the street from her apartment, fearing that someone would attack her while she bought her groceries. Her fear was not unwarranted. Three days after the presidential election, on November 12, 2016, Zafir was driving Ghada, who wears a *hijab*, and their children back from Walmart in the same Kia Sedona. They were at a red light when another car cut them off. The driver was yelling. Zafir and Ghada, who had little command of the English language, could only make out "fuck" and "home." Zafir clenched the steering wheel with his right hand and held down the horn with his left one. He was prepared to fight if the man got out of the car. He thought about the man having a weapon. Eventually, the man drove off. As Zafir put it the fear was particularly bad as his family, like others seeking refuge, had "nowhere to go." He explained,

> We escaped from our countries, from war, and we came here to find comfort and security and a future for our children. We are Muslim. My wife wears a *hijab*, and my daughter too [. . .] And Trump is a divisive person. I am afraid of what this will mean for our family's future in America.

However, the final and most pressing limitation to women's building and expression of human capital is the structure of assistance and the lack of investment. First of all, DSS did not recognize the work that women did as *work*. On one of many visits to the DSS, Rajaa and I sat, like everyone else, on chairs facing the bulletproof glass that the caseworkers sat behind. An hour into the visit, after we'd stood in a long line outside, Rajaa wondered aloud, as I'd hear almost every refugee in the United States wonder: why did the United States take in refugees if they had no intention of helping them? But then she pointed to an elderly Black man sitting across from us in a wheelchair, asking "And why aren't they helping that man? Where is the compassion in this country?" Rajaa, a particularly bright woman, recognized that her assistance and the man's assistance were linked, and that both of their social contracts had been broken.

A year after her arrival, Rajaa was required to visit DSS once a month to show them she was actively searching for work by submitting a "Work Verification" form. The form was a calendar on which she needed to document thirty-five hours a week during which she was actively working, searching for work, or preparing for work. Her English class attendance counted for twenty hours. But for the other fifteen, she would not be allowed to list her crochet work or her care for her daughter, who had an anxiety disorder. TANF only counts paid labor for which there is a paystub; none of the men's entrepreneurial activities would count either.

What's more, while DSS has limited childcare assistance for working mothers, women couldn't even access that due to their nonworking status in the eyes of DSS. And, unlike other countries where there is public childcare support and child tax subsidies to support care, there are no such programs in the United States at the time of this writing; so, when the women—Narjis, Rajaa, Sarah, Faten, and Rima—had babies, there was no support for them.

Neither the resettlement agency nor the city's English classes allowed children in the classes, as they'd disrupt other students learning. So the women dropped out of class. Sarah joked, "Trump might be able to stop the Syrians from arriving, but we're going to fight the ban from within." Having children was a way of settling down, but due to the structure of resettlement policy, it was also an obstacle to the women's ability to progress in their classes and economic endeavors. While women did experience more gains in human capital than the men, and while these victories could bring joy, they were weak reprieves from the crushing poverty that left them in a constant state of anxiety. Rajaa spent nights lying in bed awake, racked with worry about how they would be able to make ends meet. Sarah's family would at one point be threatened with eviction. Their work, and all the women's work, was helping to make ends meet, but it was an irregular top-off to their husband's bad full-time jobs.

And, in the end, the women's improvements in English were limited. Five years after her arrival, Rajaa went to a lawyer to apply for the citizenship exam, along with all of the other families who'd arrived with her. Only two women, Faten and another who already spoke fluent English before arriving in the United States due to having attended college, had enough English to apply. Everyone else did not.

———

To understand Syrian refugee experiences in the United States is to understand choices made at the intersection of the self-sufficiency imperative, their position as racialized Syrian refugees, and gender stratifications both within the families and in United States policy. Refugees in the United States are expected to be self-sufficient, to enter the labor market immediately. It is through this system and its lack of *investment* that the United States structures the human capital of refugees.

Fulfilling their role as breadwinners, men who were once contractors and plumbers and carpenters became low-income workers on the bottom rungs of a labor market that does not offer a living wage. Women, by contrast, stayed out of the labor market as caregivers and as a result were able to build new language skills and to find new uses for old skills—particularly cooking but also handcrafts. However, these endeavors were stopped short by limited access to resources and structured by federal policy, as well as racism against women who wear the *hijab*, which diminished their feelings of safety while in public.

That the refuge families in this chapter had to scramble to find ways to creatively resist their descent into poverty is a feature and not a bug of United States resettlement policy, a policy that does not *invest* in people. This policy draws on the broader social service system, which has long treated poverty as an individual failure. The experience of these once middle-class people in pursuit of refuge, who are strangers to this system, clarifies the ways in which the system diminishes human potential not just for them, but for other beneficiaries regardless of their immigration status.

4

Canadian Integration

Two months before Zafir and Ghada arrived in New Haven, their relatives, Nizar and Somaya, arrived at Pearson Airport in Toronto. The two families shared a lot in common. Nizar was Ghada's uncle, but Ghada and Somaya were closer in age. Whenever I visited Somaya, she insisted that we call Ghada with her phone on speaker, each time exclaiming loudly, "*Dooodi habibti*," punctuated by her easy, high-pitched laugh, a laugh that I could sometimes hear down the corridor as I approached her door.

In Syria, the two families were neighbors. They both lived in Homs, off of al-Qahira Street, the city's main thoroughfare, in the al-Khalidiya neighborhood. Like Zafir, Nizar owned a butcher shop and restaurant where he sold raw and grilled meats. And, while Nizar and Somaya only had three children whereas Zafir and Ghada had five, both families had a child with special medical needs. In 2012, the families fled Syria after the explosions of bombs and gunfire replaced their neighborhood's usual cacophony of beeping traffic and the calls of vendors. They went to Jordan, where they'd find respite from the fighting, but where they would also deal with their undocumented status and the emotional and financial trauma of losing their homes and businesses in war.

While in Jordan, both families received calls from the UNHCR asking if they'd like to be considered for resettlement. For Zafir and Ghada, the call came for resettlement in the United States, whereas for Nizar and Somaya it came for resettlement to Canada. And while the process for Syrian refugees traveling to Canada would speed up under the leadership of Justin Trudeau, at the time, under the leadership of Stephen Harper in Canada, and with Barack Obama still President in the United States, the two families' processes took a similar eighteen months. Nizar and Somaya arrived in Canada in May 2015, whereas Zafir and Ghada arrived in New Haven three months later.

Five hundred miles apart, under these two adjacent countries' drastically different resettlement policies, the families' otherwise parallel lives would diverge. While the United States aims for refugees to achieve quick self-sufficiency per the 1980 Refugee Act as described in the previous chapter, in Canada the goal of refugee resettlement is "integration" under a policy of Canadian multiculturalism. As the Canadian government's website puts it, "refugees often need help to settle," and to that end the government provides services to help "refugees adjust to life in Canada," including income assistance intended to cover rent and other basic expenses for the first year. The goal is for the refugee to learn both "English and French so that they have the skills to live in Canada and search for and find jobs."[1]

Nizar and Somaya were government-sponsored refugees. They were resettled alongside privately sponsored refugees, whose resettlement is financed by a group of private citizens, rather than the government. For instance, Israa and Abdelhameed, parents of four who arrived in Canada in 2016, were supported by a "Group of Five," which, as the government of Canada puts it, consists of "five or more Canadian citizens or permanent residents who have arranged to sponsor a refugee living abroad to come to Canada."[2] The Group of Five, in addition to providing financial support for the new arrivals' first six months in the country in an amount equivalent to government support, was also committed to providing moral and logistical support by helping them find a place to live and connecting them to government services.[3] Of the 29,125 Syrian refugees who arrived in Canada between 2015 and 2016, 13,460 people were resettled with half year or full-year support from private sponsors.[4] Importantly, the goal for privately sponsored refugees is the same as for those sponsored by the government: integration through language learning.

Nizar and Somaya, who did not have private sponsors, would arrange their own housing. They were placed in a hotel by COSTI, a nongovernmental organization tasked with resettling refugees who came through the country's government sponsorship program. They spent their first month searching for their apartment, settling on a modern three-bedroom high rise in Mississauga, one of Toronto's suburbs. Unlike their relatives in New Haven, Nizar and Somaya had the freedom to settle anywhere in Ontario while retaining all of their benefits. Their neighbors were other immigrants, and the neighborhood featured dozens of Arab grocers and restaurants that could be spotted from Burmanthorpe Road, Mississauga's main drag.

The couple felt well-supported in finding an apartment and settling down. Like their relatives in the United States, as government-sponsored refugees, they received welcome money in the form of a "gift" that covered their start-up costs. However, unlike their relatives, they had access to other resources. One was a loan to cover their security deposit. Another was new furniture "with the plastic still on it." The real differences came, however, in the cash assistance—unlike Zafir and Ghada, who had to rely on the welfare system immediately, Somaya and Nizar's assistance was refugee-specific and exceeded their rent. This refugee-specific assistance, combined with the Canada Child Benefit (CCB), which is allocated monthly to all families inversely to their income (including both government- and privately sponsored refugees), meant that Nizar and Somaya had their needs covered for the first year, as is intended by the Canadian system.

Supported by these benefits, Nizar and Somaya both attended state-sponsored English classes each morning, a short walk from their home. Though the family did not need it, since their three children were school age, the English classes had an adjoining free childcare facility. After a year of lessons, the couple's English remained halting, but enabled them to have basic phone conversations, an impossibility for their New Haven counterparts. Somaya, for instance, made and fielded phone calls advocating for her parents, who were living in a studio apartment in Jordan with her brother and his children. She was in search of a private sponsor to help her fund their travel to Canada. Her jovial demeanor dimmed as she explained that this was her one discomfort about living in Canada: that her parents couldn't enjoy it as well.

As a result of these differences in support, while Zafir was working as a delivery driver without a license and earning below minimum wage in Connecticut, Nizar was a chef at a restaurant in Mississauga. He was able to wait for a suitable job due to the cash assistance received from the government. He worked part-time, by choice, to avoid aggravating his bad back, for which he'd also eventually receive disability assistance. But even with his part-time pay, Nizar was making CAD 15 an hour, out-earning Zafir by one-and-a-half times. He expected the pay rate to increase to CAD 20 an hour. At first, Somaya wasn't sure whether she too would work, since like Ghada, she hadn't been employed in Syria or Jordan. But then, through the English class, she heard about free training for Syrians who wanted to become hairstylists. She was considering taking the course, and in her usual cheerful tone declared, "Somaya who just cooks and cleans is over, *khalas*."

In some ways, Nizar and Somaya's experience was typical of families who arrived in Canada to a system far more generous and welcoming than the one in the United States. However, the Canadian system was also imperfect. Wael, an electrician from Homs, would struggle to take up his profession in Canada. And Israa, a nurse from Aleppo, would give up almost entirely on her dream of regaining her credentials. What's more, as her family was in part privately sponsored through a blended visa program, she had both more support in her resettlement and less autonomy over her surroundings. In order to understand the complexities of the Canadian system—both its generosity and the ways in which it falls short—it is essential to understand it as part of a broader immigration apparatus that, like all immigration systems in a rigidly bordered world, is inherently exclusionary.

The Case of Canada

Canada's policy of *integration*, like the United States' policy of self-sufficiency, did not emerge from a vacuum. Instead, it draws on longstanding and intertwined national approaches to social welfare and immigration. First, the United States and Canada are both neoliberal welfare states, as classified by Gosta Esping-Andersen in his foundational comparative work, because they operate on the principles of a free market.[5] However, while the United States began to retract social assistance in the 1970s, in Canada, social safety nets remained intact, resulting in "differences that matter" between the two systems, as Daniyal Zuberi titled his book on this comparison.[6] Workers in Canada, he showed, benefit from stronger unions and higher workplace protections in terms of unemployment benefits and maternity leaves. The country also offers universal healthcare, tax credits for low-income families with children, and generous welfare support, which together mean a higher quality of life even when comparing people who earn a similar income or who are similarly low-income.

Refugees in Canada are no exception to this rule. They all receive a full year of financial support through the state, private sponsors, or a combination. They are offered access to free language education and free skill-building classes. Free childcare services are available, though outside of major cities these were less accessible. They also benefit from Canada's other redistributive policies such as health care and the Canada Child Benefit. All of this constitutes meaningful *investment* in newcomers' ability to gain new human capital in the form of language or additional training and thus to express their existing skills.

Refugees and other recognized immigrants are met with this generosity as a result of the country's policy of Canadian multiculturalism, which seeks to integrate state-recognized immigrants into a notion of the Canadian whole. In 1971, Prime Minister Pierre Trudeau (father of future Prime Minister Justin Trudeau) stood in front of the country's parliament to announce "multiculturalism within a bilingual framework." The policy was launched in recognition of the fact that the country, which had long limited immigration through racist quotas, and which has a majority White population, was now admitting non-White immigrants. The goal of the policy was to bring new arrivals into the Canadian fold by facilitating access to citizenship and language training, with an emphasis that immigrants should be "given the chance to learn at least one of the two languages in which the country conducts its official business and its politics."[7]

Multiculturalism has become a core part of Canadian national identity since its introduction. The policy has led to important antidiscrimination measures and to the allocation of crucial resources to arriving immigrants. There is public buy-in to the idea of multiculturalism, so much so that Canada, unlike other western countries, was found to not face the so-called "progressive's dilemma," where increases in ethno-racial diversity led to reduced public commitment to redistribution.[8] However, this policy and its centrality to national identity does not mean that Canada is a utopia of racial equality and inclusion. Like other countries addressed in this book, it sits within a framework of exclusionary systems that shape the contours of national belonging.

Multiculturalism has been criticized as reinforcing White hegemony.[9] From the perspective of the First Nations, Inuit, and Métis peoples, who are indigenous to Canada, it is colonialist because it insists on integration, including of immigrants, into French and British institutions and languages.[10] Through the vehicle of multiculturalism, the Canadian state also attempts to indoctrinate notions of the Canadian "values" that non-White, non-European, immigrants are thought to lack—as captured in citizenship guides that assumed "some newcomers may lack Canadians' multicultural perspective and commitment to gender equality."[11] Himani Bannerji[12] argues that image of Canada as embracing "visible minorities" (a census designation for the non-White, including Arab immigrants) is both essentializing and obscures the institutionalized racism that *does* exist. Meanwhile, immigrants are expected to express gratitude, and these stories, particularly of refugee gratitude, as Vinh Nguyen has suggested, are held up to say, "Look, Canada is welcoming and tolerant."[13] This feeling of a need to express gratitude is observed in the narratives of the men and women in this chapter.

What's more, as Keith Banting points out, the sustainability of the political buy-in to multiculturalism is contingent on exclusionary immigration and welfare policies.[14] Canada's main immigration system is points-based, with immigrants selected based on a measure of their human capital. The policy has been criticized as reinforcing racial inequalities, class inequalities, and gendered inequalities, which all shape access to the skills that make someone eligible to travel.[15] Selecting "skilled" immigrants, however, means that newcomers are often not disproportionately in need of state benefits.[16] And, besides these skill-based immigrants and refugees, most other categories of immigrants are excluded from these benefits. What's more, Canada, surrounded on three sides by frigid ocean, severely restricts unauthorized immigration through strict visa requirements for temporary visitors[17] and policies such as the "Safe Third Country" policy, which entitles Canada to send back asylum seekers who arrive there by crossing the border with the United States. Importantly, even with these restrictions, there was consternation about refugees receiving welfare and questions as to whether they were taking resources from nationals.[18]

Despite this skill-based focus of the Canadian system, however, the system has an issue with regard to the inadequacy of skill *recognition*. Skill-based immigrants in Canada chronically face underemployment, and are systematically overeducated for the jobs they seek out.[19] Studies show that the Canadian system struggles to recognize the credentials of non-White immigrants and women in particular, resulting in their incomes lagging behind native Canadians even ten years after arrival.[20] While the Labor Ministry has attempted to create various recognition and credentialing systems, these are imperfect.[21] In this chapter, the cases of two refugees, Israa, who was once a nurse, and Wael, who was once an electrician, attest to this issue of credential recognition.

It was to this complex scaffold of policies that the Syrians in this chapter arrived in Canada. Most were admitted in the winter between 2015 and 2016, when Justin Trudeau ran for Prime Minister, including in his platform a plan to admit twenty-five thousand Syrian refugees. By 2017 he would admit close to 49,810. Under Harper, Trudeau's predecessor and opponent, very few Syrian refugees were admitted due to the fear that they would not assimilate. There were debates as to whether a *niqab* could be worn during swearing-in ceremonies.[22] There were suggestions of setting up a police hotline where Canadians could report immigrants' "barbaric cultural practices." And in 2015, the rate of hate crimes against Muslims in Canada increased by sixty percent.[23]

Despite the continued reality of this racism, the political commitment to admit Syrian refugees under Trudeau and the national buy-in through private sponsorship—which directly involved citizens in the process of refugee selection—created a warm welcome for the arriving Syrian refugees. This, coupled with the ability of new arrivals to move within the province to which they had been admitted, and therefore to move closer to co-ethnics and other immigrants, insulated them to an extent from the kinds of racist experiences reported in the United States or, as the next chapter will show, in Germany. What's more, state investment with the goal of *integration* came in the form of a year of support, language classes, and employment training unavailable to their counterparts in the United States. However, life in Canada was not without its difficulties for these men and women. Some would struggle to have their histories recognized as meaningful, and all would have to figure out, as strangers in a new country, how to manage their new context's realities and expectations.

Arriving in Canada

The Toronto Plaza Hotel is located to the northwest of the city. Outside, men took quick, shallow, puffs off cigarettes in the hotel driveway, the vice stripped of its social pleasantries by the harshness of the Canadian winter. Inside, groups of new arrivals chatted in the warmth of the hotel lobby, standing on the burgundy and eggshell patterned carpet. A group of boys ran between them after a ball.

This scene at the Plaza Hotel towards the end of February 2016 was replicated across the country, as Canadian provinces came up with creative solutions to accommodate twenty-five thousand Syrian refugees, or "newcomers," as they are called in Canada, in hotels and government buildings. The newcomers had been admitted during the prior three months through an expedited process that was part of Trudeau's making good on his campaign promise for Canada to become a world leader in confronting the Syrian refugee crisis.

Trudeau was prompted in particular by the case of Canadian Tima Kurdi, who applied to bring her brother Abdullah's family to Canada through private sponsorship. She was denied, and a few weeks later, her three-year-old nephew Alan's body washed up on a shore near Bodrum, Turkey, hours after the family of four attempted the journey to Greece.[24] The case attracted the world's attention, and Trudeau responded to the pressure to do more, announcing that newcomers would be admitted through an expedited process. While Nizar and Somaya had been vetted for over a year under Harper, new arrivals now underwent a quick three months of interviews before they boarded a flight to Canada, often from Jordan, Turkey, or Lebanon.

The first arrivals were received at the airport by the Prime Minister himself, who teared up as he welcomed them. The women in New Haven, Connecticut swooned over the moment. "Oh, if you see him cry over us," one said, to which another replied, "you can't even compare him to this one here. An orange with yarn taped on its head." On Facebook and Twitter, a Canadian children's choir's French, English, and Arabic rendition of "Tala' al-Badru 'Alayna"—a song that originated in early Islam and the prophet Muhammad's refuge in the city of Medina—went viral.[25] It became a testament to Canadian multiculturalism.

However, not everyone supported Trudeau's decision. Refugee advocates were glad that Trudeau was admitting such a large number of refugees but questioned the priority given to Syrians at the expense of other refugees who had been waiting for decades in situations of protracted displacement to come to Canada. This focus on Syrians was seen by some advocates I spoke to as anti-Black, as many of the waiting refugees were from Afghanistan and Iraq, but also from Eritrea and the Congo. And, while refugees are typically required to pay for their travel—through an International Organization for Migration travel loan—the Trudeau administration canceled this obligation, but initially only for Syrian refugees, leading again to criticism.[26]

Another source of criticism was predicated on anti-Muslim racism. Canadians questioned whether the Syrian refugees *could* assimilate into Canada and whether they should be admitted. In 2016, a survey showed that sixty-eight percent of Canadians reported feeling that immigrants should do more to "fit into" Canadian mainstream society.[27] While initially half of Canadians reported in a poll that they supported the admission of Syrian refugees, these sorts of objections would get louder over the coming years.[28] In 2019, over half of Canadians said in a poll that Canada should *not* be accepting more refugees.[29]

In addition to these concerns, refugee practitioners felt that the government was admitting too many refugees too fast. There was no precontracted housing set aside for the new arrivals, and finding houses for families of five or six in Toronto was no easy task. Temporary hotel stays turned into month-long waits, which for the newcomers represented an unwelcome elongation of their years of displacement. Resettlement workers' requests for the Canadian government to pause the Syrian arrivals were denied, with the Trudeau administration insisting on meeting resettlement targets. At one hotel Yasmine, whose family of six had been resettled from Lebanon, explained,

> We were told by the officer that we'd come here, to a home, that we might get a sponsor who would help us navigate this country. But that wasn't the case. We've been in this hotel for a month.

Still, new arrivals, including Yasmine and her husband Omar, who were parents of four from Daraa, Syria, were hopeful even in this moment of continued displacement because other things that they were told by resettlement officers did come true. While at the hotel, they had meetings with caseworkers from COSTI—the NGO tasked by the Canadian government with managing the admission of Syrian refugees—who registered them for applicable government services. At the Plaza Hotel, these intake sessions happened to the left of the lobby, in a conference room. The caseworker, himself an Eritrean who had been resettled in Canada years prior, and who spoke Arabic due to his years of displacement in Cairo, had been hired only three weeks earlier by COSTI to meet the increasing demand for processing. On this day at the end of February, he sat across from a couple who were once farmers. The man, who spoke with a deep rasp, the result of throat surgery, told the caseworker that his wife suffered from dizzy spells, and provided the ages and various health needs of each of their five children.

Based on these responses, newcomers were registered for assistance in Canada, including health care, which is universal and free, but also for disability and other long-term social services for which they qualified. Everyone else received refugee cash assistance of CAD 768 per adult, a set national amount distributed to refugees for the first twelve months of their resettlement. In addition, the refugees were given start-up funds. Yasmine and Omar referred to this money as the *hedeya*, or gift. The amount differed from family to family, again depending on need and family size, but for Yasmine and Omar it was almost CAD 6,000, which was placed in a bank account in their name.

This amount would go to cover their security deposit, first month's rent, and any other basic one-time expenses. What's more, during the first three years, if this money wasn't enough, they could access no-interest loans from the Canadian government.

Like the other refugees at the hotels, Yasmine and Omar would spend the following weeks searching for housing with the help of COSTI officials and volunteers who came to the hotels to facilitate this search. Chatter in the Plaza Hotel lobby was all about housing: would the prices go up because all of these Syrians had arrived at once in the Toronto rental market? Which was a better suburb: Mississauga, Kitchener, or Hamilton? Should they move to the suburbs or pay more money to stay in Toronto proper?

These were all questions that each family could decide for themselves, not only due to the amount of assistance—the amount of "Welcome Money" provided in the United States was similar to the start-up money provided in Canada—but due to the *structure* of the assistance. Because it is given directly to the refugee, refugee assistance in Canada allows new arrivals to make their own decisions on things big and small: where to live, how much rent to pay, and whether to invest in expensive coats or buy cheap ones they'd have to replace. It was *their* money to spend. What's more, the money's effect was amplified in that it provided ties to the broader Canadian safety net. As Yasmine put it,

> They brought us here, and they treat us like any other Canadian. Canada has *Daman Ijtima'i* (social protections), unlike in the United States. The health care system is fantastic. Here, we get the same assistance as Canadians.

Health care access, for instance, is not relegated to clinics that accept Medicaid or Medicare—as is the case for refugees in the United States—but is provided through the universal system that all Canadians access. The policy of multiculturalism means that immigrant support organizations exist across the country, as do English language classes. These are accessible and free resources that refugees can draw on regardless of which city they decide to settle in. Further, the Canadian government has partnered with banks to offer financial tools to newly arrived refugees. While Yasmine and Omar's start-up money was placed in a bank account, the newly arrived refugees in the United States would be largely unbanked for much of their initial year—both fearful about accessing a bank and unsure how money in their account would impact their government assistance. Credit cards were also available to newcomers in Canada with low interest rates, with no background checks or credit history required.

Most importantly, newly arrived refugees qualified for the Canada Child Benefit (CCB), which, due to the large size of Syrian families, became their major source of cash support. The CCB is a tax benefit for all Canadians with children. Those earning under CAD 31,711 in 2015 received an annual maximum of CAD 5,400 per child for children ages six to seventeen, and CAD 6,400 for children under six. The CCB is disbursed in monthly installments of CAD 450 to CAD 530.

On the thirteenth month after their arrival, the refugee-specific cash benefits run out. However, since they are part of the Canadian social service system, the new arrivals have access to Canadian welfare, which differs by province. "Ontario Works," as Ontario's program is named, is, like TANF in the United States, focused on getting recipients into the labor market. And, like TANF, it monitors beneficiaries' bank accounts and activities. Ontario Works will deny cash transfers to anyone who loses a job without reason, refuses to look for work, or has too much money in their account. However, the program offers higher amounts of assistance than in the United States—CAD 617 per adult—and no lifetime limits. And the government of Canada *expects* that refugees will utilize the program, writing,

> When income support from the government or private sponsors ends after twelve months, in most cases, it is a normal occurrence for some refugees to transition to provincial or territorial social assistance support.[30]

Moreover, even as new arrivals in Canada transition to welfare and experience a decrease in their assistance, they are still firmly supported by the safety net provided by the CCB money and the other services that keep them afloat. And, as I'll show throughout this chapter, the nature of this investment in refugees structures opportunities to build skills and abilities—through language classes and other trainings—that are unavailable to their counterparts in the United States. But, while Yasmine and Omar came through the Government Sponsorship program, along with fifty-four percent of those admitted to Canada, the remaining forty-six percent were admitted with half- or a full year of support from private sponsors.[31] What is it like for refugees who arrived through these systems?

Private Sponsorship, Another Pathway

Canada's unique system of private sponsorship increases quotas for admission by allowing private citizens to participate in the work of sponsorship, creating an avenue for them to directly support refugee resettlement. As a result, the Canadian sponsorship system has become a model for governments around the world—and similar programming has been attempted in multiple countries including the United States.[32] Private sponsorship, however, is not without its complications—it selects the more privileged by design and shifts resettlement from a government benefit to a gift for which the arrival should be grateful.

Private Sponsorship, a central beacon of multicultural policy, came out of a little-known provision in Canada's 1976 Immigration Act that was added to appease a Jewish lobbying group seeking to resettle dissidents from European countries.[33] In 1978, Professor Howard Adelman, a philosopher at York University and an activist who was trying to push the Canadian government to sponsor Vietnamese refugees, was informed by government officials of this provision that allowed private citizens to sponsor refugees. Drawing on it, he launched "Operation Lifeline," which became a "Sponsorship Agreement Holder" (SAH) contracted by the Canadian government to support citizens in sponsoring refugee arrivals. Since then, three hundred thousand refugees have arrived through this system.[34] People arriving through this system receive support comparable to government-sponsored refugees, with the added benefit of the emotional and moral support from the Canadians who receive them.

The operation of the private sponsorship system is illustrated by the experiences of John, Latif, and their families. During Ramadan in 2016, I was invited by the Arab Canadian Community Center to an *iftar* hosted by an Episcopalian church. The event was attended by refugee advocates, as well as by Private Sponsoring families and by the families they had sponsored. John, a sponsor who was quick to a joke and a laugh, proudly told me that he arrived as a refugee himself through Operation Lifeline in 1979 with his mother and siblings. His family, he explained, were Vietnamese refugees who came with the "boat people" and settled in Camrose, Alberta. They were poor, he recalled, but the trauma he carried from his childhood was due to the racism they endured:

> There were a lot of racists. I mean, you don't see it, but you can see it. You always feel very inferior [. . .] we got into so many fights, so many comments against us and stuff like that. I guess it's still in my mind sometimes, but we just forget it and just continue. And luckily we came to Toronto, which is a very diverse city.

When the Syrian refugee crisis began, John, who was knowledgeable about the private sponsorship process, decided he too would sponsor a family. "I think it's just humanity," he explained when I asked him why he felt compelled to do it. At first, he sent an email to friends and employees in his office, but not all were receptive. He summarized the objections as "Why Syria? Bunch of terrorists." So, he turned to his family, who agreed that this was the right thing to do. He raised CAD 54,000 to sponsor a family of seven, and then he began the sponsorship paperwork through "Lifeline Syria," a group whose name pays homage to the Operation Lifeline begun by Adleman and which enabled John's family passage to Canada.

John completed paperwork attesting to the money he had raised and registering the Group of Five he brought together, which committed to sponsoring a refugee family. Then, he needed to find a family to sponsor that qualified for refugee status. Lifeline Syria connected him to Latif, who was already in Canada with his wife and children, but whose parents, brother, sister-in-law, and their two children were in Jordan. John agreed to sponsor Latif's family, and the Canadian government approved his application to have them recognized as refugees.

The selection of this family, however, speaks to an issue in the design of private sponsorship—in order to connect to a private sponsor, one needs to have the social capital to do so. Latif is a highly educated, fluent English speaker who had long worked in the development sector. Latif himself came through private sponsorship after wiring the money it would take to sponsor his nuclear family to his sister, a longtime resident of Canada. Though this was not technically allowed, I spoke to advocates who explained that this became a common practice as people caught in the crossfire of war looked for a way out. However, as a result of this structure, privately sponsored refugees disproportionately have stronger language abilities—four in five have some English or French knowledge, as opposed to approximately one in six government-sponsored refugees. Over half enter the labor market within the first year, both as a result of these language skills and to limit reliance on family support, or in the case of Latif, the expenditure of one's own savings.[35]

The design of the private sponsorship system also creates other points of tension. Arriving families rely on private citizens' support. While the government theoretically monitors this support, in practice, the government takes a hands-off approach, meaning the newly arrived often have to do the delicate work of managing these relationships on their own. A recent study of private sponsorship found that conflict can occur over prearranged housing, which is often in a location close to the sponsor, in neighborhoods that may be expensive for the newly arrived refugee.[36] The study also documented conflicts between sponsors and new arrivals over budgeting—how the new arrival is spending the money that the sponsor allocates. Though well-meaning, the study finds that sponsors may also not have the cultural competency or psychological know-how to understand new arrivals' experiences of racism or their choices about family life.

To examine these issues and maintain the comparative rigor of the design of this research, I included two families who are BVORs, an acronym for the more clunky "Blended Visa-Office Referred Refugees," in this project. Selected through the same system as government-sponsored refugees, they are supported by an organization or by a Group of Five that raises half of the costs needed for their first year. The Group of Five also commits to providing a full year of social and emotional support to the newly arrived family. More than two thousand Syrian refugees came to Canada as part of the Trudeau cohort through the BVOR system, and an additional eleven thousand were fully privately sponsored. In the following two sections, I return to the case of Omar and Yasmine and other families to examine how they fared as government-sponsored refugees, before I turn to the case of Israa and Abdelhameed, who were resettled contemporaneously through the BVOR program.

Making a Life in Canada

During Ramadan in 2016, which coincided with June, I drove down Industrial Drive, fittingly lined with smoke-stacked factories, and into Hamilton, Ontario to visit Yasmine and Omar in their new home. It was a quaint three-story white house with front and back yards, five bedrooms, and a large living space and kitchen. They moved to Hamilton with ten other families who all lived within walking distance of their home, forming an enclave in the otherwise White working-class town.

Before Omar and Yasmine settled on Hamilton, they were searching for apartments in Mississauga. They applied for two but were turned down by landlords both times. They didn't know whether they were turned down because they had been outbid or because they were Syrian refugees. They suspected the former, since "everyone here in Canada has been so nice," Omar explained. In the end, they were glad that their bids weren't accepted. Their rent of CAD 1,500, about CAD 100 more than what their other friends in Hamilton paid, was still substantially lower than the rent paid by the Syrian new arrivals who'd stayed near the city, and it was easily manageable between the monthly refugee cash assistance and the Child Benefit. "We feel stable again," Omar told me as I congratulated them on the place.

While there was no COSTI office near their home, there were other immigrant support organizations, which helped them register the kids at school and dispute a CAD 650 heating bill that they received. Yasmine and Omar attended English classes at a local community center. Like elsewhere in Canada, these classes were free of charge and had a supervised space for their youngest, though usually they left him home with his older siblings. At the mosque, Omar met co-ethnics who had been in Hamilton for years and spoke fluent English, on whom he could rely for additional support on how to navigate day-to-day basics like the purchase of a car.

On this day in June, I was in Hamilton for an *iftar* hosted by Omar and Yasmine and attended by an Egyptian pharmacist—one of the co-ethnics that Omar had gotten to know—and his wife. The couple were newlyweds, the wife having recently arrived from Alexandria, Egypt. As the *athan* sounded from Omar's phone to announce the sunset prayer, we broke our fast on dates, prayed *Maghreb* led by Omar, who as the man of the house had this task, and then sat on the living room floor around a sheet where delicacies like *kibbeh* and *fattah djaj* were spread before us. As the attendees quenched their thirst and hunger after the long sunup to sundown fast, the conversation began with questions about the United States election and concerns over whether Donald

Trump could win. The pharmacist then told us about his work and about how welcoming Canada had been to him, prompting Omar and Yasmine's fourteen-year-old daughter to express her aspiration to become a pharmacist herself.

After dinner, Omar went out for a cigarette, and I joined him. A blacksmith by trade, he'd owned his own workshop in Syria, adjacent to their home. Over drags of a Marlboro, he flipped through his phone to show me photographs of wrought iron doors and windows he'd welded, of precise curved metal rods joined by embellishments, all fitting the frame of someone's mansion gate. He took pride in the rarity of his work, telling me he'd be called from several cities away to do special jobs, expensive jobs. He admitted that he was getting bored in Canada without work. "But we have to learn the language first," he told me. He planned to get back to blacksmithing once he had. "I'm *ibn kaar*," he said matter-of-factly, using a slang phrase that translates to "son of a trade" and connotes that his work is as central to his identity as his ancestry.

Yasmine, however, refused to work for money. When the men went to pray *taraweeh*, a Ramadan nighttime prayer at the mosque, I sat with Yasmine and the pharmacist's wife. "Guess how old I am?" Yasmine asked us. When we couldn't guess, she exclaimed, "I'm thirty years old!" She and I were the same age. She laughed, patting her fourteen-year-old daughter's shoulder. She was married to Omar when she was fifteen and he was twenty-five, a normal age gap for marriages in her network in Syria. Yasmine was quick to say she would not marry her daughter off so young. "I became responsible for a lot very young," she explained. But, partly as advice to the pharmacist's wife and partly stating her own preference, she was clear that she had no interest in joining the Canadian labor market,

> These women come here to Canada and want to do everything themselves. She's going to go buy things for herself, and work, and drive. And meanwhile her man is going to be happy because now he doesn't have to do anything. Nope. That's not going to be me. Where's the *onoosa* (femininity)?

She boasted that when they were first married, she didn't bring as much as a pair of socks to his apartment. And, she explained, he *had* to provide up to the standards she set. "When I asked for a house," she explained, "I got a house," gesturing to the room around us. "And when I wanted a *manteau*, he knew he had to get it for me. Even though I know he doesn't really have money." As Homa Hoodfar found in her ethnography in Cairo decades earlier, women draw on interpretations of Islamic jurisprudence that declare men to be financially responsible for the household as a way to assert a *right* to support for them and their children, particularly in situations of economic stress.[37]

Even though Omar and Yasmine had made these strong statements about what they wanted for their lives in Canada, these would not hold into the coming years. By February 2017, thirteen months after their arrival, they had moved to Mississauga, feeling that the house they'd rented in Hamilton had been too big, and the city too rural. The Syrians with whom they'd moved there were nice, but they did not know them well, and they struggled to create an intimate sense of community with people with whom they shared a national identity but not strong, preexisting ties. What's more, Mississauga had a large Arab population. "Here I can go to the grocery store, and even to the doctor's office, and only speak Arabic," Yasmine exclaimed. So many Syrians were in Mississauga that Yasmine had even run into a relative of hers at the bank. "YOU!" she remembers shouting as she recognized the distant cousin. "Mountains don't meet, but people do," she wistfully reflected.

As the couple passed their thirteenth month, their refugee cash assistance was supplanted by welfare. Omar felt that welfare was enough to get by month-to-month. They had even taken a trip to Niagara Falls, he explained, where they ate out at an all-you-can-eat Chinese Buffet. "For thirty dollars a person!" Yasmine added. However, later in the conversation, Yasmine revealed to me that Omar was in debt after taking out a loan from the Canadian government to be able to move from Hamilton to Mississauga, relying on the policy that allowed refugees to access no interest loans for three years after their arrival.[38]

Despite the financial stress it caused, the move opened up possibilities for the couple. They would continue to attend English class every morning. In Mississauga, where there were more learners, Yasmine had the option of attending a women-only class, which she preferred, explaining that she felt more relaxed and comfortable to participate. While she had gotten to level two, Omar had been promoted to a level three-four, which annoyed her. "I'm better than him! I'm smarter!" Yasmine exclaimed as her husband nodded in agreement, laughing. "But the teacher who teaches me won't graduate anyone," she continued, "she teaches with a lot of *dameer* [commitment]." Yasmine had a lot of respect for her teacher, who was herself an immigrant of Indian origin.

Professionally, Omar also found the opportunity in Mississauga to become a blacksmith again. His English was finally good enough to enable him to have basic conversations. And, unlike artisans in Germany, as the next chapter will elaborate, he did not need any special credentials in Canada to have his skills as a blacksmith recognized, to be able to work in his former occupation. The pay was good, CAD 25 an hour. But Omar struggled at the job. He had always had a bad back, which was exacerbated by going back to work as a blacksmith. "I'm not young anymore," he chuckled. He went to the doctor in Canada and was finally told that he had six slipped discs in his back. Working would also mean dropping out of English classes, which Omar saw as crucial for his progress,

I'm going to need English for citizenship, a level four. And then that will be it. I'll be just like anyone else. I'll have really integrated. There will be nothing left.

Omar reluctantly relinquished what had been his trade, his *kaar*, and considered other avenues. Benefiting from Canada's educational system, he took a free three-month course for forklift training, along with other Syrian men, where he learned about the safety precautions and became a certified operator. But, with that job he would also have to do physical lifting, which with a bad back, now diagnosed, he would be unable to do. He considered becoming a long-haul truck driver, a well-paid job. However, he did not like the idea of being away from his family for too long.

As Omar was telling me about his plans regarding employment, Yasmine interjected, "I'm working too." She worked in the kitchen of an Iraqi restaurant in Mississauga, owned by an Iraqi woman, going in two to three days a week, earning CAD 10 an hour. "Exploitation," Yasmine chuckled. She found the job through a friend in her English class, another Syrian woman who had experienced a delay in her Child Benefit when the family first arrived and thus needed work. "The Iraqi woman will only hire Syrian women because we're clean and we're quick. I know my way around a kitchen," she boasted, continuing, "what I do there is exactly what I do in my own kitchen, there really isn't any difference."

I asked Yasmine what had changed her vehement anti-work position from when she first arrived. When they lived in Hamilton, she remembered, she'd been offered work as a caterer's assistant, but she was hesitant, and her husband didn't want her to take it. "We were new to Canada, and we didn't know what the world was like here. Now we're relaxing our understandings a bit." She explained that now that they're in Mississauga, where she has a lot of Syrian friends, including some who work, she has shifted her idea about it. And there were more opportunities to work in situations that are comfortable to her, with other co-ethnic women. "We're getting more flexible in Canada," she laughed.

Yasmine, who had taken a food safety course to prepare for this job with the Iraqi woman, could now imagine for herself a life in Canada where she had full-time employment. She explained, "you need two incomes here to live a good life. The kids need things—cell phones, new clothes—you need to be able to provide a lifestyle for them." Recently, she'd heard of a two-year certificate to become a dental hygienists' assistant. When she called her mom and told her that she was considering it, a game of telephone ensued that ended with a phone call from her cousin that began with, ". . . I heard you're going to be a dental hygienist."[39]

Yasmine and Omar were able to gain English language ability, develop work-related skills, and handle the turbulence of the initial years due primarily to the Canadian government's *investment* in them. This investment is a culmination of multiple different kinds of assistance. The refugee-specific cash and loan assistance meant that they could make the choice to continue to attend English classes rather than taking work that did not fit their physical abilities or interests, and that they could afford to move their family when new opportunities arose. The English classes were available due to a system that caters to all immigrants, free of charge. And they also benefited from the social system in Canada that is available to all Canadians, which offsets the cost of childcare through the CCB and which provides free, high-quality health care to all Canadians, rather than poor quality systems that cater to the poor.

What's more, in addition to this investment, once Omar had enough English and was living near a larger number of co-ethnics, he was able to use the skills he'd built over the course of his life. The same was true in a sense for Yasmine, who was able to use her skills as a cook, also gained through the course of her life, to generate an income. But perhaps most importantly, by offering new arrivals the opportunity to access loans and cash assistance directly, the Canadian system enabled them to be able to withstand the commonplace turbulence of the first years of life in a new country.

But how does Yasmine and Omar's experience fit into the broader landscape? By 2018, only forty-three percent of government-sponsored refugees who had been in Canada since 2015 had found stable employment.[40] New arrivals reported English class attendance and attempts to get their credentials recognized as obstacles to entry. Omar, who was among the twenty-three percent of new arrivals looking for work, eventually started driving for Uber in 2019 and got off welfare. Yasmine, who gave birth to a baby boy in 2019, left work to take care of her infant. Unlike her counterparts in the United States who had babies, however, she also took a break before continuing to attend English classes, which, the same study showed, was extremely common among government-sponsored refugees, with nine in ten attending language training. What's more, in the same period, nine of ten Syrian refugees in English-speaking provinces felt that they could get by in English in doctors' offices, social situations, and shopping, while eight in ten could get by to do their job.[41]

The case of twenty-eight-year-old Wael and twenty-two-year-old Hania, who are parents of three, gives additional texture to this data. Unlike Omar, who was a blacksmith, Wael was an electrician by training. He needed a certificate to practice the same job in Canada. He had a knack for language, learning English quickly and reaching a level four in under a year. To become an electrician in Canada, he'd need eight thousand hours of training, and then to pass an exam. The Canadian system recognized his years of work as an electrician towards these hours of training, and he was offered an apprenticeship where he could learn the ropes while earning CAD 20 an hour.

Wael needed to pass a written exam at the end of his apprenticeship to qualify to become an electrician. He failed. Wael admitted that the exam was complicated, and there was a lot on there he just did not know. Though schooling would be free, he would have to be retrained. While he waited for the semester to start, like Omar, he drove for Uber, a job that allowed him to "be his own boss," as he put it, echoing the refrain of immigrant Uber drivers elsewhere who take on this work as a stopgap measure.[42] Unlike Omar, he would need to reacquire credentials to find work in his field in Canada.

Wael's case also offers a second contrast to Omar and Yasmine's experience. The vast majority of refugees received at least one month of welfare after the end of their refugee assistance, but historically in Canada, the proportion using this assistance decreases over time, with less than thirty-four percent of refugees receiving welfare after ten years in the country.[43] Wael is one of the very few government-sponsored refugees who never received welfare. His hesitance to be on welfare was due to a feeling of being surveilled. He explained, "welfare knows everything." He was particularly concerned that he'd be caught for sending money home to his family, as I explore further in chapter 6 of this book.

But he also didn't take welfare because he was worried about being seen as less-than by Canadians. A Facebook post making the rounds alleged that,

> A Canadian welfare recipient [in B.C. for example] receives only CAD 3 per day for food while our government will spend CAD 15 per refugee for breakfast, CAD 16 for lunch and CAD 30 for dinner per refugee.[44]

And a parliamentary candidate suggested running on a platform that screened refugees admitted to Canada by using questions like,

> Do you recognize that to have a good life in Canada you will need to work hard to provide for yourself and your family, and that you can't expect to have things you want given to you?[45]

Wael wanted to avoid this criticism. He explained, "here there's a lot of issues around it. There's embarrassment." As soon as his friends received their first paycheck, they drove to the welfare office to get off it. But he doesn't judge anyone who does receive welfare, wondering if he got off it too early himself. "Everyone is on welfare, because one year isn't enough to get a language and settle in, and sometimes people need longer." Low pay for entry-level jobs can also dissuade new arrivals from relinquishing welfare. As Wael explained, "I can get CAD 1,300 from welfare, whereas if I make CAD 12 an hour working, I might not make that much more because then I also have to pay taxes."

Finally, Hania offered the final caveat: there is a discrepancy in men and women's skill building and employment. The Canadian government data finds that women are less likely to access employment services, and that childcare is not always available for all age groups, which impacts refugee women.[46] In Hania's case, she had two young girls at home and was pregnant with their third. The English school would allow her to bring her oldest daughter but could not provide care for her youngest. A volunteer came over once a week to her home to teach her and other women in her neighborhood, but this wasn't enough to make progress on the language. Hania did not learn to drive, though Wael had purchased a car, and she did not have plans for employment. Hania was isolated, in drastic contrast to her husband who spoke fluent English. And, while Yasmine did work, and Somaya was open to the idea of working, it was still the men who consistently confronted the labor market on behalf of newly arrived households.

The cases of Yasmine and Omar, Somaya and Nizar, and Wael and Hania are all ones of government sponsorship. But what happens to similar families who have the added structure of private sponsorship? Of the Syrians selected for resettlement in Canada, around 2,260 were resettled as Blended Visa Office-Referred Refugees (BVORs), which meant, as the previous section described, that they were selected by the government due to their humanitarian needs, just like the government-sponsored refugees, *but* they also had the support of a private sponsor. The case of Israa and her husband Abdelhameed, resettled through this program, clarifies how the addition of the private sponsor can shape the experience of new arrivals. Israa's case, too, clarifies the limitations of the Canadian system when it comes to *recognizing* a new arrival's existing skills.

Israa and Abdelhameed

On a hot day in June 2016, I drove Israa, a thirty-six-year-old mother of four, to a flea market in Mississauga to shop for *abayas* and *manteau*. All summer, Israa had worn the same zip-up velvet green *abaya*, which was incompatible with the summer heat. She had arrived from Jordan with very little, and hadn't had the chance, or money, to go shopping until then. Somaya, who loves to shop and lives around the corner from the flea market, decided to tag along. The market itself is a testament to the presence of an immigrant community in Mississauga. I felt transplanted by the wafting scent of musk incense and the mannequins sporting the latest in *hijabi* fashion—matching *abaya* and *manteau* sets. During the trip, the women, whose personalities were diametrically opposed, had a few, stilted conversations. While Somaya was always ready for a loud laugh, Israa was a woman of a few demure smiles and fewer words.

Israa was different from Somaya and many of the other women in this study in other ways, too. While she grew up in similar economic circumstances, her father had sent her, despite her protests, from their village in the governorate of Daraa to a boarding school in its eponymous capital, where she trained to become a nurse. Israa worked full-time as a nurse from 2000 until 2013, through the first two years of war. Then, as the war intensified, she fled to Jordan with her husband Abdelhameed, who was a farmer and fruit vendor, and their children. While there, like the other refugees who were resettled to

Canada, the couple received a call asking if they'd like to be vetted for travel. They agreed and found themselves in Toronto three months later.

Life in Canada for Israa, her husband, and their children got off to a difficult start. Abdelhameed's father died two days after their arrival. Their five-year-old son was battling a health care crisis that required multiple hospital visits. While the family did not come through Private Sponsorship, they were flagged as a case that needed extra support, above the usual humanitarian support offered by the Canadian government. For this reason, a Group of Five was recruited to help support their resettlement. The Group would provide half of the family's financial needs for the first year, around CAD 20,000 for the family of six.

The Group of Five sponsors found the family a two-bedroom apartment in the Dovencourt neighborhood of Toronto, near Little Italy, an expensive neighborhood close to where many of the sponsors lived. While being in the city meant that the family didn't need a car, it also meant that the family of six needed to find a creative way to fit in the tiny two-bedroom apartment. Israa immediately felt cramped in the space, where her four children shared a room. At the end of the first year, she would seriously consider moving, but by then her children had begun school and made friends. She didn't feel like it was fair to displace them yet again, and they couldn't afford to move elsewhere in the neighborhood.

The sponsors helped Israa and her husband pay their CAD 1,800 rent during the first few months. After the first six months, the couple received government-sponsored refugee funding of CAD 718 a month each. And, like the other government-sponsored refugees and all other Canadians, they qualified for the Canada Child Benefit, which for them was almost CAD 2,000 a month given that the family had four children. This support from the private sponsors and from the Child Benefit meant that Israa and Abdelhameed—who were not forced to find a job immediately—could attend English class every morning, which Israa did regularly. Already, four months after her arrival, although not yet fluent, Israa was able to complete a form for her daughter's school, writing in "English" as something she hoped her daughter could improve in the coming months.

However, as Israa advanced in her English classes, transitioning from a level three to a level four fourteen months in, Abdelhameed fell behind. Like others who sought refuge elsewhere in the world, he suffered from mental health issues exacerbated by war and displacement, but also by the struggle of putting together new lives that were so different from their old ones. Abdelhameed suffered from violent stomachaches which, Israa noticed, got worse when he couldn't get his mother, who lived in Syria, on the phone. Convinced that he had stomach cancer, he went to several specialists who all said the same thing—there was no physical explanation for the pain. He struggled to attend English classes regularly and to find work. The Group of Five, well-resourced

(White) Canadians, attempted to find him employment opportunities that fit his background as a farmer and fruit vendor, but he was not receptive.

Six months into the family's resettlement, when Abdelhameed expressed resistance to continuing with English classes, the sponsoring group found him a job stocking shelves at a grocery store known for promoting from within its ranks—its CEO once stocked shelves. However, Abdelhameed turned this job offer down, explaining to them that it was Ramadan and that he didn't want to start a new job while fasting. But when I spoke to Abdelhameed, he said that he didn't want to take on this kind of work—he was hoping for better than stocking shelves. Besides, his family still had its refugee assistance, so what was the rush? Almost a year later, when the family was transferred to welfare, Abdelhameed would temporarily lose his welfare benefits because he would quit yet another job and continue to refuse to attend English class. As in the United States, welfare benefits in Canada are tied to employment searches and performance. While there was a commitment to provide mental health treatment for refugees across contexts, there was little recognition in Canada or the United States (or in Germany) of mental health concerns when they manifested in an inability or unwillingness to perform within the country's economic life.

In conversation, Israa vacillated between sympathy for and frustration with her husband, both wishing he would take a job and reminding herself, and me, that he was struggling. When she saw homeless people on the street, she worried her family would become homeless one day too. Hearing her say this, one of members of the private sponsoring group, Sally, assured her that the Canadian government would support their family. But, Sally continued, "you should really have a plan." I was annoyed by this statement, which to me felt like she was speaking down to Israa. But Israa replied without bitterness, simply stating she *did* have a plan but that she could not control whether Abdelhameed would go along with it.

Earlier that year, Israa had another difficult moment with the group of sponsors as she and Abdelhameed transferred to welfare in what Canadian resettlement workers refer to as "month thirteen," when refugee-specific assistance runs out. Though the family hadn't received assistance from the private sponsors for six months, Israa felt judged when she shared with them that she was transitioning to welfare. "They didn't like it," she explained, echoing what Wael had said he felt. The group of middle-class Canadians hoped that Israa and Abdelhameed would not rely on government assistance. They were not the only privately sponsored refugees to express this; articles on month thirteen, as well as policy briefs, show that this was a common point of contention between refugees and sponsors.

Israa, however, after relaying this complaint, was quick to come to her sponsor's defense. "They don't meddle," she said. I noticed something similar that Abdelhameed did. Even when he was complaining about how the sponsors were pressuring him six months after arrival to take on work he didn't want, he interjected, "but they are really great people, they continue to support us." To be sure, there is no reason to suspect that Israa and Abdelhameed did not feel truly grateful to the sponsors who did support them emotionally and, initially, financially. However, the expression of this gratitude reminded me of radio coverage of refugees in Canada who spoke of the pressure to appear grateful as engrained the Canadian system—evidence that Canada was indeed the "multicultural" haven it purported it was.

On a drive home from the flea market, Israa was explicit about how she thought she and other immigrants should behave. A car passed us with a flag on its hood. "What's that? I see it everywhere," she asked. "The Portuguese flag," I responded. To which she said,

> I don't like it when people put the flags of other countries, even if they're proud of their own countries, they shouldn't fly it in the face of Canadians that allowed them to live here. The only flag one should raise in Canada is the Canadian flag.

I asked her if she felt that Canada was her country. "Not yet," she responded. She hoped to go back to Syria—she shrugged—once things got better. She was particularly concerned about her children's future. She would later explain to me that the focus on Christmas, or the constant questioning of her children by teachers when they fasted, or of her own choice to wear the *hijab*, made her worry about her ability to raise her children in Canada with her own Islamic and Arab cultural values. Certainly, Israa felt grateful to be in Canada, but underlying this outward gratitude were concerns over where she and her family fit in.

Israa dealt with other obstacles to feeling at home in Canada. As she progressed further in English, she considered getting her nursing degree and her work experience *recognized*. But she couldn't retrieve her degrees from Syria due to the ongoing war; if she sent a family member, they might be asked about her and her husband's whereabouts, which could get that family member into trouble, as the Syrian government doesn't look kindly on those who fled. However, the sponsoring group members informed her that she could perhaps have her skills tested, and that once she'd achieved a level five in English, she could enroll at a university.

The process of getting her degree recognized, for Israa, was not facilitated through the Canadian system. It would be a long road, requiring at least a few years college training after Israa gained the requisite English. Unlike Omar who could go to work immediately as a blacksmith, Israa's profession was regulated in Canada, which made the process of recognition more complicated. She considered changing course and becoming a dental hygienist, a job that would only take two years' training.

Though Israa could not pursue her career, she could pursue other interests. Through certificate programs offered by the Canadian government, she was able to take six courses free of charge. Two of these courses were training to become a mental health facilitator. After gaining these skills, Israa worked with other immigrants as a volunteer at a community center, facilitating group sessions on displacement and family life, which gave her a sense of joy to be able to give back, to feel integrated in a true sense in a group in which she was not the recipient of support, but the *giver* of support. What's more, through this certificate program, Israa gained other food handling knowledge and credentials. Through the sponsoring group, she was able to use these skills, ending up working at a café that hired refugees.

With regard to broader Canadian data, among those in Israa and Abdelhameed's group who were BVORs, resettled through the same system as government-sponsored refugees but who had the support of private sponsors, fifty-five percent found work, as opposed to only forty-seven percent among the government-sponsored refugees.[47] The social capital and connections that this group of private sponsors offers is crucial to the newly arrived Syrians, who, like Israa and Abdelhameed, face multiple obstacles to employment—including struggles with the language, with how to earn an economic livelihood, and in cases like Abdelhameed's, with mental health. These same obstacles, however, can make it difficult to live up to the expectations of private sponsors, which creates unique tensions in an already complicated resettlement process.

———

Regardless of whether the refugee was resettled through the governmental or private systems in Canada, they received a greater degree of *investment* than in the United States. As a direct result, both men and women learned more English and had more opportunity to gain new employable skills in Toronto than they did five hundred miles south in New Haven—enabling them to both express their existing skills in new ways and to gain additional ones. They were, as a result of state assistance and this ability to use and gain human capital, more financially comfortable, and more likely to express *feeling* settled, than their counterparts in the United States.

The Canadian system, however, is imperfect. Those with prior experience in the labor market worked to have their skills recognized, though not with equal success. While Omar, a blacksmith, was able to find work in his field, Wael, an electrician, found the recognition of his skillset complicated by required exams, while Israa, who was once a nurse in war-torn Syria, struggled to even begin the process of this recognition. And, though women and men benefited from the generosity of the Canadian social benefit system, as we saw with the case of Hania, childcare was not always provided, which put pressure on women, who were more likely to be responsible for this gendered labor.

Importantly, in Canada, unlike in the United States, those resettled through both governmental and private sponsorship benefited from the expansive social service system available to them as recognized refugees. Private Sponsorship, regarded by some as a gold standard for resettlement practice, and which has been introduced, following the Canadian model, in countries including the United States and Italy, also benefits from this expansive system. Those seeking refuge benefit from child benefits, universal health care, and the availability of integration courses. As the cases throughout this chapter demonstrate, these services support the difficult process of transition. In Canada, refugee-specific assistance is provided in addition to a safety net that supports not only those seeking refuge, but other low-income Canadians and recognized newcomers.

Still, even in this case of a strong resettlement and social service system built on policies of integration and multiculturalism, there were difficulties. Being a refugee in a new country is an experience of displacement, regardless of the kinds of resources that you are offered. Families struggled with being away from loved ones and with rigid processes of family reunification, discussed further in chapter 6, "Here & There." And, though in Canada the refugees had an easier time than in the United States or in Germany with regards to exposure to racism due to their greater freedom to move around the country and to having arrived under a welcoming government, there were still undertones that they had to contend with, including an emphasis on being grateful to Canadians for opening their doors.

5

German Credentialization

Imad picked me up from the train station in Essen, a city in North Rhine-Westphalia, just north of Dusseldorf. I was introduced to him and his wife, Amina, by her cousin Rajaa, who is one of the Syrian women resettled in New Haven, Connecticut. Rajaa, Amina, and their families arrived at their respective destinations in August 2015. As I walked with Imad down their tree-lined street and up to their third-floor apartment, I was struck by how different the two family's living situations were. Imad and Amina's three-bedroom apartment was spacious and well-furnished, with rugs in each room and brand-new Arab-style couches set against the walls in a U-shape. They had a large-screen television in one corner. The apartment, which they shared with their three children, was well-appointed, well-furnished, and comfortable, a far cry from the rat-infested two-bedroom apartment Rajaa, Majid, and their three children inhabited in a low-income neighborhood.

Amina, who shared her cousin's round face and dimples, welcomed me with coffee, cookies, and a blue glass, coal fired *argila* stuffed with apple-flavored tobacco. As Imad adjusted the coals, I noticed one of his hands was bandaged. He explained that he had been injured at work. When I asked if he had gotten workers' compensation, he hesitated. "I was working *fel eswed*," he explained, using the Arabic word "black," which connoted that his labor had been part of the informal economy. Imad had been working for a friend, an Egyptian who exported used car parts to Egypt. The man needed help in his warehouse and offered Imad an on-the-books training job for a month. After the short-term contract was over, however, Imad stayed on a few weeks longer, during which he injured his hand. Imad and his friend could both incur tens of thousands of euros in fines if they were caught. So, not only did Imad not receive worker's compensation, but he would also lie to the Jobcenter—the

German unemployment agency—telling them that he'd been injured doing repairs to his kitchen.

Importantly, what pushed Imad to stay on at his friend's place, an arrangement he knew was suboptimal, was not financial need. Unlike their cousins in New Haven, Imad and Amina were able to cover their basic needs and even to send remittances to his family back home because of the Jobcenter assistance. Instead, Imad took the opportunity with his friend because he was deeply anxious about entering the German labor market. When he arrived in Germany, he'd learn that his experience driving a bus and long-haul trucking—though it had gotten him arrested and nearly killed in Syria—would not be recognized in the German system, which had strict credential laws and norms for who could work in most occupations.

Drivers in Germany, in addition to going through a long process to secure a specialized license, had to be trained through the German dual system. This system, a part of the country's broader coordinated economy that links education and employment, provides those who enter one of Germany's 350 technical professions with both theoretical and practical training at companies for jobs.[1] To enter this scheme, asylum seekers like Imad need to attend Integration Courses and to secure at least a B-1 level in the German language, which seemed an impossible feat for Imad, who had dropped out of middle school in Syria. When Imad looks at job listings, he sees requirements such as the following, which I found on a job posting for "truck driver" on a German apprenticeship site:[2]

1. You are at least eighteen years old
2. You speak German at least at the following level: B-2
3. European Union Citizenship or Work Permit
4. You meet the following special requirements for this position provided by the employer: Completed vocational training, driving license class D with appropriate driving experience, driving license for passenger transport. Ideal would be a training in traffic service and an accomplished first aid training (no more than five years earlier). Your employer expects from you a clear customer friendliness and service orientation.

Imad, a man who saw himself as a skilled worker, became unskilled in the face of these requirements. To gain credentials as a driver in Germany, he would have to do at least two years of language learning and at least three of job training.

This erasure of his human capital was consequential. For Imad, it meant he'd be unable to enter the labor market in the profession in which he'd built a career in Syria. It also caused concern about his family's ability to secure legal status. To secure permanent residency and eventually citizenship in Germany, the new arrivals would have to show that they could support themselves financially and that they had the requisite German language proficiency. What's more, for Imad, finding work was also an emotional and existential issue, as he put it, "I've been working all of my life, I can't just sit at home doing nothing."

The non-recognition of Syrian credentials not only impacted the arriving Syrians, but also hindered Germany's goal of meeting its need for workers.[3] The German labor market features a low and steadily dropping unemployment rate, and the lowest youth unemployment rate in Europe. As death rates outpace birthrates, there's a need for immigrants to fill the gap. Commentators, particularly those who are proponents of admitting asylum seekers, argue that the Syrians who entered in 2015, eighty percent of whom were under the age of thirty-five, are an important boon to the German labor market that badly needs more workers.

For all these reasons, German policy makers attempted to rectify the system's inability to recognize foreign credentials even before the Syrians arrived. One strategy involved passing a Recognition Act in 2012 to facilitate the acknowledgment of foreign credentials for all workers in Germany. This policy, however, only had a mechanism for recognizing formal credentials (those requiring diplomas), which many Syrian workers lacked, particularly those who worked blue-collar jobs. Even among the Syrians who did have formal credentials, such as doctors, lawyers or teachers, the recognition rate was low. Just thirty-five percent of all Syrian applicants were recognized partially or fully through this policy in 2018, as opposed to eighty-one percent of all credential recognition requested by European Union nationals. A list of recognition rates by country shows that the top rates are for Western European countries (Netherland, Switzerland, Belgium), and the lowest recognition countries are in the Global South (Tunisia, Mexico, China).The explanation given on the government's portal for low recognition of Syrian credentials is that "recognition rates tend to be higher in the geographically and culturally closer countries than in the more remote countries"—an admission that the credential gap is shaped by culture rather than skill or ability.[4]

The Case of Germany

By seeking asylum in Germany, Syrians were entering one of the world's most generous social service systems.[5] Germany is a corporatist system, in which economic policy is shaped through coordination between employees, employers, and the public sector.[6] This system, intellectually rooted in functionalism, or the idea that actors play symbiotic parts in a societal whole, sees individuals in terms of their social roles. Those in need of cash assistance are addressed as workers. Unless there is an extenuating circumstance because of which one cannot work, assistance is distributed as unemployment support from the Jobcenter. Those offered asylum receive a form of unemployment designated for those who do not have prior work experience. This assistance is meant to cover rent and basic needs while people gain the credentials necessary for work and search for employment.

By addressing individuals in their social role as workers, this system has historically excluded women from state support. As opposed to East Germany, which was socialist and had more gender parity, in the former West Germany men were the *de facto* breadwinners, so women were left out of state support. After reunification in 1989 this exclusion persisted. Today, "sustainable family policies" have extended state benefits through "use-it-or-lose-it" parental leave for both partners, childcare for children's early years, and support for primary caregivers of infants. All of this has brought German women into the fold of state assistance in the last decade. Syrian caretakers, often women, arriving in this system also benefit from the support of young children and provision of free childcare.[7]

But, while the German welfare system invests in newly arrived asylum seekers, it also fails to recognize their abilities. Coordination between employees, employers, and the state is achieved, in part, through narrowly defined labor-market pathways. As we saw with the case of Imad, credentials are earned through a "dual educational system." One part of this system, for vocational training, pairs students with employers through apprenticeships. The second part channels high-achieving middle school students into high schools and university training. This makes the labor market impenetrable for foreigners who did not go through the German education system. People like Imad who have a history of employment outside of Germany cannot express those skills or competencies without either recognition or retraining.

Both the generosity of the German welfare system and its restrictions are a product of the country's insularity. It is a German system for Germans.[8] Until the 1990s, West Germany's immigration policy was expressed as "Deutschland ist kein Einwanderungsland," or "Germany is not a country of immigration."[9] But this statement, while a reflection of national ideology, was never factually true. The *Gastarbeiter,* or guest worker, program instituted in the 1960s and 1970s was designed to bring in unskilled laborers temporarily. This resulted in widescale immigration of Turkish laborers who stayed and brought their families.[10] What's more, between 1990 and 1994, as the Cold War ended and East Germans migrated to the West, so too did over a million people from the former Soviet bloc, though not all stayed in the long term.

"Germany *is* a country of immigration" became the mantra of reformers, who in 1999 introduced a citizenship bill that did away with the *jus sanguinis* requirement for citizenship, or the limitation of citizenship to those with "German blood."[11] Instead, the country switched a more civic-minded *jus soli* model, which created a naturalization pathway for longtime residents of Germany including Turkish immigrants, so long as they renounced their parents' nationality. Germany's first immigration law, which gave preference to highly skilled immigrants, was introduced in 2005. As part of this policy, anyone who entered Germany, even for family reunification, was required to take a language test and then to enroll in integration classes once they had arrived in the country. Citizenship also required language fluency as it does in the United States and Canada.

But even as Germany became more open to immigration, it remained committed to a notion of a coherent German identity that should be preserved. Writing about racism against Germany's Turkish immigrants, the country's largest minority, anthropologist Ruth Mandel argues that one idea of racial purity, which fueled the Holocaust, is the notion that immigrants or people with non-German heritage can never become "real Germans." This, she argues, collides with the claim of a desire to be a more multicultural country.[12] Like other immigrants in countries around the world, Turkish immigrants formed ethnic enclaves in Germany's major cities in response to discrimination. They became racialized in German media and political discourse as a monolithic mass unwilling to integrate. After 9/11 they were also Islamicized—seen as violent, anti-feminist, and antithetical to "Western Values."[13] In 2018, Horst Seehofer, Merkel's Interior Minister, said succinctly that Islam "does not belong to Germany. Germany is shaped by Christianity."[14]

Against this backdrop, the predominantly Sunni Muslim Syrian asylum seekers were seen, as Turkish immigrants long had been, as threats to German *Leitkultur*—guiding culture. Articulating and defending the concept, and referring specifically to the Syrian new arrivals, Thomas de Maizière, two-time German Minister of the Interior and a member of Angela Merkel's Christian Democratic Union (CDU), wrote in an op-ed in 2017,

> Beyond language, the constitution and respect for fundamental rights, there is something that holds us together at the core, that makes us different and that distinguishes us from others.

Listing ten tenets of *Leitkultur*, he begins with, "We shake hands in greeting [. . .] We are an open society. We show our face. We are not burka."[15] In this way, he frames *Leitkultur* specifically against Muslims, among whom there are those who do not shake hands with people of the opposite gender and some pious Muslim women who cover their face. He goes on to say, "is this [*Leitkultur*] a canon of education everyone should know and learn, for example in the hundred hours of orientation we offer in our integration course? That would be nice." He continues,

> But what about those who have come to us, have a prospect of staying here, but are not willing to familiarize themselves with it or maybe even

reject it? Well, integration is unlikely to succeed with them. Because they will not feel that they belong without knowledge and in any case respect for our guiding culture.

De Maizière was writing in the aftermath of the 2015/2016 New Years' Eve incidents in Cologne, during which men described as Arab and North African sexually assaulted German women celebrating the New Year. Though it's unclear whether Syrians were involved, the events were used as evidence that the newly arrived asylees were dangerous and that their values were not German ones. Though de Maizière's statement drew sharp criticism from some Germans, the notion that people need to relinquish their values for German ones permeates the country's integration policy.

The tension between the image of a multicultural, welcoming Germany and the commitment to *Leitkultur* is observable in the 2016 Integration Act. As a result of the law, German employers could hire immigrants without first searching for Germans to fill the role. It also removed the age cap on *Ausbildung*, or vocational training—opening it up to new arrivals who were older than twenty-one. Moreover, it expanded the Integration Courses that are both a vehicle for *investment* and a way to indoctrinate new arrivals with German values, as de Maizière's statement makes clear. What's more, the law called for the creation of one hundred thousand refugee-specific "Minijobs"—short-term contracts made possible by the controversial Hartz reforms in the 2000s. Intended to help refugees "occupy their time in a meaningful way," these contracts pay a single euro an hour. Failure to involve oneself in courses, vocational training, or a Minijob would result in a reduction of benefits.

Together, these policies made it so that, although the Syrians in Germany would benefit from the country's expansive welfare system, they would also sense a persistent message that they are not good enough. As thirty-two-year-old Mo'men put it, "The Germans see themselves here," he put his hand flat above his head. "They see us here," he said as he put his hand to the floor. "They tell us, if you want to be with us you have to get to our level." But first, to be a part of the German system, the new arrivals would need to navigate the country's notoriously complex bureaucracy, through which they became asylees.

Navigating Asylum

On August 25, 2015, Angela Merkel held a press conference outside of a refugee camp that she visited in Dresden, Saxony. She confirmed a decision her government had made the prior week that Germany would suspend its commitment to the Dublin Regulation, which would have sent the asylum seekers that arrived in Germany back to the country where they had first entered Europe and been fingerprinted. By suspending the regulation through October 2015,

Merkel was promising hundreds of thousands of asylum seekers a fair vetting for asylum in her country.

But, as she announced this suspension in Saxony, she was heckled by a jeering, booing crowd that called her a "politician lowlife" and yelled "there's money for everything but your own people."[16] Merkel, however, was adamant, stating what became the emblematic phrase of her leadership on the issue, "Wir Schaffen das," or "We can do this." She saw this admission of asylum seekers as evidence of a new cultural reality in Germany of *Willkommenskultur.* As she put it, "The world sees Germany as a country of hope and opportunity, and that was certainly not always the case."

Syrians waiting in train stations and camps across Europe chanted "Angela! Angela!" and "Germany! Germany!" in celebration of her decision. Because the Dublin regulation hinges on fingerprints, the Syrians who, like Imad and Amina, had been apprehended in places like Hungary, came to see their own fingertips, their whorls, loops, and coils, as potential chains to places where they did not want to live. While the Dublin Regulation assumes that all European countries are equally capable of processing asylum claims, the Syrian asylum seekers did not want to live in Greece or Italy, which were dealing with their own economic crises, or Hungary, which was led by Prime Minister Viktor Orban, who would later proclaim, "We don't see these people as Muslim refugees. We see them as Muslim invaders."[17] In suspending the Dublin Regulation, Merkel allowed the Syrian asylum seekers an alternative place of refuge by choosing, as the Syrian refugees put it, to "break the fingerprint," or "*Kasarit el Basma.*"

For the Syrians began the work of securing asylum in Germany, of adjusting to a new country, of securing a decent life for themselves and their families. In the next few months, they would have their first interactions with the web of institutions that would govern their lives for the coming years. These would make asylum seekers legible to the German state. In their first interaction with German authorities, Syrians would be registered at police stations or reception centers, where their photographs and fingerprints were taken and uploaded to EuroDac (the European Union database) as well as the German database.

Then they were distributed to one of Germany's sixteen federal states, where they were expected to reside while applying for asylum. This distribution was done through the Königstein Key, a system developed in 1949 as a way for financial burden-sharing in the field of science policy, which factored in states' tax revenue and number of inhabitants. When used to allocate asylum-seeking families, it was rebranded the EASY system.[18] While this system was efficient from the German government's perspective, it ignored Syrian newcomers' interest in being around family members and co-ethnics and away from a rising tide of neo-Nazi violence.

The EASY system defined family as spouses or registered partners, and their minor, unmarried children. But for twenty-one-year-old Rajiya, who travelled from Turkey, across Europe, and into Germany with her fiancé Ahmed, her parents, and her aunt's family, this definition did not suffice. While she and her parents were grouped together and allocated to Baden-Wuttemberg, Ahmed, who was not her registered partner, was to be sent across the country, as was her aunt's family. Rajiya and Ahmed pleaded with camp officials, explaining that they saw themselves as a family, but to no avail.

To resist their separation, Rajiya and Ahmed got married in the reception facility. She wore a white dress. He found a blazer in the donation bin. They got refreshments and recruited a local Sheikh to officiate. They invited camp officials. Their plan worked. Although Rajiya and Ahmed were still not officially married in the eyes of the German law, camp officials intervened to keep them together. The two were allocated to the same state, along with Rajiya's parents. Her aunt's family, however, was sent across the country, and Rajiya and her parents had not seen them since. She was too far away, and travel was too expensive.

Not only did the policy make it difficult to stay with family members, but it also disrupted reunifications with co-ethnics already in Germany. Nadine, a single mother of three who was fleeing not only a war but an abusive marriage, would find herself unable to join her brother in Hamburg, whom she had hoped could help her raise her children. Tito, who was only seventeen when he arrived in Germany, would also not be able to join his uncle's family since his uncle was not his formal guardian. He was instead placed in a camp for minors.

While Nadine, Tito, and others would experience this forced placement as jarring, disruption of reunification was a desirable consequence of the EASY policy from the perspective of policymakers. Sigmar Gabriel, a leader of the Social Democratic Party and vice-chancellor of Germany, warned that without the EASY system and a requirement to reside where one was placed "people—including recognized asylum seekers—will all move to the big cities," [and] there would be a "real ghetto problem," unreflexively using a term with a brutal history that has otherwise referred to the forced sequestering of minorities. His position hinged on the idea that without being forced to interact with others, Syrians would become insular, not learn the language, and therefore not integrate into German society.[19]

Implicit in his statement is the idea that there is necessarily a conflict between Syrians associating with their own group and their ability to deal with their new context, implying that for Syrians to assimilate they should step out of their community. However, this understanding of immigrant integration is contested by decades of scholarship showing that immigrant co-ethnic communities can be economic and cultural resources for integration, as well as vehicles to help immigrants make meaningful contributions to their host countries.[20]

Sonnenallee, a major street in the working-class neighborhood of Neukölln in Berlin, is testament to this. The longtime home to Turkish and Lebanese immigrants and a former checkpoint between East and West Berlin has become "Little Syria"—an ethnic enclave full of Syrian stores and restaurants. The very popular Aldimashqi restaurant, for instance, is owned by a wealthy Syrian from Damascus and staffed by younger Syrian men. On a summer night in 2017, it was busy with Arab families who lined up for a meal of hot *shawarma* with a dollop of *toomeya*, finished off with *kunafa nabolsi*. Lined up next to them were German clientele, mostly young, who were experiencing another culture's food.

The EASY system was not only disruptive of family life and co-ethnic resources; it was also blind to Syrians' fear of racist acts by German neo-Nazis. Syrian families expressed anxiety about moving to former East Germany, where there was a lot of anti-refugee activity by organized far right groups. Imad and Amina were allocated to Saxony, the state where Merkel had given her address, and the same state where Pegida, a virulent anti-Muslim group, had been founded. Although they found a nice home in Meissen, they would only spend a year there. As Imad put it plainly, "in the East there are Nazis." They moved after attacks on a refugee camp by White supremacists near their home.

Reham, a woman in her thirties whom I met in Bavaria, had also been allocated to Saxony. She stopped wearing her *hijab* after multiple racist incidents, including being spat on by a German man. While she had decided to wear her *hijab* again now that she lived in Bavaria, she showed me her identification card, where she had been photographed without her *hijab*, with her hair hanging just beneath her chin. "It was so difficult for me to make take off the *hijab*, like letting go of a piece of myself," she said, "but I wouldn't have been safe otherwise."

To be sure, racism was not relegated to East Germany. Hanaa, who, like Reham, lived in Bavaria, regularly received hateful, anti-Muslim messages in her mailbox from a neighbor, who marked up articles from far-right newspapers about the evils of Islam in red pen, adding long, ranting messages that left her terrified. She put a cupboard in front of the door to her studio before she slept at night. Other Syrians in her town also reported being attacked in public, berated on public buses, and spat on.

Regardless of where they were allocated by the EASY system, Syrians were first placed in makeshift housing. Accommodations varied between converted stadiums, shipping containers, or other public spaces, in both rural and urban areas. Emblematic of these camp accommodations was the Tempelhof Airport in Berlin. Built by Hitler with the goal of being the largest airport in the world, the airport was later used as a Nazi concentration camp and has now been repurposed as the largest refugee camp in Europe, with rows upon rows of cots divided by temporary white walls. Even after Syrians were recognized as asylees, they remained in transient housing until they could find permanent apartments—a tall order in big cities where vacant housing was scarce and landlords discriminated against Syrian housing applications.[21]

After being distributed throughout the country by the EASY system and placed in different camps and temporary housing situations, the Syrians applied for asylum. To do so, they went to the BAMF (Federal Office for Migration and Refugees) to submit their fingerprints, photographs, and other documents. Then, they waited for their asylum appointment, at which they were asked questions to assess their qualification. Very few Syrians were denied. In 2015, almost everyone who was recognized as needing protection received Geneva Convention recognition, which acknowledged that they had escaped persecution by state or non-state actors.

In 2016, however, this pattern of recognition changed, with almost forty-two percent of Syrians receiving Subsidiary Protection instead of Geneva Convention protection—a lesser status that recognizes that they cannot return to Syria but that assumes that they did not themselves experience persecution.[22] The issuing of this subsidiary status, upheld in the court, was combined with a federal decision to suspend the right to family reunification for Syrian asylees who were offered Subsidiary Protection. This decision mattered for the many asylum seekers, mostly men who had spared their family the dangerous journey across the Mediterranean, hoping to reunify with them through formal channels after arrival.

After navigating all the legal obstacles, Syrian asylum seekers, whether they had Geneva Convention Status or Subsidiary Status, could stay in Germany, work, and access social services. Those with Geneva Convention Status got a three-year renewable stay, and those with Subsidiary Status could renew their residency after one year for another two. Both also had the right to eventually apply for permanent residency, provided they met, as stipulated on the BAMF documents, "preconditions [. . .] such as the ability to make a secure living and adequate knowledge of German."[23]

Within the context of these preconditions and the requirement to apply to renew their residency, Syrian asylum seekers in Germany were terrified of their legal status being revoked. As Rajiya put it,

> Say the regime in Syria has a ceasefire, they might say, ok, your residency has expired, whether they gave you a year or three years [Subsidiary Protection or Geneva Convention Status]. What if the Germans send us back?

Imad expressed another concern regarding Syrians legal status, asking rhetorically, "if you are here for five years and have nothing to show for yourself, why will they keep you?" He and others felt that they would have to prove themselves worthy to have their asylum applications renewed, to be able to remain in the country, particularly, as Imad put it, "if Angela goes." Securing asylum in Germany represented another hurdle passed for the Syrians who went there. But a long-distance race lay ahead, one that required them to learn a language that was "hard on their tongues" and to enter a labor market that did not recognize their work histories while also dealing with all the other difficulties of adjusting to a new country. The silver lining was, however, that as they did this, they'd be supported by the strong German Jobcenter system—something their counterparts in the United States were not afforded.

Jobcenter Support

Once asylum was adjudicated and the asylum seeker was recognized under the Geneva Convention definition or Subsidiary Protection, the asylee was entitled to the same kinds of assistance that unemployed German citizens receive. Germany has two unemployment systems—one for those with employment histories, which is tethered to one's previous salary, and a second for those without sufficient employment history, which is federally funded. Most Syrians, as new entrants to the labor market, accessed the latter. Syrians who had chronic health issues that prevented them from working more than three hours a day were instead entitled to state welfare. The unemployment assistance was offered through the German Jobcenter.[24]

The amount of assistance was intended to cover necessities and "to a reasonable extent also relations to the environment and participation in cultural life," according to the Federal Employment Agency. This assistance, along with childcare specific help, *did* exceed refugees' living expenses. As Imad put it, "the situation here, in terms of money and financial support, is excellent. And no one is in need of anything." In addition to offering an amount to each individual, the Jobcenter also covers rent for families and provides a one-time transfer for furnishings, which covered the costs of Imad and Amina's nice apartment in Bonn.[25]

Families fared better than individuals in this system, due to the higher amount of assistance provided each month. For young single men, money was tighter. For example, Mustafa, a twenty-seven-year-old bachelor who lived in Stuttgart, whose parents I knew because they were resettled in New Haven, received only EUR 404 a month in addition to bus benefits and rent coverage. He said of the assistance,

> It's good. You're on a budget but its good money. You can take care of yourself, but there isn't much leeway. Sometimes my friends and I will run out and have to spot each other around the 20th of the month, but that's only if we go out too much.

The problem, Mustafa clarified, was that even if you have cash and rent assistance, renting a home was difficult because of xenophobia and racism.

There is racism here, not everyone, but you will find it. Here in the city [Stuttgart] there are lots of *Auslander*, Turks, Poles, people from everywhere. So there's less racism. But still, landlords don't want to rent to people on the Jobcenter; because the idea is you are taking our taxes, and you're abusing our system. So, they don't want to rent to people who get the Jobcenter income. But what they don't understand is the Jobcenter is going to help me for one to three more years, but I'm going to end up paying them back.

Tight rental markets coupled with discrimination resulted in many remaining in what they referred to as *Heims*—refugee camps that had private rooms, bathrooms, and kitchens—for much longer than they wanted to, particularly if they lived in large cities. And, when they did find housing, they often had to agree to subpar living conditions, such as homes that were unrenovated or that were below ground level. Multiple homes I visited in Regensberg fell into this latter case.

What's more, support from the Jobcenter came with a series of requirements. First it came with the stipulation of attending classes. These Integration Courses, described in detail in the following section, were both an investment in asylum seekers by the German government that allowed them to learn the language and a mechanism through which the government sought to assimilate Syrian refugees into the German system by teaching cultural lessons about what it meant to be German. When the person receiving support reached a B-1 level of language ability in conversational German, they are required to actively search for work and to take the jobs that they are offered.

All of this is monitored through regular meetings with Jobcenter staff, which Syrian asylees were also required to attend to keep their benefits. These meetings weren't always pleasant. Ali, a twenty-four-year-old single man who lived in Stuttgart, described feeing disrespected by Jobcenter staff,

When we learn German in class, they teach you also about German culture, and they tell you that officials like at the Jobcenter are supposed to treat you with respect. They're supposed to use the respectful "Sie" but instead you're barked at, "what do you want?" [in the informal *du*], "sit here," "give me your paperwork."

The expectations tied to Jobcenter assistance were enforced at these meetings. For instance, if one didn't attend Integration Classes, their funding would be cut—which Imad was threatened with when he was working with his friend rather than attending classes. And if one were fired due to something that was considered their own fault, or if one quit, they would no longer be allowed to access Jobcenter assistance. Zaid, a twenty-five-year-old, found himself, along with a few other friends, financially supporting a friend who was fired due to a clash with what the man described as a racist German boss.

Furthermore, the Syrians described their experience with the Jobcenter staff as being invasive. Tito, the now twenty-year-old who arrived in Germany as an unaccompanied seventeen-year-old minor would learn the hard way that any money earned needed to be reported to the Jobcenter when he was paid EUR 160 for participating in a photoshoot while playing soccer. He spent the bonus quickly, splurging on a nice dinner with his girlfriend and his friends. When the Jobcenter asked for him to pay the money that he had earned back, he no longer had it. He was also taken aback that the cash he had earned was counted against his social assistance. Tito decided then and there to relinquish the Jobcenter assistance, beginning a complicated pathway into the labor market, which I describe in the coming sections of this chapter.

Overall, the Syrians in this study felt well-supported by the cash aspect of German assistance. They could pay their rent, buy food, and furnish an apartment. However, this investment in refugees came with caveats. Not securing work within this system could result in a loss of benefits. And, as described in the previous section, since entering the labor market was tied to the possibility of securing permanent residency and citizenship in Germany, Syrians' whole futures were riding on their ability to navigate this system into the labor market. But first they had to learn German.

Language and Integration

On a hot day in the middle of June 2017, I met Mustafa outside of the Stuttgart central train station on the Konigstrasse, a pedestrian walkway lined with international chains including H&M, TJ Maxx, and McDonalds. I recognized him immediately because he resembled his brother who worked around the corner from me in a pizza restaurant in New Haven. He guided me expertly back down into the station, to the platform for the train that would take us to the *Heim,* or camp, where Ali lived with Om Ali, Nermine, and Nermine's one-year-old son.

Mustafa was more than twenty-one years old when his family was resettled in the United States, which made him ineligible to be included in their resettlement file. Ali's family became a sort of surrogate family for Mustafa in Germany. As Stuttgart's suburbs streamed past through the window, Mustafa recalled how, for the first few months in Germany, he struggled with navigating the public transit system. He had never lived in or visited a country that had one. But what made things more difficult for him is that people would not always stop when he asked for directions in his mixture of broken English and German. He recalled, chuckling, that one time a man did stop, only to admonish him for not knowing German before continuing briskly on his way.

The expectation that refugees should quickly learn the language came from rude Germans, but it was also a fact of the system. As Mustafa put it,

> You need [the German] language here for everything. To do anything. It's not like they will let you learn on the job; you have to do language training before you get the job. Any job.

More than a tool of human capital, language was a *prerequisite* for any other sort of skill. To apply for any apprenticeship, or any job at all, one needed to be certified up to the required language level—at least a B-1, but up to a C-1 for higher skilled jobs.

There was also a moral imperative to learn German, which was captured in the stranger's admonition. Speaking German is a core tenet of what it meant to belong in Germany. In de Maizière's treatise on *Leitkultur*, he writes, "Beyond language [. . .] there is something that holds us together at the core," thereby treating the German language as a taken-for-granted part of national culture, so obvious it's unnecessary to list. This moral imperative to learn would be felt by refugees in their day-to-day interactions, particularly the racist ones in which their presence in German public space was questioned. It was also, as the previous section clarified, a requirement of the Jobcenter through the Integration Classes.

Integration Classes require a commitment of 430 to 1,000 hours, depending on existing language ability. The course begins with the ABCs, progressing to A-1 and A-2, which teaches the basics of German vocabulary and grammar, ending at B-1. At this level, the learner should be able to "produce simple connected text" rather than complex sentences. Refugees who achieve the B-1 level were expected to begin to enter the labor market, although this level of German offers limited employment opportunities. The bus driver jobs Imad was applying to, for instance, required a minimum of a B-2.

In addition to language study, Integration Courses were also a place for Syrians to learn about "German culture." Specifically, the courses focused on the laws of Germany, rights and obligations, forms of community life, and "values that are important in Germany, such as freedom of religion, tolerance and gender equality." Alisha Heinemann, who conducted an ethnography of these courses, argued that there was an implicit assumption underling the instruction that the asylum seekers—who come from Muslim and Arab countries—did not believe in these same values and needed to be instructed.[26] This was at the heart of de Maizière's statement that these Integration Classes were a way to bring the new arrivals into the fold of the *Leitkultur.*

When Syrian refugees spoke about the classes, they expressed that the difficulty was in learning the language, particularly for people like Imad and other Syrians who had dropped out of school at a young age. It was hard, he explained, to pay attention in class. Besides, he said, the classes were geared towards teaching *Hochdeutsch*—formal German—whereas the work that he would do would be with people who speak in a dialect. However, as opposed to her husband, Amina was excited to be in German classes. "I've gotten very good," she boasted. "But you can't speak," Imad responded to his wife. "Yes, I can," she said, to which he retorted, "but not in colloquial."[27] But even for younger refugees, like Mustafa, Ali, and Nermine, learning the German language was considered terribly difficult.

After a twenty-minute ride from central Stuttgart, Mustafa and I arrived at the *Heim* where Ali, Nermine, their mother Om Ali, and her one-year-old son lived. It was a beige prefabricated two-story building with a bright orange and yellow railing on its second floor. Outside, there was a group of children from a mix of backgrounds playing soccer in the parking lot. A man stood under a tree, smoking a cigarette and yelling at the children in Arabic to watch a parked car. On the second floor, to the left of the narrow staircase, the door opened into the suite that the family shared. The room where we sat was tight, with two cots forming an L-shape along the walls. As they do in overcrowded homes of the poor around the world, the cots served double duty as couches by day and beds by night. The family was actively looking for a home to rent, which the Jobcenter assistance would cover, but they had not yet been successful, having been turned away by multiple landlords.

The conversation began with Nermine's divorce and traumatic separation from an abusive partner, the father of her son. But soon, it turned to her plans for her future in the country, which all hinged on learning German. But learning German, to them, like to Imad, felt so arduous. To make this point, Ali shared with us a joke that was making the rounds on Syrian WhatsApp chains about a Syrian woman who got pregnant and needed to have an abortion. By the time she learned to say "abortion" in German, the joke went, she'd already had the baby. Ali did not know how to say abortion in German, but he assured me it was lots of consonants strung together.[28] Ali continued,

> In English you only have "the," but in German you have like nine articles depending on what comes after it, you've got the *der*, you've got the *die*, you've got the *das* and so many more. And the pronunciation, it's so far from the Arabic tongue.

The "difficulty" of a given language is understood by linguists to be a function of factors such as grammar and pronunciation, but also social proximity. Though English and German might be equally dissimilar to Arabic, due to the widespread use of English in songs and movies and the teaching of basic English in school, the language felt much more socially proximate, whereas German felt heavy and foreign.

But the difficulty wasn't just shaped by the language, but also by the conditions in which the learners found themselves—conditions that differed by gender and obligation. By happy coincidence, while we sat together, Ali got the news that he'd passed his B-1 exam. *Mabrook!* we all cheered. Ali responded joyfully, "I don't know how it happened! *Alhamdullilah*. It was a really hard exam." I asked Ali if he would look for work now that he'd passed his B-1 exam. He responded that he planned to go on to B-2, and then C-level classes. "Each level has ten thousand words to learn," he explained, excited. Ali wanted to make something of himself in Germany, to get a good job, and B-1, the level required by the state as a basic criterion, would not ensure that. Though B-1 is all that is required of refugees for Integration Courses, the Jobcenter staff had approved him to take additional courses.

As a woman and caregiver, however, his sister Nermine faced different obstacles to her language learning, and she had different goals that she intended to achieve. Nermine, unlike her brother, was still in A-level classes. Her progress was hindered because she was both a single mother and navigating an ongoing court battle to get alimony from her ex-husband, whom she'd married just before departing from Syria to Germany with the hope that they'd build a life together in this new country. However, the man was physically and emotionally abusive and turned out to still be married to his first wife in Syria. This made Nermine unrecognizable as his partner by the German government, which did not acknowledge bigamous unions.

Nermine, however, could benefit from a stipulation in the German system that gave an exception to the Integration Course requirement for caregivers during the first three years of a child's life. Child caregivers, mostly mothers, could begin to send their children to preschool as early as one year old. Many of the Syrian arrivals, however, including Nermine, were hesitant to send their children to German preschools so young. This was also the case for many German mothers, as Caitlyn Collins explains in her comparative study, particularly in former West Germany, where there was still an expectation that a "good mother" is the sole caretaker of young children.[29]

Nermine, however, did not feel that she had the luxury to wait three years. She needed to find a job, as she was the sole provider for herself and her son. What's more, she felt that securing this education was important for her own sense of self,

> When you get an education, you feel like you are stronger, like your brain is stronger [. . .] I have ambition, I feel like we can do everything. If a man can create and fly a plane, can I not learn a language?

Nermine could afford to attend the language classes because her mother, who did not intend to build a new career in Germany after a long one as a salon owner in Syria, volunteered to be listed as the one-year-old's primary caretaker, which freed her up to watch the boy during the day while Nermine went to class. Still, Nermine struggled to attend when her mother's chronic back pain flared up or when her son was sick. She explained that since she was a student and her mother was the caretaker, the Jobcenter would deduct from her assistance if she stayed home because her mother needed extra support.

For Nermine, who wears a *hijab*, the language wasn't only a pathway to work, but also, she imagined, a way to shield herself from racism. On a bus trip, she asked a woman who was standing in an area that was designated for strollers to make way for her son's stroller. The woman responded *nein,* that she would not move. Nermine was furious but felt tongue-tied, lacking the ability to respond. A boy, who looked about high school age to Nermine, said something aggressively to the woman. The woman acted surprised, as though she had misunderstood what Nermine wanted from her, and she moved. Nermine continued,

> I wished I could speak the language so I could tell her off myself. Sometimes they look at you like, how is it that you are sitting while I am standing? And you are Syrian and I am German? Some are still imprinted by their history of racism.

The idea that the language was an antidote to foreignness was also explicitly relayed in the Integration Classes themselves. If she constructed a sentence perfectly but missed a final article or pronounced something wrong, her teacher would correct her, telling her that she sounded like an *Ausländer,* a foreigner. Nermine was not offended by her teacher and explained,

> They want you to pronounce everything like you're from here, and people who have been here a while, who are trained through this system, sound like they're German. People will think I'm a convert to Islam, not that I'm a foreigner by the end of this.

But while Nermine experienced racism due to her *hijab*, which she imagined might go away or be lessened if her German was better, her brother also experienced what he felt was racism because he did not speak the language fluently. As he put it,

> The language is very important to the Germans. They are frustrated when you cannot speak as well as they want you to. They'll say things like "you must speak German." I want to say to them, why are you belittling me? I'm trying to learn. But people aren't always nice when you are trying to say something, even if they understand you. At the Jobcenter, sometimes I can't say things perfectly because I'm new at the language, and she'll say "What?" and make you repeat what you said, even though she knows what you said. Not everyone is like that, but there are definitely people who *are* like that.

Mustafa too wondered if it was the chicken or the egg: would he feel less alienated if he learned the language? Or was he unable to learn the language because he was alienated? "Maybe if I had German friends I'd learn faster," he hypothesized. Indeed, those who *did* make connections with Germans saw improved language results. The strongest language learning outcomes came from romantic relationships, which in my study were between Syrian men and German women. Tito, for instance, in his early twenties, had a long-term German girlfriend whom he met at a mixer at a refugee camp, and he credits her with helping him learn the language. Hesham, a thirty-year-old law student who recently passed his C-1, also credited his dating life and his German friends with his quick acquisition of the language. Given the importance of alcohol to German culture, Hesham, who identifies as an atheist, wondered what his experience would have been like if he didn't drink, as is the case for many Syrians who are practicing Muslims.

Regardless of how comfortable they felt learning the language, the next step for the Syrians after learning German was to try to enter the German labor market. This would mean that they would be forced to navigate the German corporatist system, which featured strong links between the educational system and the labor market. This system, structured around indigenous learners and workers rather than foreign ones, is difficult for new entrants to permeate, as the next section demonstrates.

A German System for Germans

Tito arrived in Germany in April 2015 as a seventeen-year-old unaccompanied minor, making his case an outlier in this study. However, his pathway into the labor market demonstrates the structure of the German educational system, how it is intertwined with the country's labor market, and what happens when someone tries to traverse it. It also shows how this system obscures not only Syrian qualifications but also the dreams they held for themselves.

Tito is not an Arab Syrian but a Kurdish one, whose parents had long experienced oppression as Kurds—their language, Kurmanji, could not be taught in schools, written in publications, or used to name children or businesses. For this reason, as the war got closer to where they lived and as ISIS began to appear, they decided to smuggle their conscription-aged son out of the country. In the span of two months, Tito went from sitting at a high school desk to being smuggled into Europe.

Tito dreamed of arriving in Germany, where he imagined he'd have a physically and economically safe future. He was always planning to go to college, and now he dreamed of going to a German university to become an engineer. He fantasized about being employed in the world-renowned German automobile industry—at BMW, Porsche, or Mercedes.

When Tito got to the refugee camp, however, he learned that he didn't qualify to enter a German high school that prepared students for college. His grades in his eleventh year, during the war, were assessed as subpar, and he didn't have a high school diploma because he had to leave Syria before he could earn one. To get back on track for college, he was told, he would need to take enough German and then take an exam to qualify for a college-track high school. This process would take the seventeen-year-old at least four years and require that he be held back educationally, starting over in class with fourteen-year-olds. Tito was devastated. As he put it,

> The system here is great. But it's a German system for Germans. For us, it's a very difficult system, because they're saying to us that the German system is for you too. There's no recognition that I'm coming from Syria, that I have an eleventh-grade education, and that I want to continue to finish my education. Why can't I just continue on? It's racist. We left war and we came here to be met by this racist system.

German pathways into the labor market begin in secondary school. If a student wants to go to university, they need to attend a *Gymnasium,* or a high-level high school, where they will earn an *Abitur,* a diploma that qualifies them for entry to university. A student who does not have the interest or grades to enter a *Gymnasium* attends a *Hauptschule* or *Realschule* that offers vocational training. Students then enter the dual-training system, a federal system that involves cooperation between small- and medium-sized companies and publicly funded vocational colleges through a system of apprenticeship or *Ausbildung* in each vocation. Then, those who have the *Ausbildung* can secure jobs in that field, often at the same companies where they trained.

This path-dependent system is crucially consequential for economic mobility, especially for the Syrians in this study. Across Germany, eighty-six percent of workers attain upper secondary credentials. Just over half of those between the ages of twenty-five and sixty-four have a vocational education, and another third are estimated to have a university degree.[30] Unsurprisingly, the distribution of children across these different kinds of secondary schools reflects class inequalities, with lower income children more likely to enter vocational tracks or, worse, to end up in the ranks of the "low skilled," without any of these secondary degrees.[31] These inequalities increase as those children become adults with jobs that offer different earning potentials, since degrees are highly determinant of lifetime earnings.[32]

For Syrians who are unable or unwilling to be credentialed—who owe money to smugglers, need to send remittances home, or simply feel resistant to sitting in a classroom again, there are limited jobs available. These include jobs in the service industry that require little language skill, including cleaning jobs. A respondent in Regensberg described taking a job through a temporary agency, a *Leihfirmen,* on an eighteen-month contract in accordance with German laws. Though he was working at an automobile factory, he got paid less than colleagues who had an *Ausbildung,* and the work had a clear end-date. What's more, the temp agency charged a fee for each hour worked.

Another option for those who wanted to work without the requisite credentials was to take on a Minijob, a job that pays a maximum of EUR 450 a month. When I met him, Tito was working for a bicycle delivery service in such a Minijob. When he decided to relinquish Jobcenter assistance, this was the only work he could find. I had seen the company's bright orange packs and white lettering on the backs of bikes zipping up and down D. Martin-Luther-Strasse, the street that ran perpendicular to the Regensberg *Banhoff.* Tito gestured to his thick calves, exposed underneath his shorts, as evidence of the forty kilometers he rode each day delivering food from the city's restaurants to its residents. "One time I took ten pizzas together," he boasted, arms wide mimicking how high they were stacked. Though Tito did not mind the job, delivering pizzas was a stopgap measure, taken up after the future he had imagined for himself in Germany evaporated in the face of the logistics of the nation's education and employment systems. After applying to a few temp agencies that hired people to work in car factories and being denied, he was waiting to start an *Ausbildung* in the fall in house painting, something he admitted he had little interest in.

Altogether, this German system effectively creates a tightrope for new arrivals through which they could potentially secure a middle-class life if they're willing to go to vocational training. However, there were obstacles to this pathway. As the previous section showed, learning German wasn't easy. But even when armed with this tool, as Tito was, figuring out next stages wasn't easy either. The process of entering the German labor market would be harder for women who wore the *hijab* and who experienced discrimination. And it was also harder for people—predominantly men, but also women—who had long labor-market histories that they saw erased at their entry.

Like a Newborn Baby

Ali and Nermine's mother, Om Ali, a woman in her fifties, was widowed while her children were infants. To support her children as a single mother, she scraped together the money to start her own hair salon in her native Damascus. Nermine's earliest memories were in the salon, where their mother created a room for them to hang out in during the day, and where she would cook their meals and help them with their homework. "My mother suffered a lot," Nermine said, as her mother, who sat across from her, looked on.

> There were some beautiful, happy customers, but there were also the snooty girls who would never be pleased with even the nicest hair styles or the most perfect nails [. . .] My mother had to be a father and mother to me and Ali.

Despite her experience, Om Ali was not seen as a qualified hairdresser in Germany. Like most jobs in Germany, hairdressing required training in the dual-education system. Nermine and Ali also didn't qualify, though they grew up in the salon and had cut hair alongside their mother. If they wanted to become qualified after they learned German, they would need to enter years of training as a *Friseur*, a hairdresser.

Faced with these prospects, the three family members would make different decisions. Om Ali stayed out of the labor market and helped Nermine take care of her son. She did not anticipate rejoining the labor market, explaining matter-of-factly, "it's now time for the children to take care of me." Besides, the prospect of learning German seemed impossible to the woman who had little formal education in Syria and couldn't imagine learning a new language at her age.

Nermine considered taking the path to become a hairdresser, but she worried about her *hijab* hindering her opportunities. She explained, "I feel like [my *hijab*] might be seen as a negative thing for my clients, and particularly potential male clients coming in to get their hair cut." She explained that public interactions with Germans were always awkward for her as a Muslim woman,

> They all shake hands here, but I don't like it. I know they don't mean anything by it, but I just don't like it. But they judge you for it. If you don't kiss or you don't hug, they think that you are very ignorant and that you're super conservative. So, I don't give my hand immediately, but if someone puts his hand out, I will shake his hand.

Other women experienced the discrimination Nermine feared. Manal, who lived as a Palestinian refugee in Syria until she was made a refugee again by war, knew that although she would not have imagined working in Syria, staying out of the labor force would not be an option for her in Germany. "Both need to work," she explained referring to her and her husband, "it's how it's done here." So, she went to apply for an *Ausbildung* that would qualify her to work at daycares. However, she was discouraged by the Jobcenter staff who explained that Germans would not want a woman wearing a *hijab* educating their children.

While a Federal Constitutional Court ruled in 2015 that a blanket ban on *hijabs* in schools was not permissible, prior to that it was banned across eight states, including Bavaria. The majority of states where it was banned allowed crosses and Catholic nun's habits to be worn. A Human Rights Watch (HRW) report on this practice found that parliamentary debates and explanatory documents "emphasized the need to recognize the Western cultural tradition shaped by Christianity (and Judaism)." Reviewing these documents and laws, HRW found that Germany was failing to protect individuals' rights to freedom of religion and equality by discriminating against Muslim women, and that the ban also discriminated by gender. They state, "the measures effectively force women to choose between their employment and the manifestation of their religious beliefs, violating their right to freedom of religion and equal treatment."[33] Despite the 2015 decision, court cases continue to be brought by Muslim women who are denied positions due to their *hijab*.[34]

Manal was not the only woman denied a work opportunity due to her *hijab*. When Manal's sister-in-law, a pharmacist who graduated from a Syrian university and had her degree, went to apply for a training job at a pharmacy, she was asked if she would take off her *hijab*. When her answer was no, she didn't get the training position. A 2016 audit study found that these experiences are likely common for Muslim women. An applicant with a Turkish name needed to send 1.4 times as many applications as an identical applicant with a German name to receive a callback, and an applicant who wore a headscarf needed to send 4.5 times more applications than an identical applicant with a German name and no headscarf.[35] Though the notion of *Leitkultur* and the training manuals for integration emphasize a need for gender equality among new arrivals (assuming a lack of commitment to it), with these policies and practices it is German employers that discriminate against Muslim women.

Even with these obstacles ahead of her, Nermine knew that she wanted to enter the German labor market as quickly as possible. "I have to be a mother and father to my son," she said, complaining that her ex-husband was dodging his child support responsibilities. Nermine contemplated taking on a cleaning job, which could be secured without vocational training. She abandoned that idea in favor of steady work that could provide a good living for her son as his only parent. She settled on beginning training as a home health aide, explaining, "it's like a humanitarian job here, and I like the idea of helping people." This job had been suggested to her by a Jobcenter employee. As she explained,

> They ask what do you want to become? What job do you want to work? You give them your preferences. Then they tell you that you have to do x, y, and z training to get that job. Or sometimes they tell you we have a demand for certain kinds of work, and they encourage you to do that.

In addition to coordinating benefits for asylum seekers as well as monitoring their income and their attendance in the Integration Courses, the Jobcenter's main objective, as its name alludes, is to connect asylum seekers to jobs. Once asylees like Nermine, who did not have recognizable qualifications in the German system, reached a B-1 level of German, they were expected to begin to look for entry level jobs or for an *Ausbildung*.

Asylees were pushed towards occupations where the German government had identified a shortage, among which were geriatric nurses and home health aides. The German population was rapidly aging, which created a huge need for this kind of labor. Nermine would have to apply, and if accepted, her *Ausbildung* would begin the following fall. Once an applicant is accepted to an

Ausbildung, they sign a contract with the employer offering the job. Then they are enrolled in a *Berufsschule*, the school where they do their theoretical training. Trainees are paid a salary by the company while they attend the training, which lasts two to three years depending on the profession.

Ali, like Nermine, no longer wanted to work as a hairdresser. He would have to get retrained anyway, so he took it as an opportunity to explore other work. He wanted to continue with German classes and was hoping he'd eventually be able to get a job in Germany working with automobiles. Since he made quick progress through to his B-1, the Jobcenter employee told him he'd be able to continue with his German classes. His hope was to find an *Ausbildung* where he could work in automobiles, the lifeblood of Bavaria. For now, however, he took on a Minijob at a hair salon, a job that came second nature to him. He also confided that he cut people's hair at their *Heim* for extra cash.

Other young men who, like Ali, had a work history chose to reskill in their professions. This was the case for Zaid, who, like his friend Tito, was Kurdish. He grew up stateless because of a census by the Syrian government in 1962 that stripped ethnic Kurds of their citizenship. In 2011, three hundred thousand Kurds had their citizenship reinstated, including Zaid's family's, to discourage them from joining the tempest of national protest and to make their men eligible for conscription. Zaid's parents, who tried and failed to leave Syria by boat in the 1990s, decided that the time had come to leave for good. They made their way to Turkey, abandoning the carpentry business that Zaid's father began before Zaid was born and that was registered under Zaid's mother's name, since she was "Arab" and therefore not stateless. Zaid dropped out of school in the ninth grade to work in the carpentry shop. "Bedrooms, kitchens, couches, frames for the windows, doors, we made it all," he said with pride.

Zaid's father made the dangerous journey to Greece and then Germany alone, leaving Zaid and his brother in Turkey where they continued to work in carpentry. After Zaid's father was granted asylum in Germany, he was able to bring Zaid, his sister, and their mother over through the country's reunification program. His brother, who was too old to be eligible for family reunification, remained in Turkey.

Zaid and his father arrived in Germany with forty years of experience between them in carpentry. However, because they lacked formal credentials, neither would be seen as skilled carpenters in the German system. Zaid's father would not be able to own his own shop with his own apprentices as he had in Syria, as this required a *meister* status, a degree after the *Ausbildung* is secured. For Zaid's father, the idea of retraining was exceptionally difficult. As Zaid explained,

In Syria, my father was just taking the measurements, saying here's where you have to cut the wood. But we were the ones who cut, we were the ones who put the pieces together and finished the product. My father was the boss, the one who told us what to do, that was it. So, it is really hard for him here. He has lost his place.

Zaid, however, was willing to take on an apprenticeship. Through the help of the Jobcenter, he was able to find an *Ausbildung* in carpentry. He attended a *Berufschule* where he took classes on the principles of carpentry while also doing practicums. While Zaid aced the practicum—he was the best in the class—he struggled in the theoretical components because they were in German. "I failed my B-1 exam," he explained sheepishly. Zaid, who had been out of school for over a decade at this point, struggled with retaining information. As Tito said of his friend, "For those who didn't go to school in Syria, who were working, it is really hard for them to learn. Their tongue is heavy." Zaid was worried that he would fail out of the *Ausbildung*. "They won't let me stay if I can't pass the exams," he said.

For those with established careers, like Om Ali, Zaid's father, or Imad, restarting was too much. They thought of the *Ausbildung* as something for the young to do. As Rajiya's brother, Mazen, who arrived in Germany after her, put it,

> I want to work, but in order to work, I need to study for three years. And language learning will take about three years too. So they won't let me work in my field until I have six years of learning. It means that I have to spill six years of my life. I'm thirty, pour another six years on top that makes me thirty-six before I can start working in this country.

When I encouraged him, saying that he was, in fact, young, he said, "war added fifty years to my life, I do not feel young." With a background in tailoring and having worked multiple jobs when he was displaced in Egypt, including at restaurants and in grocery stores, he had both the will and, he thought, the ability to work. He just needed the opportunity. But, as another man, Mo'men, put it, "When you get here it's like you're born new. I came here like a newborn baby."

Those who were more highly skilled, who had the paperwork to prove their positions, had a better chance vis-à-vis this system, though they were also systemically underemployed and required retraining. Hesham, for instance, who had a master's degree in law from Cairo University, qualified to be retrained as a lawyer in Germany after he passed his C-1 exam. He would also have to attend an additional two years of classes. And Bassam, a doctor in Syria who was in his sixties and who had already retired and moved to a farm outside of his native Damascus, also qualified for retraining. Bassam learned German quickly, reaching a C-1 in just under a year, which he attributed to already speaking three other languages—English, Arabic, and Russian. However, despite his years of work and his independent practice, he had to restart as a resident. After two additional years of training and passing exams, he was assigned to a rural area in the former East Germany, where no other doctors wanted to work.

Even for the highly skilled, however, pathways to the labor market could be unclear. Reham, who was an Arabic-language teacher in Syria with a long career, and her husband, who was a lawyer, did not have this luck. They lived in Regensberg, where he worked for one of the temp agencies at an automobile factory, a far cry from his former training or occupation. He, like many others, found himself underemployed and struggling to work his way up as a stranger in a strange system.

———

At the time of this writing, 800,000 people in Germany, or over one percent of the country's population, are Syrian, the majority of whom arrived as refugees. Through their asylum these Syrians came face-to-face with a German system designed for Germans, a system enabled by the country's limited history of admitting immigrants with the intention of their long-term integration. Syrians entering this system would find the German state generous and their needs met. However, they would also find their histories and their potential as people unrecognized.

By not recognizing new arrivals' abilities, the German government structured their human capital. Three years into their asylum, seventy-two percent of Syrians remained unemployed, despite a need for them in the German labor market. In 2020, half were reported to have either an internship, a Minijob, an apprenticeship, or a full-time job, although they were often underemployed.[36] In 2021, an integration summit was held to discuss a hundred-point plan for immigrant integration, with calls to combat discrimination, include political representation of immigrants, and move beyond a focus on language-learning in the pursuit of inclusion. Gonca Türkeli-Dehnert, who heads the foundation Deutschlandstiftung Integration, spoke directly to the issue of valuing newcomers, saying of immigrants, "They don't have to stay here, and they won't if what they have to offer isn't recognized."[37]

The non-recognition of credentials and the system of credentialization meant different things to different people. For those, often men, with long labor-market histories and who lacked formal paperwork, non-recognition meant an erasure of those histories. For younger people and for women who didn't have work histories, being in Germany opened new possibilities. While they too felt the harm of having their labor-market experiences and aspirations erased, there were pathways to middle-class lives set out before them. However, living in Germany and entering its labor market was also an experience mired by racism, particularly for women, whose *hijabs*, markers of their identity, were deemed incompatible with Germany's *Leitkultur*, and who were constant targets of discrimination.

Despite dissimilarities in the incorporation policies of the three countries included in this book—the United States, Canada, and Germany—the Syrian newcomers themselves had similar concerns and hopes for their futures. More still, they had the same fear for their relatives who had not made it to countries of asylum and resettlement and were concerned about supporting them. The following chapter follows these concerns, examining how refugees who arrive *here*, in the United States, Canada, and Germany, attempt to help their loved ones *there*, in Syria and the broader diaspora, within the constraints of their state-structured resources.

6

Here and There

In the summer of 2016, Abo Mahmoud, Om Mahmoud, and their six children were living in a bungalow near Hyde Park in Toronto. Their white siding-clad home was perched on a hill. Driving up to it I could see two flags taped up in the window, in front of disheveled blinds. The larger was the Canadian flag, and the smaller was the flag of the Free Syrian Army—three red stars in the middle of two thick parallel stripes, the top green and the bottom black. Inside the house was a second similar display of three dried maple leaves taped-up to the wall above another Free Syrian Army flag. The juxtaposition of the two flags, one of their heritage and revolution, the other of their refuge, was a shrine to the families' journey and allegiances.

Abo Mahmoud was standing outside his home when I came to join the family for *iftar*. The sun was still up, but he was smoking a cigarette, which is prohibited during the Muslim fast. Though I said nothing, he shrugged in explanation, saying, "there's no one to monitor my religion here. I never liked to fast." Though he wasn't fasting, he put together an elaborate meal, which he prepared on a grill in his driveway. There was chicken, *kofta*, and fish that he caught in a local pond. Om Mahmoud, Abo Mahmoud's wife, made the sides: rice, potatoes, and *mahshi*. After the *athan* sounded, announcing the end of the fast, we sat on the floor of the living room and ate together from large communal plates as the television broadcast news from Syria.

Finishing my meal, I leaned back onto the couch behind me, noticing for the first time a laptop in the corner. The screen had a Skype window open, and in it was a little boy climbing onto a couch. As Abo Mahmoud saw me noticing the boy, he yelled to him, "Say *assalamu alaikum* to Madame Heba." The boy giggled and waved, and I waved back. Then, a man joined the boy on the screen and waved to me as well. The man was Abo Mahmoud's brother, who was living with his family in Mafraq, Jordan. They were having their *suhoor*—their pre-dawn meal in preparation for the day of fasting—while we were having our *iftar*. As Om Mahmoud poured us tea in Toronto, we sat together with the family on the screen. My accent gave me away as Egyptian, and everyone, online and offline, tried their hand at Egyptian banter learned from old movies.

While the rest of the world would learn to sit with loved ones on Skype or Zoom in the context of the COVID-19 pandemic, refugees, separated from loved ones by manmade borders, were already experts at the task. On the night of their arrival in New Haven, the resettlement agency gave each arriving family a flip phone that lacked internet access. The next morning, they invariably sought out a data plan and a smartphone. Though that may seem like an extravagance to an onlooker, to the men and women in all three countries it was a necessity that enabled them to communicate with those who mattered most. Phone calls, videos, presence on speaker phone, as well as video attendance of formal events—of weddings and funerals and baby's celebrations—were crucial and deeply meaningful ways to keep up family ties.

If we were to trace these online connections between those who resettled or were given asylum and those who lived in countries of immediate refuge, or who live in Syria, we'd draw refugees' social network. These transnational ties tell us something about who Syrians are—their kin networks, who they love, and for whom they feel responsible.[1] They would also show us remittance pathways. While better-resourced immigrants use transnational networks as sources of business ties, with money going back and forth, for those whose contacts are less-resourced, like the men and women in this book, there is a unidirectional transfer to those in dire circumstances elsewhere in the diaspora.[2] This network is also a blueprint for potential avenues for mobility—the nodes of the network that are in safer countries become anchors, possibilities for family reunification.[3]

Opportunities to send remittances or petition for reunification, however, are contingent on one's resources, and particularly on one's economic and language ability, which are shaped, as I've argued throughout this book, by state *investment* and *recognition*. As we learned in the last three chapters, in the United States, where there is an expectation of self-sufficiency, there is scant *investment* in newcomers, including a lack of support in learning the language and in time and money to adjust existing skills or gain new ones. In Canada, state funding does support newcomers in these same pursuits, while in Germany, despite generous *investment*, the system fails to *recognize* newcomer abilities, hindering their entry into the labor market and the German system built around it.

In this chapter, I argue that, by structuring new arrivals' human capital, these national systems are also shaping their ability to help their loved ones elsewhere—a brother in Syria who was considering joining a paid militia to feed his family, a sister in Norway trying to flee her abuser, and a father in Syria felled by a stroke. Since prospects for family reunification in all three countries are also contingent on the resources of language, finances, or both, the same systems shape the ability of refugees to petition for family reunification. But sending money out of the country or reunifying with family was not only determined by refugee resources—it was also shaped by other state policies on cash transfers and immigration laws.

While sociological work emphasizes the benefits of immigrant networks both local and transnational, this chapter tells a story of depletion, of poor people trying, and sometimes failing, to help their poorer relatives at great personal cost. The takeaway is not, however, that transnational social networks are bad for refugees. The takeaway is that this entire network links people who are struggling under systems that could do more to support them. The resources within this network are shaped by the investment in and recognition of refugee potential *here*—in the United States, Canada, and Germany—but also by the resources denied family members *there*—in Turkey or Lebanon or Syria. Refugees in this book are shouldering the burden for people whom the world has neglected—a reality in which the wealthy countries where they reside are complicit.

Remittances and Connected Lives

Across all three countries, when the men and women in this book created a budget or considered taking on new work, they factored in both the expenses of their own households, in terms of rent and bills, as well as their support for their families in the diaspora. They felt responsible to provide for loved ones who were living in camps, in tight quarters in Istanbul or Amman, or who were still back in Syria, suffering under astronomical inflation and constant threat of violence. The ability to send money back, however, varied depending on the country they were in, which determined their expendable cash from state benefits and their overall earnings prospects.

The case of Sarah clarifies both the importance and difficulty of sending money home—particularly under the constraint of United States self-sufficiency. Sarah's parents and siblings remained in Syria, moving around the country to escape bouts of intense violence. They lacked the resources or opportunity to seek refuge outside of Syria. On the day the Trump administration bombed a Syrian airbase in Homs in April 2017, Sarah called me to recount a joke which captured the precarity of her family's situation in the country. "Do you know *Om Arba'a we erbe'een*?" she began. I understood the literal translation—"mother of forty-four legs"—and through some explanation deduced that it's the Syrian word for centipede. She continued,

Anyway, the joke goes there's an abusive centipede who married a chick. When they fight, the chick doesn't know where the beating is coming from—an arm, a leg, what exactly is hitting her. This is what Syria is like. We're the chick that doesn't know where it's coming from, the beating.

At the same time as the bombing, her parents and brother were being displaced yet again. Sarah's loss from war was steeper than that of many of the other families in this book. Two of her younger brothers were killed within a year of one another earlier in the war. She regularly posts photos of them on her Facebook page. The round face and big cheeks of her younger brother seemed mismatched to the blank expression he wore in the photo and the machine gun he held. Sarah, in her caption, referred to him by his *laqab,* or nickname, of Abo Ahmed, for the son he'd never get to father. He was killed after joining a local militia. Militias were a way to fight against the Assad regime's onslaught, but they also offered pay in the absence of any other economic opportunities.

When Sarah's mother, father, and remaining brother were moved to an internal displacement camp near Aleppo from their home in Homs, around the same time as the Trump air raid in 2017, she worried that her remaining and youngest brother would join a militia to secure an income for his family and follow his two siblings to an early death. Their mother, who shared Sarah's fears, threatened impotently to kill him before he could do something stupid that would take yet another of her babies. Sarah felt that it was incumbent on her, the one who "made it" to the United States, to come up with the cash to keep him from joining.

Sarah, however, was struggling herself. She has a chronic illness, a nerve disorder, which limits her ability to work any manual jobs she'd be qualified for. Her husband, Atef, whose income was already low—he worked at a pub as a dishwasher—had been hospitalized a few months prior due to a mental health crisis, with seizure-like symptoms.[4] Like many other displaced people he struggled with post-traumatic stress disorder, and anxiety over the fate of his own nuclear family in the United States, as well as that of loved ones back home. Though the family was selected for resettlement by the United States government *because* of their experience of war, Sarah's chronic conditions, and their overall humanitarian need, these needs were not supported upon arrival.

Even though Sarah did not know if she could pay her own rent, helping her family and potentially saving her brothers' life became her top priority. She scrimped and saved from the money her husband brought in and made and sold cookies at a fair to attempt to put a small amount aside, but it wasn't enough. Sarah reached out to a charitable group that offered help to Syrian families, which, after fact-checking the situation, raised money to add to the few hundred dollars Sarah had managed to save. While Sarah, as a result of this assistance, was able to help her family at a critical juncture, she knew more difficulties would come. She was racked with worry about how her family would manage and whether she'd be able to help keep them alive, sheltered, and fed.

Sarah was not alone. All of the men and women in this book dealt with continuous family crises. Rajaa would need to send money home to help pay for her father's medical care after a series of strokes left him immobile and nonverbal. Jamil would send money to his sister-in-law in Turkey to pay for her smuggler fees into Europe when his brother was diagnosed with terminal cancer shortly after his arrival in Germany. Zafir sent money to Jordan to help with his father-in-law's funeral expenses after he died suddenly, shortly after seeing a YouTube clip that showed the home that he had built in Homs destroyed by siege.

In the face of scarcity, these crises could sometimes result in arguments between couples as to *whose* families back home deserved support, arguments shaped by gendered expectations for breadwinning and remittances.[5] For instance, when nineteen-year-old Narjis, who was living in New Haven, wanted to send money home to her sister, whose son was chronically ill, her husband Zachareya demurred. Narjis received pin money from Zachareya, a monthly allowance that she could spend however she wanted and that she intended to send to her sister in Turkey. However, when she asked Zachareya for help sending the money to her sister, he kept dodging her request. He did not want her to send the money, Narjis realized, because his mother, who lived near Narjis' sister, would be offended that he had not sent it to her. He was the man, Narjis explained, and his mother felt that she was more deserving of what she considered her son's money. Eventually Zachareya helped Narjis send the money, but only after her sister promised to keep the cash a secret from his parents.

Men and women in Canada and Germany faced similar crises to Sarah and Narjis, but in the context of less financial scarcity. They were also better able to set aside meaningful amounts that went home each month.[6] In Germany, for instance, where the Jobcenter benefits were generous, Imad was able to send home a few hundred euros each month to help support an extended network of family members who were suffering greatly. He explained,

> I know people who are dying of starvation, people who have not had an apple in five years. I can't eat while I know people who are starving with no food. If I didn't have to send anyone money, this assistance from the government would be enough, we don't need anything else to live. We could go to Italy for vacation, or we could go to France. It's like EUR 200 round trip, it isn't a big deal, and it wouldn't impact us negatively at all, we can afford it. But we can't because we send that money home instead.

Like Imad, Abo Mahmoud in Canada also sent money to family members, drawing from the state assistance that he received from the Canadian government as a refugee and on the Canada Child Benefit (CCB) for his seven children. On one of my early visits to Canada in 2016, I received a call from him asking if I could accompany him to the bank. Once there he wired CAD 500 to his sister in Norway. He explained on the drive to the bank that his sister had gotten married to a man she met on the journey between Turkey and Germany. She thought that this marriage might keep her safe from the "dangers of the road"—sexual violence that single women migrants face. But her husband, it turns out, was the danger. He physically abused Abo Mahmoud's sister, and when she tried to leave him, he attempted to keep her from accessing the state benefits to which she was entitled. The money her brother sent her allowed her to rent a room while she figured out how to reinstate her assistance from the Norwegian government. It saved her from homelessness in a country where she knew no one while she dealt with this traumatic ordeal.

While those seeking refuge in Canada and Germany (as opposed to the United States) had easier access to money in their initial years because of more generous social benefits, across all three countries sending money to loved ones in dire circumstances meant working around government oversight over the financial transactions made by those receiving social benefits. The external transfer of state benefits—welfare in the United States, Jobcenter support in Germany, or refugee assistance and welfare in Canada—was prohibited by the state. There was also another concern for refugees who were sending money directly to Syria, that the Syrian government would be able to trace the funds and harass the relatives who received it.

These men and women navigated the restrictions creatively. In Germany, due to the presence of over half a million Syrians, a *hawala* system emerged. *Hawala* is a method for cash transfer that has been around since the eighth century, in which a representative in one country receives money and authorizes their partner in another to disburse money to the recipient, for a fee.[7] *Hawala* is preferred over formal channels such as bank transfers or Western Union because the transactions are not observable by any governments, including the Syrian one. It also offers better rates than formal cash transfer markets. Conversion rates from euros or dollars to Syrian pounds can vary widely, with government rates at about half of what black market rates offer.[8]

Without a *hawala* system, families in the United States and Canada had no choice but to use formal channels. Abo Mahmoud, desperate to get money to his sister, used a bank transfer, though he admitted that it was a risky decision. Meanwhile, families in New Haven used Western Union to transfer money out of the country while they were receiving state welfare or TANF payments, which was less visible than a bank transfer but still could potentially be tracked by the United States government.

The men and women in this study tried their best to hide these transfers. Asad, in his early twenties, asked me to go with him to the CVS near his house in West Haven to help complete a money transfer. Though there was an Arabic language option on the Western Union call, the automated list for selecting a language was long and confusing. On this day, he was sending USD 100 to his sister, who had recently had a baby and who lived in a suburb of Cairo in

Egypt. But because his sister and her husband were undocumented in Egypt, he was sending the money to their friend who had a formal identification card and could receive the transfer. Western Union charged Asad USD 10 to send the money. As I helped him navigate the transaction, I recognized there was a second and more important reason he had asked me to come with him—he was hopeful that I would transfer the money under my name so that he could avoid oversight by the United States government.

Not knowing the person to whom he was sending money, and having grown up with horror stories like that of Mahmoud Reza Banki—an Iranian man who, after sending remittances home, was accused of violating United States sanctions and imprisoned, I apologetically declined. Other immigrants have over the years been targeted by United States authorities for aiding terrorism after sending a remittance payment to the wrong person or to an organization deemed unlawful by the United States government. This experience with Asad, however, revealed another strategy that these newcomers employed: that of using different senders, preferably co-ethnics who are not on welfare. Another technique was to send small amounts. Rajaa explained that she had heard that one should send less than USD 1,000 because the government doesn't check small amounts. She couldn't be sure because she never had that much money to send.

Once the money was out of the country, on its way to family or an intermediary in Jordan or Turkey, the sender in the United States or Canada could then use a *hawala* broker to transfer money further to Syria. This was an expensive process. Rajaa, who often struggled to decide whether to send money to her elderly parents in Syria or her brother in Turkey, explained, "Between the Western Union fee, the *hawala* fee, and the conversion rates between dollars, Turkish lira, and Syrian pounds, half of the money is lost in the process."

But perhaps the most drastic strategy to prevent monitoring of money transferred to loved ones in need was one taken by Wael in Canada, who sent money to his family in Lebanon each month. He decided to never accept welfare, despite the Canadian governments' express expectation that those resettled would require welfare support after their refugee-specific assistance ended a year after their arrival. In part, this decision, as described in chapter 4, was motivated by the stigma he felt welfare recipients faced in Canada. But it was also motivated by a desire to avoid government oversight in these remittance transfers. As he put it,

Welfare is restricting. You can only have CAD 5,000 in the bank, you can't get caught sending money back home to your family. You are limiting yourself in the kinds of jobs you can work because you need to earn under a certain amount. But I want to build a future, and progress in work, and start settling here, so that I can help my family in Lebanon, too. That's not something you can do on welfare.

During the initial years of resettlement and asylum, those who sought refuge in the United States, pushed by the self-sufficiency imperative, entered the American labor market, while those in Canada, supported by state assistance, were just beginning to earn an income, and those in Germany who were working to re-credentialize, were not yet earning an income. Those who *did* work in Canada, however, including Wael, had higher incomes than people in the United States—due in large part to *investment* in his human capital by the Canadian state, particularly with respect to language skills. This too shaped remittances. Even after they reached the limit on welfare benefits (two years after arrival), Rajaa, Sarah, and others continued to insist on sending money home and continued to struggle to come up with the money. By contrast, Wael felt freed by his non-reliance on welfare and was earning an income that allowed him to send more money home.

Even when they sent money home, however, men and women in the United States, Canada, and Germany carried with them tremendous guilt over the fates of family members. This guilt is captured in an afternoon conversation with Nermine, Omar, and their children in Canada. In April 2017, the family took a trip to Niagara Falls. "It was an incredible trip," Nermine gushed. "The best ever," her son chimed in. They went to an all-you-can-eat Chinese buffet while there, where all of the children got cotton candy for dessert. But, in the midst of an excited retelling, Nermine paused. "What's wrong?" I asked. She explained that whenever she thinks about the outing and how much fun she had, the memory is accompanied by a pang of guilt. "My parents struggle to get basic necessities, and look at how much we spent on fun," she said. Omar chimed in. "Even when we're smiling, there's a dark spot in our hearts."

Because families in the United States, Canada, and Germany were responsible for so many others, the assistance that they received in destination countries, the *investment* and *recognition* of their skills and capacities, and their ability to earn money shaped not only their lives but also the lives of their loved ones. The money that was at the disposal of refugees was hugely consequential not only *here* but also *there*, sometimes making the difference in life-or-death situations. But sending money home was treating a symptom, rather than the problem, of their family members' displacement. The real goal of many of the families in the United States was to remove their loved ones from harm's way by bringing them from *there* to *here*, a prospect that also depended, in part, on their language skills and financial resources.

Reunification

Immigrant families have long been anchors for their relatives to join them. Scholars of immigration have shown that social networks facilitate immigrant mobility—moving to a new country and imagining oneself living and working there becomes easier when someone you know, and particularly a family member, has done it, can tell you how, and can support you in the process.[9] Not only does migration through social networks matter for the individual immigrant, but it also transforms the makeup of cities—like Dearborn, Michigan, the main Arab enclave in the United States, or Berlin's Sonenallee, a Turkish enclave, towards which Syrians have also gravitated.[10]

The ability to immigrate however, varies for different categories of immigrants. Borders in the United States, Canada, and Germany are designed to keep out non-White migrants from the Global South. Legal prospects for reuniting with loved ones, therefore, are often contingent on whether those who have made it to destination contexts can petition for family members to join them. In all three countries, this legal petitioning requires language ability and financial resources—which are structured by the state's incorporation policies.

For those resettled in the United States, the possibility of reunifying with relatives in Syria or Turkey or Jordan is drastically curtailed before one attains citizenship. There are only two legal ways to petition for reunification *without* citizenship. First, family reunification policies allow for spouses and children under the age of eighteen to join a resettled refugee, an important policy for people whose nuclear family remains trapped in perilous circumstances, but a limited one that does not apply to other family members. The second is the remote possibility that the United States government independently selects your family members for resettlement. This is exceedingly rare, given that only one percent of the world's refugees will ever be offered resettlement.

Even if a family member *is* independently selected for resettlement, their ability to travel is subject to political whims. Afaf, a mother of twelve who arrived in the United States with only four of her children, dreamed of bringing two other children who, along with their families, were living in particularly bad circumstances. Her daughter, a newly married eighteen-year-old living in a camp with her young child and husband, *did* receive a call from the United Nations for potential resettlement in the United States. Over the coming year, she and her husband completed all of their interviews. However, in January 2017, then-President Trump signed Executive Order 13769, which suspended Syrian refugee resettlement and limited travel from Muslim majority countries. Afaf collapsed upon hearing the news, knowing that her daughter would no longer be able to join her. The Trump administration slashed the refugee resettlement program further from an anticipated 110,000 people in 2016 to just 18,000 in 2020. While the Biden administration increased the quota, at the time of this writing, Afaf's daughter remained in the camp owing to a backlog of cases.

If a family member is neither eligible for family reunification nor selected for resettlement, the other option, only available to citizens, is to bring them to the United States through a "Petition for an Alien Relative." These petitions can take years, if not decades, to come to fruition. Family-based migration, however, is the basis of the United States' immigration policy. In the United States, the 1965 Immigration and Nationality Act was written to end a quota system in place since the turn of the twentieth century, which limited immigration from outside of Western Europe. However, policy makers, in an attempt to maintain the country's Whiteness, wrote the 1965 Act to give preference for family-based immigration, assuming that since people from Western Europe were the ones admitted in the United States, these petitions would limit admissions to their (White) relatives. The unanticipated consequence of the 1965 Act was that immigrants from outside of Western Europe, long denied this prospect, used this system to bring their families. The coming decades saw a rise in non-White migration to the country.[11]

To secure the American citizenship required to petition for an "Alien Relative," however, one must be able to read and write English sentences and sit for a civics exam in English, answering correctly six out of ten questions selected from a list of one hundred possible questions. Except for one woman who already spoke English when she arrived in the United States and another who was able to attend English classes at a community college early on, none of the men or women in this book had the English proficiency required to sit for the citizenship exam once they were finally eligible to apply five years after arrival.[12] The reason for this is clear—the United States failed to support them or invest in their language skills.

Indeed, resettled refugees in the United States are not the only ones that struggle to gain citizenship. According to the Pew Research Center, only forty-two percent of Mexican immigrants who qualify for the citizenship exam are planning on taking it, citing financial barriers (a cost of more than USD 975) as well as language barriers. This contrasts with more than eighty percent of immigrants from India, who tend to be wealthier and better resourced.[13] All low-income immigrants, refugee or not, must figure out how to study for the exam while working long hours at multiple jobs that do not necessarily expose them to English speakers. Benjamin Franklin and Betsy Ross feel extremely distant to those working the backs of bars or cleaning hotels.[14] In short, the citizenship process, as well as the limited support for immigrants to acquire the linguistic and financial tools that it requires, both discriminates against the impoverished *here* and denies their families *there* a chance for travel and reprieve.

Historically, Canada's immigration policy parallels the one in the United States. Like in the United States, racial quotas were in place until the 1960s to curb the arrival of non-White immigrants. However, as described in chapter 4, rather than supplant this system with family reunification, as was the strategy in the United States, the Canadian immigration policy selects based on an immigrant's skills, using a point system to recruit immigrants who will contribute to the Canadian economy.

While the Canadian system does not require citizenship for family petitions (a permanent resident can also submit one),[15] it limits possibilities for
family reunification. Familial sponsorships in the Canadian system are limited
to partners (spouse, common-law partner, conjugal partner), son or daughter,
or parent or grandparent. Only in special situations can an immigrant sponsor another category of relative, and then the possibility is limited to just one
relative. What's more, you must show that you have the financial means to
sponsor your relative when they arrive in terms of food, shelter, and clothing,
to "make sure that the relative does not need social assistance."[16] This means
that your ability to bring your family is contingent on income, which in turn is
shaped by the *investment* of the Canadian government in those seeking refuge
and the ability to use and develop their human capital.

Beyond family petitions, there are two other possibilities in Canada for
refugees to petition for family reunification. First, there's a "one year window"
to bring one's spouse or dependent children who are listed on refugee forms
but who did not arrive with the refugee—a provision similar to that of the
United States for immediate family. Second, and unlike the United States, as
part of the country's private sponsorship program, there is also the possibility
to privately sponsor family members as refugees. However, this too requires
that the petitioner raise money to support the arriving family.

Somaya, who lived in Canada with her husband Nizar, was working tire-
lessly to bring her mother and brother from Jordan, where they lived in an office
space shared with two other families. She visited an Arab-Canadian NGO to
ask about her options. They told her she would need to raise CAD 40,000.
Through Somaya's husband's employment, the couple was able to put aside
CAD 10,000, but not the full amount. Somaya wrote an email to Lifeline Syria,
an organization that supports private sponsorship, and they confirmed that the
chances of bringing her family over would increase if she raised more money.
"But everyone is trying to raise money for their families," she explained. The
prospects of her being successful in finding someone to match and exceed
the amount she had raised were slim. What's more, even if she did, there were
quotas that limited how many refugees could come through the private sponsorship program. Five years later, Somaya had not brought over either her
brother or mother.

While Somaya's nuclear family was sponsored by the government in
Canada, those whose resettlement was supported through private sponsors
had better prospects. For instance, Abdelhameed, who was resettled along
with his wife Amina and their three children in Toronto through government
sponsorship, were also supported by a Group of Five as part of Canada's hybrid
Blended Visa Office-Referred Program.[17] This well-resourced group was able
to advocate for Abdelhameed and to raise money through their network to
bring his brother to Canada. For Abdelhameed, who struggled with mental

health issues, his brother's arrival made his life in Canada more tolerable, and it protected his brother, who was living in a camp, from many more years of legal liminality.

Finally, in Germany, where half a million Syrians were admitted, family reunification was complicated and a major political flashpoint. Unlike the United States or Canada, outside of spouses and children, applications for family reunification in Germany are limited to cases of proven "extreme hardship." And there are a lot of stipulations. A non-EU spouse must pass a German language exam to secure the visa—an issue faced by Mustafa, a man in his early thirties who became engaged to a Syrian woman he courted online. As he describes in his contribution to the afterword to this book, his fiancée had to take and pass A-level German language exams. Mustafa, as the petitioner, also had to prove that he had command of German *and* a sufficient income and that he was not himself reliant on public benefits. Mustafa took a low-wage job at a café at the train station to be able to prove he could support his partner. He also had to sit for the B-1 exam. As we saw in chapter 5, and as Mustafa elaborates in the afterword, he had to navigate the pressures of non-recognition of his credentials on the one hand and needed to learn the language and earn an income on the other.

Those unable to learn the language and find work had limited prospects for family reunification. For instance, Mo'men, a thirty-two-year-old man who was engaged to a woman in Turkey, remained on Jobcenter assistance five years after his arrival. He was at an A-2 level in his language classes, not yet admitted to the B-1 that is necessary to qualify for most jobs, permanent residency, and eventually citizenship. Like many other people in this book, Mo'men struggled with his mental health, and he admitted to me that he often felt depressed. Mo'men felt that the German system's unwillingness to *recognize* his years of college education left him in a downward spiral. He was depressed and discouraged—feeling, as described in chapter 5, that he was being treated like a "newborn baby" rather than a grown man. This discouragement was exacerbated by his separation from his partner. But he was unable to petition for her to join him *because* he was not making progress in the German system. Mo'men told me of people who, in a predicament similar to his, had simply gone home to Syria or to back to Lebanon, Jordan, and Turkey, to situations that were extremely precarious. After all, he explained, his permanent residency and citizenship in Germany required him to speak the language fluently, be able to take an exam in it, and earn a regular income that allowed him to pay taxes—and he could not imagine being able to accomplish all of that.

The one exception to these requirements of proving financial ability or language skill concerns recognized asylees who are reunifying nuclear families—children under eighteen and preexisting spouses (Mustafa or Mo'men did not qualify because they were both newly engaged and married). Unlike those resettled in the United States and Canada, where nuclear families arrived together, many asylum seekers, often men but also sometimes also women, travelled to Germany alone to protect their families, and particularly their young children, from the dangerous sea journey and to bypass the very expensive cost of smugglers. Being able to then reunify with their partners and children was crucially important to them—it was the whole point of seeking asylum.

Musa, a father of five, traveled to Germany alone, fearful of putting his children, the oldest of whom was eight, on a smuggler's boat and lacking the money to pay the passage for the family of seven—a cost that would easily exceed USD 10,000. When Musa arrived in Germany in August 2015, desperate to reunify with his wife and children whom he had to leave behind in an unsafe Turkish refugee camp, he was told he'd have to wait for several months. There were a hundred thousand other people applying for asylum at the time. Once his asylum was processed, it would take another six months for his petition for family reunification to be processed. Musa's family arrived in Germany a year after he did, a year in which he thought each day about returning to Turkey to be with them.

But, even with this wait, Musa was one of the lucky ones. The German government, fearful that allowing family reunification would increase the number of refugees fourfold, wanted to prevent their arrival. So, as described in chapter 5, they stopped recognizing Syrians under the Geneva Convention—as people who had escaped persecution by state or non-state actors—instead recognizing them under "Subsidiary Protection"—a lesser status that recognizes that they cannot return to Syria, but that assumes that they did not themselves experience persecution.

This change was coupled with a decision to suspend the right to family reunification for those given Subsidiary Protection. As Thomas de Maizière, German Minister of the Interior, put it, "We're telling them, 'You will get protection, but only so-called subsidiary protection—that is to say, for a limited period and without family reunification.'" Beginning in 2018, those with Subsidiary Protection would only be allowed to reunify with family on a limited basis, with a maximum of one thousand people allowed to travel to Germany through family reunification each month.

Caught in this net was Hanaa, a woman in her thirties who was separated from her husband and children for two years. Her family remained in Saudi Arabia, a country whose immigration system is predicated on a *kafala* or sponsorship system—where one's residency is contingent on the endorsement of a Saudi employer who can withdraw it without prior notice. When the Syrian war began, her husband's Saudi employer began to mistreat him more than usual, recognizing that the family was now completely reliant on the residency and thus the job. Originally from Hama, Hanaa and her husband toyed with the idea of returning home. But home was far too violent.

Hanaa and her husband faced a conundrum. They did not want to put their two young children on a boat, a terrifying prospect, particularly after the death of three-year-old Alan Kurdi. But Hanaa and her children could not stay in the country without her husband—their residency was contingent on his. So, Hanaa decided she would travel alone. When she reached Germany and petitioned for asylum, however, the German government, classifying Saudi Arabia as a safe third country where she could've chosen to say, would not recognize her. Instead, they offered her Subsidiary Protection. What's more, they would not allow Hanaa to petition for her families' reunification, because Saudi Arabia, in the eyes of the German government, was safe. Hanaa found herself battling this decision in court. Meanwhile, her husband was repeatedly threatened with deportation, along with her children, to Syria. These stressors debilitated her. Some days she couldn't leave her bed, and when she made it to German class she couldn't focus. Hanna had made it to safety, but what did safety mean if those who mattered most remained in danger?

Bringing family *here*—to the United States, Canada, and Germany—from *there*—countries of immediate refuge or Syria—was the only way to truly extract them from the protracted conflict that promised to rage for years to come. However, prospects of reunification were limited by the rigidity of borders, which prevented the admission of refugees' family members. They were also complicated by the linguistic and financial resources refugees needed to petition for family members, which, as I have argued throughout this book, are structured by the incorporation policies of each of these states.

———

At the time of this writing, although some of the violence has abated, the Syrian war has not stopped. The humanitarian crisis caused by the war has not ended. Meanwhile, there is a dearth of resources available to those who have been victimized by the war and subsequent displacement.

The men and women in this book who have sought asylum or been offered resettlement are the minority—the people who "make it" among the millions who do not. And, from this position, they step in to protect their loved ones. They try to support them financially through remittances. And they try to bring them *here*—a task that requires navigating complicated immigration laws, gaining linguistic ability, and expending financial resources.

For men and women trying to construct new beginnings in the United States, Canada, and Germany, this need to help their loved ones strains their meager resources. As sociological work has shown, particularly for people of color, having low-income loved ones can greatly deplete one's ability to build assets.[18] However, connections to loved ones are also hugely meaningful for those who are displaced. They are a reminder that even when one is *el-ghorba*, a stranger in foreign lands, there are those to whom one remains *ahl*, or family.

Refuge is a global story. Surrounding the war and the pursuit of refuge from it is a bordered world whose purpose is to hoard resources for the few at the expense of the many. Those offered resettlement and asylum in wealthy countries are attempting to fill a gaping chasm that requires a *structural* solution— one that helps the millions who are displaced and in need of support. By shaping the resources of those offered refuge within their borders, the United States, Canada, and Germany are shaping these individuals' ability to help their loved ones. And by shaping the borders of the world and the distribution of resources within it, they are also complicit in the humanitarian crises that the men and women and this book are trying so desperately to fix.

7

Refuge

The men and women in this book described the descent into war as slow, until it was not. At first, the protests were just protests. Some of the people in this book supported them and even participated. Others disagreed with them, either because they harbored sympathies for Assad or preferred the devil they knew. With any situation of political violence, it is impossible to know what is coming next.[1]

The people in this book could not know that their neighborhoods would be cordoned off as part of their city's no-go zone because of the havoc reaped by a government siege. They could not know that the days of sitting for Friday lunch in family homes were numbered, that the people who sat with them would soon be dispersed beyond borders that are impermeable to those without the right legal documents. They could not know that even if they *could* regather around the table, many would be missing—killed, or worse, disappeared into prisons nicknamed "slow death" and "the slaughterhouse" for their unfathomable brutality.

They became "refugees" in the legal sense of the term—people who have been displaced from their country due to persecution and generalized violence. With this legal designation came a series of social realities. The designation was a formal recognition of what they already knew—that they could not return to their physical homes, to their streets and neighborhoods, to the places where aspects of their identity such as their family name or occupation had weight and could be carried with pride. It meant that they would now be forced to navigate the legal liminality, political disdain, and social nonbelonging that comes with being seen either as an interloper, or at best, a recipient of charity.

From this position of loss and marginalization, they had to rebuild. Those who are resettled or who sought asylum are a small minority of the world's refugees. Access to these legal "solutions" offers an opportunity to try again in well-equipped wealthy countries with full legal status. However, the destination countries, including the United States, Canada, and Germany, are not saviors. They are complicit in the conditions that instigated the very wars from which refugees are fleeing. And, within their borders, they too are capable of violence—the violence of minoritizing, of denying living wages, of non-recognition of people's humanity. *Refuge* captures how countries equip new arrivals for their pursuit of a good, stable life through the same systems that have long shaped the contours of national belonging.

In these final pages, I reflect on the importance of centering the experiences of human beings and of taking a critical eye to the unequal systems through which they're offered "refuge." I end with a call for a fundamental rethinking of the borders that deny refuge and create these displacement crises in the first place.

A Human-Centric Approach to Immigrant Economic Lives

Scholars of immigration have long asked whether and how immigrants fit into an image of a national whole. The answer to this question, particularly in the United States, has always revolved around questions of economics and race. In the 1920s and 1930s, the Chicago School focused on whether and how low-income, predominantly European, immigrants assimilated into middle-class Protestant Whiteness.[2] Over the last several decades, sociologists have continued to pursue the same central question of how immigrants fit in. Some have asked whether, given an immigrant's race, legal status, social networks, and, of course, their human capital, they are likely to move "downward" into racialized poverty or "upward" into the middle class.[3] Others have attempted to reprise the concept of assimilation, asking whether immigrants are moving towards notions of the "mainstream."[4]

Recently, however, a new generation of immigration scholars have abandoned measures of "assimilation" or "integration" and questions of whether immigrants fit into a (White) mainstream or are "contributors" to a capitalist system. Instead, they are shaping what I'm calling a *human-centric* turn in immigration, by asking how immigrants *experience* the destination countries and whether those countries offer opportunities for self-realization, economic and emotional comfort, and belonging. Among these scholars is Neda Maghbouleh, who asks, for instance, how immigrants from Iran experience shifts in racialization as Islamophobia ebbs and flows in the national conversation and national policies.[5] Angela García also focuses on immigrants' perspectives when she asks how their experience of their undocumented status differs within their local context.[6] And, in her work, Joanna Dreby centers how parents experience being separated from their children and loved ones by borders.[7] These studies, by shifting the focus to human experiences, clarify that race, legal status, and social capital are not just determinants of immigrant trajectories but dynamic *outcomes* of destination country inequalities.

This book identifies and builds on this human-centric approach. It centers the understudied early years of immigrant life, during which newcomers' histories collide with systems within the receiving country to coalesce in their first designations of "race," "legal status," and, of particular interest to this book, their "human capital."[8] It is from this vantage that we can see why the existing conceptualizations of human capital—as attributes of an immigrant measurable in years of education or occupational history—are insufficient. Instead, the theory of *state-structured human capital* advanced in this book underscores that it is states' recognition of immigrant skills and abilities as capital and their willingness to invest in them as people that augments, diminishes, or transforms that capital. This *recognition* and *investment* occurs through systems of social welfare that are shaped by understandings of *who* is worthy of investment and *who* is recognized as having the potential to contribute to the country. These understandings are structured by inequalities in all three countries.[9]

Inequalities of gender and race are intertwined in these notions of worth. Across all three countries, Syrian men and women arrived with divisions of labor that assumed that the men would be breadwinners and the women would take care of the households. However, as these assumptions interacted with the three systems, we saw different results. In Germany and Canada, where social welfare systems included *investment* in child benefits, assistance targeted for caregivers, and childcare centers, men and women were both supported in their pursuit of education. But in Germany, where newcomers' existing skills were not *recognized* by a system that privileged German and more "culturally proximate" Western European credentials, the men, who were more likely to have histories of employment in Syria, experienced erasure. And, in the United States, where the welfare system and workplace regulations are driven by racism and unfettered capitalism, the family as a whole went unsupported. While the Syrian men in this book entered the lowest rungs of the labor market to try to make ends meet, women repurposed culinary or handicraft skills for the market and attempted to stay in English class. Despite these efforts, families struggled against the brutality of American poverty.

Refuge, through its human-centric focus on the initial years of resettlement and asylum, cannot speak to whether those seeking refuge will successfully rebuild a semblance of what they have lost or whether they'll triumph against systemic constraint—people often find a way against what seem like impossible odds. It cannot tell us whether they will ever achieve economic comfort, or even whether they will stay in the United States, Canada, or Germany if the war in Syria abates. What it *does* tell us, however, is how national systems equip newcomers in their personhood and particularly in their pursuit of new lives and ambitions. It also tells us whether systems leave refugees to the ravages of poverty—the threat of hunger, eviction, and the stress of not having enough—or whether they recognize their humanity and support their transition. By observing these national systems from the perspective of these newest arrivals, we see these systems from a new vantage and learn something more about how they have formed and sustained inequalities long before the Syrians arrived.

State-Structured Inequality

Policies for incorporating refugees are, as I have shown throughout the book, rooted in social welfare systems that are shaped by national notions of who belongs. We cannot understand the goal of self-sufficiency for refugees or the assumption that people who have just lost everything should become self-reliant in a few short months without understanding the weakness of the United States' social safety net due to anti-Black racism and xenophobia against non-White immigrants.[10] We cannot understand Canadian "integration" without understanding it as a part of the country's broader commitment to social benefits, but also to "multiculturalism"—the integration of people through language learning—which exists within an otherwise exclusionary immigration system.[11] We cannot understand German "credentialization" without understanding the historical relationship between the country's unions, employers, and the state, the hesitance among some to policies that create Germany as an immigrant destination, and the resulting "German system for Germans" that feels impenetrable to newcomers.[12]

By observing the contemporaneous experiences of men and women in this book, strangers to these three systems, we can also better understand the experiences of other immigrants. For instance, showing how *investment* mattered for newly arrived refugees in Canada speaks to the finding that immigrants there are more likely to experience a sense of belonging and to become citizens than in the United States.[13] At the same time, the uneven *recognition* of people's abilities in Canada, seen in this book in the case of Wael, who was an electrician, or Israa, who was a nurse, have also been documented for other categories of immigrants—who, although skilled, are systematically pushed into unskilled jobs, which has been described as the "taxi driver" phenomenon.[14] Examining credential requirements in Germany and their connection to a broader demand for assimilation adds to literature asking why Turkish immigrants (the largest minority group) have outcomes that lag behind other Germans despite decades in the country. It also helps explain why they, like the Syrians and other immigrants around the world, form enclaves (seen by the German government as a sign of their "ghettoization" and non-integration) to resist the experiences of discrimination they face, including in the labor market.[15]

In the United States in particular, noninvestment in refugees speaks not only to the failure of the system to support immigrants, but also other minoritized people. I have argued extensively in this book that the policy goal of "self-sufficiency" for refugees does not work—it compels entry into the labor market and a descent into poverty at the expense of the expression or formation of new skills. However, self-sufficiency is the bedrock of American welfare policy—rooted in decades of denying Black Americans in particular, but also non-white Americans, access to public resources. As such it is largely unquestioned by proponents of resettlement who advocate for the program by emphasizing how quickly refugees enter the labor market or that they contribute USD 63 billion more than they cost to the national economy.[16] Equating people to their dollar contributions obscures the actual *cost* of those contributions—the health toll of poverty, the alienation of not belonging, the emotional trauma of financial insecurity.

This centering of self-sufficiency, and unquestioned virtue of labor market entry, not only impacts refugees but all poor Americans. The hustle of refugees in the United States, who enter a labor market that offers meagre protections and no living wage to those it deems low-skilled, is not unique. The men and women in this book stand side-by-side in the backs of kitchens, the employee locker rooms of hotels, and in markets selling goods with other immigrants from the global south and with Black Americans, who are often also denied opportunities to flourish. Low-income people in the United States attempt to resist their descent into poverty by working multiple jobs, some off the books, in an attempt to make ends meet and to secure the (very limited) government benefits for which they are eligible. They are victims of the idea that the poor do not value work and that they must therefore be nudged towards work.[17] While the Culture of Poverty hypothesis, or the idea that it is the values of the poor that maintain their poverty, has been intellectually dismissed, it continues to animate American poverty policy.[18]

Reforming American refuge requires abandoning this idea. It requires a reforming of the American safety net—adding family benefits and child tax credits, introducing a minimum wage that is a living wage, and assuring a minimum basic income. It would mean extending those benefits to everyone who needed them, including immigrants, rescinding the 1996 welfare restrictions passed under former President Bill Clinton. It would mean properly funding schools and providing free health care and restricting American capitalism by regulating companies and passing legislation that protects unions. It would mean recognizing the human potential of all people as being much more than a net assessment of dollars and cents and investing in them as such.

Resettlement and asylum are not panaceas. It is not enough to admit someone if, as the men and women put it in the United States, the system "isn't going to help" them. As we call for refuge, for solutions to displacement, we need to call for *humane solutions*, systems that recognize people as people and that build their capacity rather than destroy it. The pursuit of humane refuge includes a reimagination of our domestic inequalities and policies, but also of the borders that surround us and create the global inequalities that generate crises of displacement in the first place.

Towards Humane Refuge

The use of the terms "migration crisis" or "refugee crisis" to describe the events at the US-Mexico border, on the Greek island of Lesbos, or for the Rohingya in Myanmar, conjures the image of a swelling number of people knocking on the doors of a country or a continent, demanding to be let in. It is the same imagery that fueled the anti-Semitic reception of Jews in the United States after World War II, the diasporic reality of Palestinian refugees expelled by the Israeli occupation, and the limited opportunities of the so-called Boat People who fled a ravaged Vietnam in the 1960s, 1970s, and 1980s. This imagery blames people on the move for generating the crisis.

From the perspective of those who are moving, however, including those in this book, it is the national borders that are the cause of the crisis. It is at these national borders that they must wait, sometimes for years, for the green light to travel to refuge. It is at these borders that asylum seekers board inflatable rafts and "put their children in the arms of death." It is here that they face violent border policing tactics—expulsions, pushbacks, and endless waits. If immigrants are allowed entry, it is only after their bodies are subjected to prodding and measuring, their histories to investigation, and their traumas to interrogation. Inherent in the structure of these borders is the assumption that those who reside outside of them are, at best, unworthy of admission until proven otherwise or, at worst, invaders who will take away opportunities and resources and reshape the destination country in their image.

These assumptions, however, deny the historical facts of colonialism, exploitation, and capitalism that generate the inequalities that compel these movements. They deny that those seeking refuge are often moving towards countries in Europe and North America that, while only containing seventeen percent of the world's population, account for fifty-five percent of its wealth—a wealth gained at their expense.[19] Harsha Walia, observing this fact, has called for a world of "No Borders," which, as she explains, is more expansive than one of open borders: "it calls on us to transform the underlying social, political, and economic conditions giving rise to what we know as 'the migration crisis.'"[20]

Although we are far from this vision, one step towards humane refuge is to follow activists' call for a divestment from borders as part of a divestment in a national security apparatus disproportionately weaponized against people of color.[21] Since the founding of the Department of Homeland Security in 2003, the United States has spent USD 333 billion on border security and enforcement—including the creation and maintenance of ICE detention centers.[22] In Europe, Frontex, the European Border and Coast Guard agency, saw its budget increase from EUR 143 million to EUR 322 million in 2020 as it expanded its outsourcing and offshoring of immigration deterrence to countries like Turkey, which prevented potential asylum seekers from making the journey to Europe in the first place.[23] This is in addition to billions spent on digital surveillance. Those who do make it to Europe are left at its boundaries, in conditions deemed "insecure and undignified" by Amnesty International.[24] While Canada is imagined as a safe haven for immigrants, as Tony Keller put it, "surrounding the Canadian welcome mat is a bed of nails."[25] Canada relies on the US security apparatus and the "Safe Third Country Agreement" that allows it to send asylum seekers back to the United States. Its 2019 budget included CAD 1.2 billion in border funding, including for the "removal of failed asylum applicants in a timely manner" and funding increases for the Royal Canadian Mounted Police, which intercepts asylum seekers. Meanwhile, it also included a commitment of CAD 1.39 billion to Canada's "Middle East Strategy," which continues airstrikes in Iraq and Syria.[26]

These systems make no one safer.[27] They make migration routes more dangerous, requiring immigrants to take higher risks. They destabilize the countries, such as Turkey, Libya, and Mexico, to which the violent protection of borders is outsourced. Politically, they expose destination countries, including the United States, Canada, and Germany, as inhumane and unethical.[28] Furthermore, this focus on borders does not recognize that the global forces that compel migration are by definition borderless. Carbon emissions stop for no border, as environmental degradation claims land and livelihoods from millions of climate refugees.[29] The capitalist drive for cars, electronics, and fast fashion relies on the hard labor of people who work for a pittance across the globe and who are denied a decent living. Local armed conflict is the direct consequence and long-term manifestation of global hegemonic meddling (see Vietnam, Iraq, Syria, Cuba, Haiti, Somalia, Democratic Republic of Congo, Guatemala, etc.). In our interconnected world, territoriality is navelgazing at the expense of investment in clean energy, combatting pandemics, a commitment to global labor standards, and a mitigation of violence in all forms, all of which would protect human life.

What's more, and to reiterate the argument at the core of this book, this focus on border security suppresses human potential. Immigrants are human beings, and like all human beings they are creative, dynamic, and capable of innovation. The myopic focus on security and the resulting denial of a safe future for them thwarts their possibilities for their own exploration, and in doing so constrains our possibilities as a world. The concept of state-structured human capital first came to me when I was volunteering to teach inside a United States prison where men were being held for lifetimes. Preventing the men from participating in our society struck me as a gut-wrenching loss. I found myself wondering who they could have been had their lives not been deemed expendable.[30] Indeed, denying people the right to life, to leisure, to passion and curiosity, because they were born on the wrong side of a city, with the wrong skin tone, or on the other side of a border, is equal parts inhumane and socially destructive. By denying one another the tools to explore our full personhood and potential, we're denying ourselves the fruits of each other's creativity.

That the countries in this book and others around the world have established opportunities for resettlement and asylum is commendable, given the dearth of opportunities for the world's millions of displaced people. However, in the context of states' complicity in a harshly bordered world and given the violence from which refugees are fleeing, admission is necessary but insufficient.[31] Globally, there must be a reckoning with the brutality of borders and the obsession with security. Within countries, there needs to be a commitment to *see* those admitted as full people who are, by virtue of that humanity, worthy of *recognition* and *investment*. This means establishing ways to recognize their skills and credentials systematically. It means investing in them freely. It means inviting their families to join them and extending support to their families back home. It means a true attempt to reform the policies, the borders, the capitalism, and the environmental degradation that caused their displacement in the first place. The pathway to humane refuge, to humane immigration, requires divesting from policies that treat immigrants as threats to national security in favor of ones that embrace them as people.

Five Years In

This book focuses on the experiences of men and women who sought refuge in the United States, Canada, and Germany between the summers of 2015 and 2016. The ethnography took place between 2015 and 2018. As a result, by the time the book was written, many of the families had been in these countries for five years.

I reached out to those who feature in this book to ask if they wanted to contribute a statement on their experiences to date and to reflect on refuge in each of these three countries. The purpose of this afterword is both to include a statement on their initial five years and to amplify their voices, unfiltered by the analysis necessary for an academic text. The first-person accounts also offer an opportunity to explore themes outside of the purview of this book—including anxiety over children's well-being, the role of the co-ethnic community, and the roles of volunteers in refugee lives.

What follows are their words, translated as they were relayed to me, edited only for length or clarity, and with the express consent of the author. I used the same pseudonyms as in the book, to link their words to their experiences.

Rajaa

"I RETURNED TO LIFE"

New Haven, Connecticut
January 14, 2021

(Five years, five months after arrival) My story begins in America five years ago, as a Syrian refugee with my family of three children and my husband, who used to work as a chef of Arabic cuisine and who had expertise in *shawarma*. We came to the United States with high hopes, but with our psychological well-being already damaged by the prior years of war and three and a half years in Jordan.

Our new life began in debt from the first day we put our feet on United States soil. We needed to pay back the tickets for our flight in five years' time. Immediately we owed rent and had bills to pay. Meanwhile, there was little by way of financial support. I wish that there was help offered, support in paying rent and bills for a year to give my husband and I an opportunity to fully dedicate ourselves to learning English, but no such help was available.

My husband and I quickly recognized, as we began to get settled, that life here was not going to be easy. The first order of business, before anything else, was to find work—or life is not possible at all. My husband began to search, and with the help of some people that we got to know, he found work at a pizza restaurant owned by other Arabs. The hours he got were little and so was the pay. But we needed an income, so he accepted the job.

With the help of other friends, I too started to work. I started to make meals in the house to sell, to help him out financially. People really loved my cooking, and they loved the taste of Arab food—particularly the Americans. But, because of my inability to speak the language, I did not feel like I could effectively communicate with them. Friends who spoke Arabic and English would help translate in the beginning, but they have their own lives and got busy. At the same time, I was also using crochet to make and sell clothing. But, here too, language got in the way of being able to market my business.

There were a lot of opportunities that we recognized, but because we did not speak the language, we could not pursue them.

In the midst of these experiences and financial anxieties, a friend of my husband visited us. He told us that there was an academy in another state, five hours away from our home, that gives scholarships to Syrian refugee students. Going, he explained, would mean that my children could get into the best universities in the United States with a scholarship.

My children and husband were immediately on board. But I was worried— my son was not yet seventeen and my daughter not yet fifteen. How are they going to live far away from me? I was worried too about what our Arab community would think—the idea that children the age of mine should live away from their parents, and particularly a girl, was unacceptable. This was a violation of our *adat we taqaleed* [norms and traditions].

But when my children called their grandparents, my mother and father in Syria, and told them, to my surprise, my parents were joyful at the news. They agreed that my children should be allowed to go. They encouraged me to send them, saying it was an opportunity for a better future. My parents have always loved education. So, after a lot of discussion, I sent them. I couldn't find it within myself to stop them—particularly since everyone else was on board.

And when the day came to send them away, it was painful, it wrung my heart. It's still painful recounting it. It takes me back to another trauma, the day I left my own parents and my own siblings in Syria to enter into the unknown, to become a refugee. I hate goodbyes. I left them to God. Maybe my eyes don't see them, but God will watch over them. That's how I felt too about my children. When my husband drove them to the school and came back without them, I wept.

But I knew too I had to be strong for their younger sister, then only nine years old. As a result of the war, my youngest daughter struggles psychologically. She has intense separation anxiety. She needs to sleep in bed next to me, holding my hand so that she knows I am not going to leave her. Her situation got worse because of her siblings' departure. She would tell me, "I will never leave you mama, I will never be far from you or from my dad. I don't like travel."

I took her to see a mental health specialist. But we could not continue the treatment. While they provided Arabic translators, they did not speak in a dialect that was close enough to Syrian. Every appointment there was a different translator, from a different country. Sometimes even I could not understand the translator, myself.

There were other difficulties. Other community members could not understand my decision to send my children to boarding school. "You have been here less than a year," one said to me, "but you've become more American than the Americans." And, because my children had moved outside of the house, our welfare payments for them also ceased. Though they were under eighteen and we were still supporting them, if they did not live with us, the Department of Social Services explained, our money would be reduced.

I would complain to my friend Heba, who is writing this book, and who was the most understanding person of my situation—a sister in *El-Ghorba* [foreign land]. I will never forget that Heba and her husband once went to pick up my children from school because my husband did not have an official driver's license at the time, as the exam for the license was not in Arabic. So, it was dangerous for him to drive to go get them.

All the while I was attending English classes on-and-off at the agency when I could find time to go around my work and childcare. We had to move from our apartment that the resettlement agency rented for us because it was overrun with mice and in a bad neighborhood. The new house was further from the agency, so I couldn't get there regularly. I found another English language school that was closer to the house and that I could get to using the public bus. However, the public bus was unreliable, and on one occasion I found myself stranded for hours in a torrential storm.

The pursuit of English class is difficult. I wish that there were more places to take English classes, and better public transportation in general. Or at least, public transportation to help people get to English classes, like school buses.

In the midst of all of this, I began to notice exhaustion appear on the face of my husband. He had pains in his back. He had since changed jobs, to another restaurant, where the hours were more regular, but the work was even harder. I knew that there were some days when it felt impossible for him to work. And finally, his back gave out; he woke up one morning and could not move. We took him to the emergency room. We learned that he needed surgery. But, if he stopped working, even for a few days, we would not be able to pay rent. We wouldn't be able to pay our bills. And where would we get the money to send to our family back home who relied on our support? We send them money every once in a while, a very small amount, but for them it's huge.

My husband began his physical therapy and began to manage on pain relievers. Because he had to reduce his hours, our financial situation got worse, and we found it hugely difficult to pay rent. The emotional exhaustion was even harder than the physical pain.

We are not alone in our struggle. All of the Syrian families I know are poor, and their quality of life is low. Among them are people who have it worse than us, like people who do not know how to read and write even in Arabic, or who were older when they arrived. When we get together with these families, I hear of their struggles, and we are doing okay in comparison to them.

There are also a few who had volunteers that were helping them, that helped subsidize housing, and volunteer teachers who came to their houses to help them with English, to help them with transportation and with day-to-day translation. These families, in a short period of time, were able to really integrate into American life. They were able to truly become self-reliant, and they were no longer a burden on the American people, and they do not need government help.

But this is not true of the families who arrived with us, who, like us, went uncared for. Who, five years later, do not speak the language. Many of them are unemployed. And a large number of families have left the state of Connecticut, hoping that they'll have access to more help.[1] They are in America, but, in the end, they feel that they are still displaced, and they continue to move from place to place in pursuit of a better life.

But in the past five years, nothing has changed—we can barely speak the language. And, because of it, we cannot apply for the citizenship exam. And, recently, they made the questions harder, which has made the exam more difficult.[2] My husband remains working at a restaurant for very little pay. We keep pushing back his surgery, for fear that if he does it, he will not be able to work, and we'll not be able to pay rent.

My son, however, is in college in his second year. And my daughter is in college, in her first year. I am so proud of them. This is where my husband and I derive joy in our lives, and the one thing that eases the pain that we otherwise feel.

I am exhausted. However, I will stay optimistic. And I will try every way I can to finally learn this language. And to become citizens. And to achieve our dream of owning our own little home. And owning a restaurant that my husband and I have decided we will call "New Homs." We continue to pursue our dreams despite our circumstances.

Israa

Toronto, Canada

January 12, 2021

When I asked Israa to participate in the book, she asked me if she could relay her responses via WhatsApp. I translated the recordings that she sent. She also asked me for some question prompts to help her organize her thinking. I offered her the following: Tell me what it felt like to come to Canada, and how your arrival matched (or didn't match) your expectations. Tell me what the positives and negatives have been of your experience. And, if you were a policymaker, tell us what you would do differently. Israa used some English in her responses, which I put in italics.

In addition, as we spoke to arrange how she would send her comments to me, I asked her for an update on her family's current situation. Her family is still receiving Canadian welfare and is still living in the same tight two-bedroom apartment where they lived when they first moved to the country.

When they told me that I was going to move to Canada, at first, I felt scared of the future, of the unknown. I asked myself what was it going to be like there? I didn't have any idea about the country. When we got here, until now, *alhamdullilah*, my feeling is that of contentment—to a certain extent. We are happy in this country, but not a hundred percent because there are obstacles, you know? As you know, every country has obstacles. And human beings too have a lot of obstacles in their lives.

When we first got here, I was surprised by the weather. It was so cold. It was February, and it was one of the coldest days of the year, I found out later. But the second thing I noticed was something really positive—the way that people treated us. It was truly kind. I can't describe how it felt to be treated so kindly. The people of Canada offered my family and I safety and security. And there was hope I had for my life, that I could think again of my future, of a future for my kids. I felt like my family and I were part of this country, humans with worth. It felt immediately as though we were nationals that belonged to this country. I felt like I was a person who was capable, who had rights and who also had responsibilities.

This does not mean that there aren't negatives, and I will tell you about those in just a second. But, first, the positives that I've seen in this country. For me and my family, first, Canada is a land of possibilities. For me, or for any human being who has a dream of leaving their country, of getting out of the Middle East and the situation of war we fled, it is an excellent opportunity. As I said before, it's a land of safety and security, but it's also a place where they recognize the rights of individuals, that considers the rights of human beings as human beings, irrespective of their religion, or ethnicity, or race, or color.

But I particularly feel like there's a good future here because there are a lot of opportunities to build your skills, to develop yourself—there is time to build on your abilities and to learn. I also like that there are opportunities for comfort—like opportunities for social support and community.

But one must be ready to do the work to benefit from these opportunities. And this is something that I see as perhaps an individual issue—I have a lot of responsibilities towards my children, towards my household. I feel like that's an obstacle for me. I try really hard to learn, to get ahead, to benefit from the opportunities, but something is holding me back. And that's the responsibility that I have towards my family and household.

My husband too is the type who didn't really integrate. He wasn't willing to go out into the labor market and find work. I didn't really feel like he was cooperative in this process.

Another thing that I want to say about the positives about Canada, is that it's beautiful here. The summer is short, yes. And the winter is six months (laughs). But in the spring and summer I try as much as possible to enjoy nature, the forests, the trees, the rivers, the lakes—these things really make me feel comfortable in Canada and attract me here. And that I find positive.

For things that are negative, though, it is hard to find work. Here, *if you want* to find work, it has to be through a *network*. Through friends, maybe, or through acquaintances. The most important thing too is language—which is an obstacle for [Syrians]. To be able to learn, but at the same time to manage everything else.

There also is luck involved to be able to take the first step into the work-force. For someone to find a job. *For example*, for me, I need someone to support me, to encourage me, to take me by the hand, so that I can find work like I used to have as a nurse. I feel like I need encouragement to take my first steps towards this goal.

An even bigger obstacle is the responsibilities that I have. I try to think of myself, but I struggle to be selfish. If I go look for work, or if I go try to take advantage of the opportunities for studying—I'm still learning English till now by the way, *alhamdullilah*—I feel like I don't have the time. I don't feel like I can properly put in the time that the language needs, or try to find opportunities in my occupational stream, because it would require me to abandon my responsibilities towards my children and my family to a certain extent.

Another thing that is a negative is that you can't work with your old occupation in Syria, or in your *background* country. One has to forget, or learn all over again, or work something else. There isn't recognition for my experience.

For other Syrians here, I think their experiences are similar to mine. Or, for some, their experiences are even better than mine. The obstacles for everyone are language and work.

But another thing too, and I think I told you this before, and I don't know if you remember. But really, this is a major question for me. How do I teach my kids my culture or religion? How can I teach them my traditions? This is hard here. In a country where there are lots of religions, lots of traditions, where there's democracy and freedom—it makes it hard to control this, or to be able to keep the kids in line with what we believe. It's hard to teach *culture*, but even language—to teach them Arabic. I signed them up each Sunday to go learn Arabic. But they try to get out of it. They don't want to go.

Now, you asked me what I'd do if I was a policy maker. I feel like more can be done for embracing difference. So, for instance, religious difference. When there's Christmas here, there's an incredibly popular celebration. So that impacts those who have other religions. It impacts our children, they get drawn towards [Christmas]. I would love for there to be actual recognition of religion where there is a light that's shone on other religions, too. For Jews, or for Muslims, or for any other religions. So there can be equality.

Also, in terms of refugees who have had to leave their countries and come here—I wish that there would be an end to the use of the word "refugee." I want to abolish this word. This word, *it hurts me*. When we first came here, we were refugees, for sure. But now, we're here, we're people in this country—but we're still being called "refugees." I want this word to be erased, maybe to be exchanged for a different kind of word.

I voice messaged her to ask her to elaborate on why she does not like the word refugee and what she would like to exchange it with. I also asked her to talk more about her experiences in the labor market. Here is what she responded.

The word refugee for me means a disability, as though you're unable to do anything. I feel like a better word is *immigrant*. There are a lot of people who are immigrants—why, for Syrians in particular, is the word "refugee" used? In the beginning it was for Palestinians, and now it's for Syrians. There are a lot of people who did well for themselves and who are Syrian. So, "refugee" means to be disabled to me, and we should use the word "immigrant" instead, maybe. I'm not sure.

In terms of work, when I first came, I attended groups for emotional support for newcomers who had also just arrived. I did three rounds, and I really enjoyed it and it was beneficial for me. I also did a session to become a facilitator in the group. That encouraged me to work. I tried from there to translate that training into getting back into nursing, but there's a lot of obstacles—I need stronger language, I need my children to get a bit older. But I really want to work.

Meanwhile, my husband cycles in and out of jobs. He's not integrated in this country, I'm not sure why. He keeps finding jobs and quitting them.

My English classes were going well, and I was really taking seriously again the idea of figuring out how to re-credentialize as a nurse. But then, with the Coronavirus, I couldn't really get back into it seriously. I'm attending, but not as seriously as I was before. The children are taking their classes are online, so it's hard to focus in the house. So, now I'm looking for work, or even for a volunteer opportunity. I feel like I'm stuck in a cycle that I am not able to progress from.

I also want to say, I worked for a year and a half in a café, I was a chef, and working on the checkout. It was part of an initiative that supported refugees. We were mostly Arabs who worked there. There were also Ethiopians and people from other nationalities. I was really happy there, but it was also tiring. The pay was not great, fourteen dollars an hour, and I was doing three employees' work. I was preparing all of the food downstairs, and then going back upstairs to serve and mind the register.

I did this work until early 2020 and I thought I would go back and rejoin school—and I thought maybe I could improve my language and return to nursing. This was my ambition, and still is.

She adds a voice message the next day.

Also, my English is now at level 7! My teacher just surprised me with this news. I was going to give up, but this is really an incentive for me to keep going. So, I am going to go back in February, and now I have renewed hope. *Alhamdullilah.*

Mustafa

Stuttgart, Germany
January 26, 2021
When I called Mustafa to ask him to participate, he responded that he was working long hours and asked if we could talk on the phone instead. The following is a transcript of Mustafa's description of his life in our conversation.

So, why don't we start with you telling me how you've been since we last saw each other.
When I last saw you, I had just started school. I was in A-2 German class. I was looking for work. I had a friend who was working in a cafeteria that sells sandwiches and coffee. I tried three or four times to meet with his boss, submitting my CV. But here, they hesitate to give employment to someone who knows someone else—you know? It's the opposite of anywhere else in the world.

So the first time I applied I was rejected, and the second time I applied I was rejected. I gave up hope. But then, one day, I went by my friend's work to buy some food at the train station, and I bought a coffee. I saw someone stealing a drink. I confronted him and brought back the drink he had taken. My friend's boss saw, and she was really pleased with that, you know? So my friend told her, "this guy has applied for the job several times, and you rejected him." So, she decided to give me a go.

That day I gave her my identification card, and she told me what documents I need: residency document, a document that indicates I can work, a health document that's necessary before you work with food—it's a four-hour training about how to be clean and how to treat customers. Then I went to the *Auslander* office to get the other documents to prove I can work. I went back a week later to start.

In the beginning I was working for EUR 1,300; my hourly rate was EUR 9.20 an hour. It wasn't much higher than the Jobcenter—only EUR 150–200. But I took it because I wanted to integrate into society. I wanted to be able to finally settle. I didn't want to live on the Jobcenter assistance. And be subject to questions: "What have you been doing? What are you up to?" I wanted to be able to establish my life myself. I wanted to find my own way.

But when I first took the job, it was on the condition that I would be traveling. I had to work ten days straight in a new city, and then I got four days off. Now I work in Stuttgart, but I began this way. I started work in March 2018. From then to August 2019. I was traveling like that. I had to go between six or seven cities, the closest of which was an hour and a half. I would go for ten days—they have company housing in all these cities—and then I'd come back for four.

My language was still bad. I just had the A-2. When you're in a country with a new language, you're fearful to speak. There were some really great people who helped me out. But I also interacted with people who were against me. The world is not all the same—there are good people and people who want to show their dominance over you.

The beginning is a twenty-day trial period. So, the first twenty days they put me in the kitchen to prepare food. I was silent. I would only respond when spoken to. But after a few days I felt more comfortable. I had memorized what I needed to do. With time, I learned the words in German for the things we used in the kitchen.

After my first ten days, I met again with my boss. She asked me if I was ready to try using the cash register. The travelling person has to work all three jobs—at the cashier, getting stuff from storage, and also working in the kitchen. So, she left me for another week in the kitchen, and then she transferred me to the cash register.

My language being so bad, I was really anxious. My colleagues also didn't like that I was working on the cash register without strong language. They would make fun of me, and I felt really lost. To add, the manager who was in charge of the supplies and all of our work hated me. He was very racist. When we were changing out bags of milk, he would do things like open up the refrigerator and say, "you, pick up this bag of milk." So I'd do it, then he'd spill it on the floor and tell me to clean it up. He was trying to humiliate me. So I was really upset, and I told the boss what happened when I saw her. After that, things got better, she had him apologize.

Alhamdullilah, I feel integrated in the society. And I've met a lot of great people who are kind and want to help. But racism is definitely there. Not always, but it's there. It is a thing with customers. For instance, there was an Italian man, he's Italian-German I mean. He asked me for a cup of coffee, and he asked if I'm Italian. I asked why he's asking. That's how I knew he was Italian by origin. I said, "no, I'm not Italian," and he said, "so where are you from?" I told him that I'm Arab. He asked from where, I said Syria. And so he said, "what did you come here to Germany to do?" But he said it really nasty. Like he's saying, you don't deserve to be here, he wanted to get a rise out of me. So, I responded to him, "it's not your business why I'm here, I'm working, and minding my business." So, he had a cup of coffee and a beer. He opened his beer bottle and took off the cover and threw it on me. This sort of thing happens a lot, I'm just giving you one example. I was going to fight him, but my colleagues calmed me down and kicked him out.

Do you think the work you're currently doing is something you want to continue to do in the future?

I took this work, rather than waiting for an *Ausbildung*, because my language ability was still quite low, I was only an A-2. It did not qualify me for retraining. I also couldn't find anyone to help me traverse the system. I would go to the organizations, and they'd tell us you need to have at least a B-1 or B-2 to even be considered. But I wanted to find work, I wanted to feel integrated, I wanted to be able to speak. So I thought I'd do that first and then try an *Ausbildung*.

Eventually I really want an *Ausbildung*. Because if I have an *Ausbildung*, I will make the same amount as anyone else with an *Ausbildung*. But if you work the same job as someone with an *Ausbildung*, and you do all of the same work, and you have all of the same skills, the person with an *Ausbildung* is going to have a higher salary than you. Regardless of whether or not you have the expertise—as a worker, anyone with an *Ausbildung* is higher than you. Your expertise is irrelevant.

But when I got this job, this was the only opportunity that I found. I really held onto it. With time, after I worked and met people, I learned that there were other opportunities to work, too. But I still won't leave my job because I am not sure if they are open to me—there are other Syrians who haven't found work at all. But, as I'm trying to bring my fiancée here, I need to have a steady source of income in order for them to approve her travel. I need to have a permanent contract until she gets here. After she gets here, I hope to try to apply for an *Ausbildung* to become a bus or a train driver, which is a really good job here. You do a three-year *Ausbildung*, but if you're good, it could even be two years and two months.

Since starting to work, I haven't been able to go to German classes at all. But I went to take the B-1 exam, without taking the class, just the exam, and thank god I passed. I would need one more course to qualify for the *Ausbildung*. But I was really glad that even without courses, just through work and interacting with people, the language became easier, and I surprised myself that I passed.

This work I am doing now, it doesn't have a future. It's not terrible. But it's not good. You can live off of it, but for the future, I cannot continue. I will have to find something else when my fiancée gets here. I might try to become a DHL driver, or something. I might be able to get a loan, to do a business that they call a *gewerbe*, a small company. That might be a solution if the *Ausbildung* doesn't work out, maybe to open a small restaurant or something.

So, now that you've been here for five years, tell me about the good things in the German system, and the things here you're still worried about.
Here in Germany, you can do anything you set out to do. But everything needs patience, needs time. Nothing is easy. And it's going to be a struggle. Because no one here tells you how to get there. You have to really figure out what to do. The goal that you have, you go ask them a question. Some people don't give you the answer, very few are helpful. It is all a bit opaque. Yes, I have contacts. But the Germans, the culture here, is very private. They don't want you to ask them questions: what they did, how they began, how you should begin. And, of course, there are people who are exceptions, who like to help.

What's interesting to me is the program you have in the United States. When people come, they have housing, that's important because it gives comfort. When I took you to the camp, to see Ali, the density was very high. In this high density, one is smoking pot, one is drinking, one is trying to study—you are seeing the entire community in one building. The good person, the bum. People sometimes lose their way. Some guys who had good morals got here, and in these situations, they lost their way. And for women in particular—the divorce rates are very, very high.

Also, there are people who spend four years in the first four classes [of German]. And they just keep failing and going to the Jobcenter, who reinstate their assistance. And I wonder if these people wouldn't do better if they had a limit to their assistance, like you do in the United States.

Anyway, to me, the German system, like the one in the United States, is good because everyone is seen in the same way, and the person who has talent is the one who gets ahead. No one's rights are lost, in front of the law. And there are opportunities that are much better than our countries. And you can express yourself, you're not afraid, you know? You can say what you think out loud. And I really like that.

Tell me about your residency status, what's the situation now?
A year ago, I renewed my residency. As of December 2020, I've been here for five years in Germany. So I can apply for permanent residency. I had an

appointment coming up to answer three hundred questions to get the permanent residency. But they shut down the testing sites [due to COVID] so I couldn't take the test. You get thirty questions out of the three hundred. You need to pass this exam once, and then this is the basis for your permanent residency—it asks questions about the world wars, about the constitution, about how it's changed, questions about German history. There are also four questions about the State you're in.

My German still isn't a hundred percent, but I have downloaded an app for the test. And maybe I can understand sixty percent of the material, but what I'm doing is just memorizing the questions and responses. So it's second nature to me—whether or not I understand.

Once I have permanent residency, I can then apply later for citizenship in six years. There's no other test then, after you've taken this one, but when you apply for citizenship, you have to make sure you're not taking a single cent of assistance, you've covered all of your expenses, you are paying for taxes, and health insurance. For me, it's been since March 2018 that I haven't been receiving assistance. You also have to have a B-1, which I have. So, I'm ready.

For your fiancée to get here, is it an easy process?
I'm bringing her from a third country, so I went to Saudi Arabia and got married on paper. Then I recorded that there, sent it to Syria, got it stamped by the Syrian foreign ministry, got it translated in German, then they ask for my documents and hers—birth certification and the marriage certificate—they need to be translated and stamped by the German embassy in Beirut. The one in Damascus is closed due to the war. My fiancée lives in Saudi Arabia. So, the papers went around the world—Saudi Arabia, Germany, Syria, Lebanon, and then now back to Germany.

She also needed to take a test for her German, to pass the A-1. I helped her study for it and *Alhamdulillah* she passed. So now our paperwork is with the *Auslander* office. The paperwork got here on December 12, 2020, and they told me it might take a week or two, or [up to] two months. But with the corona I don't know if there are delays.

As we ended the call, he encouraged me to come visit Germany, and I encouraged him to come to the States. He said he might want to move here eventually, to be with his parents and siblings. "I love an adventure," he told me. "Well, your life has certainly had a lot of adventure, so I guess that's a good thing?" I said. "Yes, that's true," he laughed before we ended the call.

ACKNOWLEDGMENTS

This book is possible due to the kindness and support of so many people. To begin with, I am grateful to my Princeton community. During graduate school, I relied on the support and guidance of Margaret Frye, Alejandro Portes, Paul DiMaggio, and Miguel Centeno. Special thank you to Mitchell Duneier who believed in me and pushed this project forward in myriad ways, and who talked me out of a dissertation on women bodybuilders that seemed like a good idea that summer I got into weightlifting.

Princeton is also where I met the incomparable Viviana Zelizer. From the first moment I sat in her office, I felt seen. Our connection became even more powerful over the next decade, as she became my advisor, my hero, but also my friend. That Viviana brilliantly pioneered the concept in economic sociology that the "economic" and "intimate" are not separate things is not surprising to anyone who knows her—she creates space for the people around her to be the full complexity of who they are. This book, and honestly, my career, would not have happened had she not supported it with her brilliance, generosity, and nurturing encouragement to "just be Heba," which I take with me into the world beyond graduate school.

I am also deeply grateful for the friendship and support of Angela Dixon, Cheng Cheng, Sarah James, Jean Nava, Sarah Brayne, Rourke O'Brien, David Pedulla, Maria Abascal, Erin Johnston, Janeria Easley, Alfredo Garcia, Cary Beckwith, Linsey Edwards, Vance Puchalski, Vivek Nemana, Liora Goldensher, Leah Reisman, and Jason Windawi, and Sharon Cornelissen, an amazing source of support throughout graduate school. Special thanks to Victoria Reyes for her guidance during graduate school and in the process of writing this book. Thank you too to Cindy Gibson, Donna DeFrancisco, and Christine Nanfra-Coil.

At Columbia, where I did my postdoctoral fellowship (and where I once got my MA), I benefited from the support of Denise Milstein, Shamus Khan, Yinon Cohen, Andreas Wimmer, and Van Tran, who, though he did not know me, took the time to help me develop the argument that you see in these pages, as well as Kiamesha Wilson, who was a constant source of joy. Thanks too to other Knox Hall comrades at various times, including Kiran Samuel, Asya Tsaturyan, Dialika Sall, Jose Atria, Sarah Sachs, Ryan Hagan, Brittany

Fox-Williams, Antony Ureña, Elizabeth Adetiba, and Devon Wade, who was taken from us all too soon. My MA students at Columbia were an exceptional joy to teach, and my first solo class; I am thankful to all of them for easing my transition into teaching.

I am deeply grateful to be a member of an amazing department at Boston University, and for the support of all of my incredible colleagues, particularly Jessica Simes, Saida Grundy, Cati Connell, Ashley Mears, who is my formal (and informal) mentor, and Japonica Brown-Saracino. Thank you too to my colleagues Debby Carr, Nazli Kibria, Alya Guseva, Sarah Miller, and Susan Eckstein for your constant encouragement, and to Ayse Parla, Noora Loori, Julie Dahstrom, Rob Eschmann, Kaija Schilde, and Jake Watson for your continuing support. I am also grateful to the incomparable force that is Natalie Russo. Thank you to my immigration class at BU in Fall 2020 for reading parts of this manuscript, and to my students for encouraging me and exuding positive energy as I tried to balance writing and teaching. Thanks to Ethan Collier for early research assistance on this project. And a special thanks to Kelley Gourley for reading and helping with final touches for this manuscript, and for taking the lead on managing the Citizenship Hub that emerged from this project.

I am truly spoiled to have had a thoughtful and brilliant network of amazing people supporting me as I wrote this book. This project would not have emerged the way it did without the friendship and support of Neda Maghbouleh, whom I met through her husband, the wonderful Clayton Childress, and who has become a true ally in sociology and in this project. Her constant support, including reading this manuscript multiple times and giving me incredible feedback, is an immeasurable gift. I am also forever indebted to Mary Waters, Filiz Garip, and Rhacel Parrenas for taking the time to read the manuscript and give me comments on it as part of my book conference. Thank you too to my dear friend Edna Bonhomme, who took time out of her own busy writing schedule (of two books!) to offer me feedback on this manuscript. I am also grateful to Nina Bandelj, Fred Wherry, Rene Almeling, Max Besbris, Forrest Stuart, Kristen Schilt, Caitlyn Collins, Sarah Damaske, Dan Hirschman, Atef Said, Angela Garcia, and Rawan Arar for their support of this project at various points of my career. Carla Shedd has been a true friend, supporter, and confidant throughout.

This study would not be possible without the support of others working in and on issues of resettlement in the United States, Canada, and Germany. In the United States I am grateful to Kate Wood, Chris George, and Barbara O'Brien, who supported my entry and research at IRIS. In Canada I'm indebted to Michaela Hynie, Anna Oda, and the members of York University's research team for allowing me to observe focus group discussions, and for their support on this work. Thank you to Eva Tache-Green for hosting me and feeding me and hanging with me during my stay, and for being a great friend. I am grateful in Germany to Claudia Diehl, Daniel Degen, and their team at Konstanz University, for supporting my work and inviting me to collaborate. Thank you to Muhammad Al-Kashef for your friendship and guidance in Berlin. Across all three countries, I am grateful to the many people in government offices and NGOs who agreed to an interview.

Travel and other expenses of this research were covered by grants from the National Science Foundation and the Horowitz Foundation. What's more, generous funding from Ruth Moorman and Sheldon Simon created an opportunity for me to carve out the time to write this in my initial years as an assistant professor.

I am deeply indebted to the advocacy and hard work of Meagan Levinson, editor at Princeton University Press, who believed in this project and me as a first-time author, and who worked to quell my anxieties. She is supported by a wonderful team, including Jacqueline Delaney and David Campbell. I am also grateful for Jill Harris, the production editor, and Michele Rosen, the copyeditor, for their diligent work, flexibility, and kindness.

Then there are many, many friends to thank. There's Sofy Solomon, who I befriended in the second grade and who has understood me in ways no one else can. There is Lenka Benova, whose friendship is formative to my understanding of self, and who, along with Hania Sholkamy, Kristina Hallez, Mohamed Hussan, and Ali Atef, was my first foray into research. There's Allison Kenney, without whom I would not have gotten through graduate school. There's Kevin Loughran, who drove across the country to be at my wedding, and his wife, my dear friend Caroline Graham.

Then, there are my pillars, Catherine Tan and James Jones, who together comprise PhDesign. I text them constantly throughout the day: when I need cheering up, when there's something to celebrate, when I want to spam people with TikToks. Every day I feel tremendously lucky to have such loving friendships. Along with Efrain Guerrero, Joshua Tan, Janice Gallagher, and my own Nicholas Occhiuto, we form our Harlem Crew, among whom I've had the most fun in my life.

I am lucky too to have the comradery and support of so many others, including Luciana de Souza Leão, Elizabeth Nugent, Mellissa Valle, Menna Tarek, Aaron Rock-Singer, Michael Sierra-Arevalo, Phil McHarris, Stephan Andrade, Adam Chekroud, Molly Offer-Westort, Peter Tinti, Jen Wu, George Wood, Danielle Gerhardt, Asu Erden, Mathew Archer, Liat Kreigel, Michael DeLand, Sarah Brothers, Sarah Efronson, Matteo Spera, Ryan Piccirillo, Alex Gavurin, Gillian Gavurin, Chuck Graves, and Devon Avallone-Graves, and Susannah Cunningham, Raphael Cormack, and Adaner Usmani. Pedro Regalado and Lindsay Blauvelt have become family. And meeting Tara Menon will always be the silver lining of the COVID-19 pandemic.

I'm grateful to my family, my parents, Nadia and Yasser, who moved to this country, insisted on teaching me Arabic, and supported my development as a person and scholar. I am grateful to my brother, Omar, his partner Azusa, and my grandmother, Magda, an accidental feminist, who has been calling me "Dr. Heba" since before I got into graduate school. I am grateful to my aunts, uncles, and cousins, including the ones I won through marriage. I am particularly grateful for my mother-in-law Beatrice, an icon with a natural compass for right and wrong, and my father-in-law Joe.

This book is dedicated to two men whom I love. To my father, Yasser Gowayed, who is my role model—brave, kind, and brilliant. And to my husband, Nicholas Occhiuto, my best friend and the most generous person I know, who has given me a sense of place after a long time of feeling out of place. This book would not have been possible without him.

Finally, and most importantly, I am indebted to the Syrian men and women who opened up their homes to me, fed me their food, and shared their lives and stories with me. I am sad that the world is a place where I have to keep them anonymous, because I would like to thank them one by one. Instead, I will resign myself to having told you, in the preceding pages, who they are. This entire book is a testament to them.

On Methods

I am an immigrant, an Egyptian-American, and an Arab-American woman. Although there are many good critiques of hyphenated identities, I believe that mine is an apt descriptor of who I am. It also gives me an insider/outsider status through which I was able to do the fieldwork for this book.

First, in some ways I am an insider. I was born in Cairo and grew up in a practicing Muslim household. Even after we moved to the United States, we still went to Cairo every summer for break. I spent my sixth-grade year there and went to college there, at the American University in Cairo. After graduating, I worked there for three years in poverty alleviation policy before I decided to come back to the United States for graduate school. This background gave me a lived understanding of the religious and cultural proscriptions held by mainstream practicing Sunnis, which includes the majority Syrians in this study. And I am a native speaker of Egyptian Arabic, which is a dialect that is close to the Syrian one.

What's more, my time spent in Cairo during and after college was consequential for relating to the participants of this study. I lived in Cairo in what became the last years of the Mubarak Era. The Egyptian revolution began on January 25 and ended on February 11, 2011. On the final day I stood alongside other Egyptians in front of the presidential palace when Mubarak stepped down. Though the country progressed into an even worse authoritarianism in the years that followed, February 11 remains the best day of my life.

The position the Egyptian revolution has in my life, and my attention to Syrian politics (I even had the privilege of visiting Syria in 2008), made it clear to the men and women in this book that I was a political ally. This is important, as many people from the region, particularly people who come from backgrounds like my family's—my grandfather was in the Egyptian military—sympathize with the region's authoritarians, whom they see as the only antidotes to an Islamic takeover.

On the other hand, I am certainly an outsider. I have not been a refugee. And although I am culturally Muslim, I am not practicing. I was open about this, and could not hide it anyway, as I am married to a non-Muslim man, which is prohibited for Muslim women by mainstream interpretations. I believe this outsider status was also helpful. I was seen as accepting of things that happened and that people went through that did not conform to *adat we taqaleed*, or norms and traditions. Because I grew up in the United States, I also understood how systems in the United States worked.

Finally, I also must reflect, as this book does, on my human capital. I, too, am the product of *investments* and *recognitions*. Our immigration journey began when my father was recognized for his qualifications by Drexel University, which admitted him for a PhD and invested in him through a scholarship. His human capital shaped mine.[1] I am the product of a strong American public-school education, the kind offered to middle-class kids in university cities. I am also the beneficiary of Arabic language learning at home, led by my mother. And I am the product of various accolades—recognitions of "merit"— including admission to Princeton, funding from the Horowitz Foundation and the National Science Foundation, and eventually, the tenure-track job from whose comfort I wrote this book.

Entry, Consent, and Boundaries

I began my research for this project in the United States. I had just been unceremoniously excluded from what I thought would be my dissertation field-site in Cairo, a downstream effect of that authoritarian retrenchment. Following this expulsion, I found myself back in the United States with no dissertation project. It was the summer of 2015, and I returned to New Haven where my husband, Nick, who was doing his PhD at Yale University, was living. That summer, the United States began to admit Syrian refugees. One of the agencies that resettled those newly arrived refugees was a local resettlement agency in New Haven called IRIS.

I approached IRIS through a booth they had at an outdoor fair that was staffed by their lawyer. She introduced me to the head of the agency, and I explained to them my idea for the project. They welcomed me in, on the condition that I volunteer as an interpreter to support agency work. I was helpful to them because my native fluency in both English and Arabic meant that I could help in public-facing events and with facilitating journalistic coverage. What's more, my flexible schedule and eagerness also made me a good person to call for refugee arrivals, which often happened late at night and could be delayed by several hours as planes frequently were delayed. Although this early access to new arrivals was wonderful insight for the project, it raised two interconnected methodological issues: I was interacting with families prior to raising the question of whether they'd consent to be part of the project, and I was gaining access to the site through gatekeepers, which, as Clifford Geertz reminds us, could impact how I was perceived.[2]

To the first point, consent, particularly in an ethnography, is not just a question asked and answered. It is a relationship based on mutual respect. It can be withdrawn at any point and for any reason. And, because ethnography entails a long relationship, the nature of consent can shift over time. As others have argued, consent is negotiated.[3] I asked for the consent of the families who are in this project within our first weeks of interaction. They agreed.

However, as the months progressed, I felt that my position—interacting with them as an interpreter on behalf of the resettlement agency on which they relied—did not support a fully consensual relationship. I did not want to be perceived as a gatekeeper or be needed to conduct certain tasks. Over the course of the coming months, I distanced myself from the resettlement agency. Although I maintained a good relationship, I took my name off the list of interpreters so that I would not be called by agency staff. By that point, the men and women had my number, and if they wanted me to interpret for them, they knew that they could call me. There were many other local Arabs that they could also call.

As a result of this reorientation, my relationships with my participants shifted in a number of meaningful ways. This exit from the agency made me privy to some of the negative feelings that the men and women had about agency assistance. It also allowed me to see different interactions; I was called to accompany them on visits to employers, health care providers, and other social service agencies. And the relationships became more personal. I was invited to homes for birthday parties, teas, and dinners, and out for barbecues and picnics. I had people over to my home.

Getting close to the families meant also that my family was involved. Most of the people in New Haven have met my father. My husband Nick frequently attended functions with me, even though he spoke very little Arabic. Of course, there were some embarrassing faux pas—like the time he walked in front of a group of praying men, or when he forgot the cardinal rule to not shake a woman's hand unless she extends hers first. Not to mention, as those of you who speak Arabic have probably already considered—his name means "fuck" in the language. Nevertheless, he endeared himself to them with his well-placed Arabic pleasantries and his strong backgammon game.

The closeness I developed with the families presented other methodological issues on boundaries in fieldwork. Ethnography blurs boundaries expected in other kinds of work, which presents ethical dilemmas. For instance, I thought a lot about my decision, which I described in chapter 6, to not wire money on behalf of Asad to Cairo. Certainly, even if there were repercussions, they would be less for me as a citizen.

But, beyond these sorts of moments, I grappled with the question of impacting my field site. Early in the project, it became clear that I could not impact the power structure that I was observing. I could not prevent the men and women from falling into American poverty. If I could, I would have.

I did do what I could to support those in this book. As examples, in addition to the support through interpretation, I advocated for the driver's license exam in Arabic. I helped them sign up for reduced price internet, I started a GoFundMe for coats for the children and laptops for refugees (not just those in this group). I organized a protest march and demonstration against the Muslim ban. I helped raise money when someone's family member was in a life-or-death situation (in one case due to a health crisis and in another due to a sudden displacement). I gave rides and helped students with studying where I could. And now, years after the conclusion of the project, I have launched a program at Boston University to teach folks studying for the citizenship exam.

There is sociological guidance for thinking about issues of consent, entry, and boundaries. However, there is also a lot that the ethnographer must figure out herself. I drew on my training to do this work. But I was also guided by the principles of dignity and respect. People had opened their homes and become vulnerable to me. I owed them a book that reflected their realities to the best of my ability. But I also believe that I owe them my support where I can give it as someone who has the luck of access to resources.

Constructing Comparison

This project began as a grounded ethnography in the classical sense, in that I did not have a driving question when I entered the field in New Haven. Trained as an economic sociologist (for my failed dissertation project), it is perhaps not surprising that I became immediately interested in the economic policies that I observed as dictating the material circumstances of these newly arrived refugees.

This interest in structural forces shifted the project from an inductive one to one with a driving theoretical interest. Writing about deductive ethnography and elucidating his extended case method, Michael Burawoy explains that it's a way to reveal how society works by focusing on *process* and linking it to structures of power.[4] The interest is not in whether a single case is representative of a whole, he suggests, but whether it tells us something we didn't know about the society in which that person resides.

Although the case of the United States revealed a lot, as Guy Swanson wrote, "thinking without comparison is unthinkable."[5] The macabre reality of diaspora created a quasi-experimental situation: men and women who fled the same country, in the context of the same war, were starting their lives in different countries contemporaneously. How were they doing in other places? Were they struggling the way that men and women were struggling in the United States?

How to construct the comparison was the next question. I drew on my sociological training and practical experience of designing impact evaluations of public policy programs in my pre-graduate school life. I decided that I needed to compare similar people, varying the federal context in some meaningful way. It was only through this that I'd be able to link the microprocess of experiencing refuge to the macroprocess of refugee and welfare policy.

It was clear to me that Canada was a good comparative case. As a result of a campaign promise, Justin Trudeau was resettling Syrian refugees there in large numbers. And the US-Canada comparison has a long sociological tradition showing the variations in the welfare policies of the two countries despite having similar economic systems. My first visit there in February 2016 was short, followed by a monthlong stay that summer and then a two-week stay every six months for the next two years. I got to know the families well, through teas and dinners and regular calls and texts while I was stateside. Balancing two ethnographic field sites felt overwhelming at times—but the longitudinal vantage felt necessary for this project centering the experience of resettlement policy.

In addition to the case of Canada, however, I also wanted a European case— which is where the process of selection became a bit messy. That summer of 2015, I watched as people crammed into boats and trains, trying to get to Europe. European countries had different approaches to social welfare, and many of the Western European and Scandinavian destinations for asylum seekers had very generous social service systems. However, initially, I began with the case of Italy. One of my advisors had a contact there and was able to help me find some funding for my flight for an initial monthlong visit that April. It was a convenient place to start, as Italy is a longtime destination for asylum seekers.

However, the case of Italy, as you have seen, did not make it into the book. I excluded it, even after two years of research, because it is too different from the cases of the United States and Canada—the economy was not as robust, resettlement was very new and was done exclusively through private organizations, and the system overall was highly decentralized. The sample I had was of four Syrian families resettled from Greece by Pope Francis with the help of the Community of Sant'Egidio, a Catholic lay organization that was attempting to create a resettlement program in Italy, as well as two other families resettled by the Italian government.[6] The Italian case was an outlier case, albeit one that reveals the importance of the labor market and that I hope to write about in a different moment.

Finally, I added the case of Germany in 2017. I visited twice, each time for six weeks, once in the winter of 2017 and again in the summer of 2018. It was because of the Italian case that I secured the Horowitz Foundation and National Science Foundation funding, which I was then able to redirect to the case of Germany. The German case made much more sense. Germany had just admitted hundreds of thousands of Syrian asylum seekers. The country had a strong economy, and it differed with respect to my variable of interest: its approach to social welfare.

Doing a four-country study was not easy. It meant constant travel. I was in either Canada or Italy, or later Germany, for at least ten weeks out of the calendar year, and for even longer during the first year. I was maintaining connections even when I was in the United States, where my primary field site was located. I was also keeping track of macrodevelopments in each of these contexts—in terms of politics, refugee-related policies, and incidents of racialized violence.

However, these cases were not entirely distinct. I benefited from my immersion in the primary case of the United States, which developed my knowledge of what it meant to be a Syrian refugee—what countries of immediate refuge are like, what the situation was in Syria and continues to be, how people understand themselves as Syrians from different regions. It was also the richness of this case that clarified my questions about the mechanisms by which policies impact people in the other cases. Drawing from Mario Small's idea of case study logic, each additional case I added needed to reveal what I did not know—how policy works elsewhere.[7]

Before arriving in the countries of comparison, I did in-depth research about the laws and reception policies for refugees. I also set up informational interviews. In Germany, I spoke to people in the federal government, local governments, refugee and immigrant advocates, and people at NGOs to learn about the issues that they saw as mattering for asylum seekers. In Canada, I interviewed academics, resettlement practitioners, employees at Sponsorship Agreement Holders, as well as private sponsors who were involved in the resettlement of the families in my study. These interviews gave me crucial insight into the cases, insight that helped me triangulate what I was observing with the men and women I included in my study.

Beyond selecting the countries, however, I needed to find people who shared a similar background to those in the United States for the comparison to work. If people's socioeconomic origins were too disparate, I couldn't be sure if their experiences were shaped by policy or other resources at their disposal. For this, I attempted snowball sampling, hoping that homophily would work in my favor—the sociological insight that the people in the United States would have relatives or friends who shared a similar background to them.

In Canada, I found respondents by asking the men and women in the United States whether they had any contacts who had ended up north of the border. Ghada connected me to her cousin Somaya. And, through a longer grapevine that began with Nabil in New Haven, I was connected to the family of Omar and Nermine. However, the more I read about the case of Canada, the more I recognized the similarities between it and the United States due to the very similar selection criteria of humanitarian need. Like the families in the United States, the ones in Canada tended to be younger, not as highly credentialed, and also to have multiple children. I met Wael at one of the hotels I visited—he was standing in the lobby, and we began to chat. I connected to Israa's family through an old friend of mine whose mother was involved with the group resettling them. Finally, I connected to Abo Mahmoud's family through a party I attended, hosted by the organization sponsoring them.

Focusing on these five families and their networks of friends in Canada over the period of two years, I was able to observe how they grappled with state services and with the transition, at the end of the first year, from state resettlement assistance to welfare assistance. There were certainly variations in my observations—between people who really benefited from the system and people, like Israa's husband, who struggled. These kinds of variations, however, do not detract from the central reported finding—that the Canadian system offers more opportunities for people than the one in the United States because it *invests* in them. And, to a greater extent than the German case (I would later discover), it *recognizes* their skills. Here, remaining true to the extended case method, I was able to center and reveal the state-structured *process* of human capital development.

Finding the right cases in Germany, however, of people who shared a similar background to the ones in the United States and Canada, was a bit more difficult. I was able to connect with Mustafa, whose parents are in the United States, and Amina, whose cousin Rajaa was also in the United States. However, because I was not doing a longitudinal ethnography, I felt that I needed more respondents.

Most of the cases in Germany came when I connected with Claudia Diehl's team at the University of Konstanz. She was doing a national project in Germany using government rosters. Her respondents reacted positively to a leaflet sent to random sample of asylum seekers throughout the country asking if they would participate in this national study. She needed someone to pilot her research instrument with Syrian asylees, and I wanted to do qualitative interviews.

The cases in Germany, however, do not "match" in the same way the cases in the United States and Canada did. This is because there is no administrative selection prior to arriving in Germany—any Syrian with the funds, will, and physical ability to apply for asylum in Germany could go. As you will see in Appendix C, there was thus more variation in my sample. In this book I focus on those who were similar to the cases in the United States and Canada. However, and importantly, non-recognition in Germany had even more of a dire impact on those who did have advanced skills. I spoke to a lawyer whose degree was unrecognized and to an Arabic translator who was starting over again, trying to find a new degree to pursue.

There are some things that are obscured through this comparative design and this project's focus on federal policy. For instance, it does not take account of local resources and politics, which are important given the strong regional systems of all three countries. In Canada, for instance, Quebec stands out as having special requirements for refugee language learning. In Germany, there are meaningful variations, as I wrote in chapter 5, between people resettled in the former East and former West. I have not anonymized the location of the men and women for this reason and have attempted to explain the specificities of these local contexts. I also believe that despite these regional specificities, what I do report on reflects federal realities across these countries. Second, the book does not attempt to address human capital outcomes—a question better asked through survey research or a larger number of qualitative observations. Instead, I can show what ethnography is able to show best: how power impacts processes.

Writing *Refuge*

This project generated a lot of data, including recorded interviews with respondents in all three countries and copious fieldnotes. In approaching the data analysis, I did not do a line-by-line coding. This would not make sense, as it would in an interview-based project. Instead, I relied on thematic analysis, which is pattern-focused—allowing me to center process rather than any individual incident.

As anticipated by Braun and Clarke, this involved a process in which I first familiarized myself with the data.[8] I transcribed recorded interviews in Canada, Germany, and the United States. I listened to them and read over the transcripts many times. Throughout the data collection and analysis, I also wrote many memos about the themes that emerged. I wrote memos about race and how I saw it unfolding differently in the three countries. I wrote about how gender shaped the experience of interacting with policy. I wrote about remittances.

What's more, I spoke to people at my field site about these memos, getting their reactions to my initial analyses. Eventually, I recognized how states shape skills and abilities, and I identified the mechanisms of recognition and investment. This memo-ing, revealing these themes, allowed me to look at my data differently when I revised it. Then, the write-up involved linking memos and fieldnotes to theory and analysis.

As I wrote, I faced other issues. I struggled with the use of the word "refugee," for instance. As you read in Israa's afterword, the term "refugee" is disliked by many of those who are legally classified by it. It is a flattening term denoting their legal status and evokes the imagery of victimhood, as I write in the conclusion. Throughout the book, as a result, I have attempted to use the verb "refuge" rather than the noun "refugee." This began with the title of the book, but is attempted, though not always successfully, throughout the text.

Additionally, I worked in Arabic. The entirety of the research for the book was conducted in Arabic, my mother tongue and the mother tongue of my respondents. The translations are mine—and I have attempted to be true to both the words used and the meanings of the words as they are relayed. Translation, however, is never perfect, and something is always lost. So, I have also included Arabic words where I feel that they capture the feeling of the moment. In some cases, I translate these into English for the reader; in other cases, where the word is not necessary for understanding the meaning of the section, I do not—I think of this as a small intimacy with my Arab readers.

Finally, I decided to end the book with the voices of the men and women seeking refuge. I asked Rajaa, Israa, and Mustafa to write because they are thoughtful people who had many reflections throughout the process on their experiences, and because I had spoken most often to them about the themes I was considering. I include this afterword to provide the reader an update on their lives, but also to create a space for them to speak about their own experiences. It felt only right that their voices should end this book that their journeys began.

Interview Protocol

In Germany, in addition to observations, I used this protocol as a guide to conduct my interviews. Interviews were semi-structured, and the main guiding questions were asked out loud, though not sequentially. The bulleted questions were only there for me to make sure that I got the information that I needed—I asked them as follow-up questions if they were not answered by the main guiding questions. I also asked these questions to the families in Canada at the end of the two-year period. Interviews were recorded and transcribed into Arabic.

Tell me about your family background. What was it like growing up in Syria?
- Where in Syria are you from?
- Occupational background
- Number of children
- Demographic info

Walk me through your process of leaving Syria (without focusing on the war).
- Where you first internally displaced?
- When did you leave Syria?
- How did you get out (legally or not)?

Tell me about your life in [*country of immediate refuge*].
- Which country was it?
- Legality of work?
- Were your children in school?
- Did you have access to health care?
- Did you receive UN or other assistance?

Walk me through how you were resettled/sought asylum in terms of the process.
- How long did it take?
- What were the steps in the process?
- What kinds of questions were you asked?

- Were people friendly?
- Why did you choose to come to this country? Did you have other options?

How did you find the reception in [*country of refuge*]?

- What kinds of services does the government provide? Cash assistance? In-kind assistance?
- Are these the services that you expected?
- What do you think of these services? What do you like? What do you wish would be different?
- Tell me about your typical day since resettlement.
- Have you made friends?
- Have you found co-ethnics? Mosques?

What is your hope for the future here in [*country of refuge*]?

- For yourself?
- For your children?

What are your biggest concerns about your future here?

Is there anything we have not talked about that you would like to add?

APPENDIX C

Respondents

TABLE 1. United States Respondents, 2015–2018

Men	Age	Former work	Women	Age	Former work
Karam	37	Driver	Amira	30	Not employed
Khaled	50	Carpenter	Iman	41	Not employed
Zafir	33	Restaurant owner	Ghada	26	Not employed
Amjad	33	Contractor	Rima	27	Not employed
Majid	43	Restaurant owner	Rajaa	34	Not employed
Saad*	57	Carpenter	Sawsan	53	Not employed
Abdulrahman	34	Store owner	Faten	24	Not employed
Nabil	42	Carpenter	Najlaa	35	Not employed
Zachareyah	29	Tailor/Farmer	Narjis	18	Not employed
Jamil	43	Shoemaker	Sawsan	31	Not employed
Basil	55	Construction	Afaf	52	Not employed
Amr	44	Glass artisan	Taghreed	29	Not employed
Hesham	27	Carpenter	Marwa	21	Not employed
Ahmad	34	Cosmetics sales	Yara	28	Not employed
Ayman	33	Restaurant owner	Sarah	28	Not employed
Fawaz	49	Government staff	Wedad	45	Not employed
			Madiha	28	Cleaner
Adam	19	N/A			

*Asad is Saad and Sawsan's son

TABLE 2. Canada Respondents, 2016–2018

Men	Age	Former work	Women	Age	Former work
Omar	43	Blacksmith	Yasmine	30	Not employed
Wael	31	Electrician	Maie	21	Not employed
Abelhameed	40	Fruit vendor	Israa	35	Nurse
Abo Mahmoud	42	Farmer	Om Mahmoud	36	Not employed
Nizar	53	Restaurant owner/Cook	Somaya	38	Not employed

TABLE 3. Germany Respondents, 2017

Men	Age	Former work	Women	Age	Former work
Imad	45	Long-haul trucker	Amina	35	Not employed
Hassan	28	Tailor	Rajiya	22	Not employed
Majdy	53	Beekeeper	Nahed	45	Not employed
Basil	55	Doctor	Basil's wife Manal was a lawyer, but I did an individual interview with him		
Mustafa*	25	Grocer/Student			
Ali	24	Hairdresser	Nermine	21	Hairdresser
			Om Ali	45	Hairdresser

TABLE 4. Germany Respondents, 2018 (in-depth individual interviews)

Name	Gender	Age	Employment	Others present?
Nadine	F	40	Not employed	Yes, husband, Iraqi refugee from 1990s, restaurant owner, and children
Reham	F	30	Arabic teacher	Yes, husband present, lawyer, Mohamed
Ola	F	20	Not employed	No, but carrying her young child
Manal	F	21	Not employed	Yes, sister-in-law Yara, sister, and mother
Hanaa	F	34	Daycare worker	No
Lamia	F	36	Not employed	Equal parts her and husband, a house painter
Kareem	M	39	Architect	No
Medhat	M	28	Student	No
Ashraf	M	32	Lawyer	No
Hani	M	28	Tailor	No
Musa	M	33	Plumber	Whole family, wife & children
Tamer (Tito)	M	20	Student	No
Mo'men	M	31	Farmer	No
Oday	M	31	Mechanic	No
Zaid	M	26	Carpenter	No

NOTES

Chapter 1. Finding Refuge

1. All names are pseudonyms. This is to anonymize the identities of participants in this study, to protect their privacy and experiences, and to prevent targeting.

2. Abouzeid 2011

3. Conduit 2017

4. Fisher 2012

5. I have made a concerted effort throughout the book to not use "refugee" other than as a legal designation. As Israa describes in the afterword, the use of the word "refugee" to describe an individual outside of the legal experience can be reductive. Where possible I have used adjectives/transitive verbs (eg. "person seeking refuge") rather than refugee. I doubt I have been able to accomplish this task perfectly, however, but it is important to recognize that those seeking refuge are also just people—parents, citizens, workers, friends, etc.

6. Beaubien 2017

7. Fee 2021

8. UNHCR identifies voluntary repatriation to the home country, resettlement, and "local integration" in the first country of refuge as "durable solutions" to the problem of displacement. For the men and women in this book, asylum is being sought out not in that first country, but in another, third country, where they can secure legal rights.

9. Katz 2013; United States Congress 1980

10. Breitkreuz and Williamson 2012

11. Katz 2013; Orloff 2009

12. Gans 1992

13. Becker 1964

14. Portes and Rumbaut 2014; Sanders and Nee 1996

15. There is other literature that emphasizes that human capital is not always transferable between contexts (see Basilio et al. 2017; Borjas 1985). Recent work has also argued that no one is "unskilled," even if their skills aren't directly transferable in the immigration process, and that existing skills open-up possibilities for reskilling (Hagan et al. 2015).

16. Reitz 1998

17. Zuberi 2006. Banting 2010 also points out that the country's generosity when it comes to refugees and admitted immigrants is enabled by its selection of skilled immigrants, who are perceived to not disproportionately need state support, and its extreme restrictions on unauthorized migration. For more, see discussion in chapter 4, "Canadian Integration."

18. Betthäuser 2017

19. No one in my study identified outside of these gender categories. I have chosen to use "men and women" here as a way to avoid using "refugee."

20. Sanders and Nee 1996

21. Lindley 2009

22. Castles 2003

23. UN General Assembly 1967

24. Zolberg, Suhrke, and Aguayo 1989

25. Fildis 2017

26. Human Rights Watch 1996

27. During a visit to Syria in 2009, I was sitting in a coffee shop with a group of English-speaking foreigners. We were at a public health conference and were discussing the presentations of the day. The man who owned the coffee shop came up to the table and pulled me aside, identifying me as the only Arabic speaker in the group. "Please Madam, the walls have ears," he said. This term, common in Egypt as well, denotes a fear of informants to the regime. However, in Egypt, a conversation about basic trends in unemployment or health would not have caused the same reaction.

28. Conduit 2017

29. McCoy 2014

30. Devictor 2019

31. As quoted in Omar 2019. Ellipsis in the original. The original was not accessible through a digital platform; however, according to Omar, Du Bois wrote this in a piece entitled "The sympathy of Black America" published in the *Crisis*.

32. Menjívar 2006; NASEM 2015

33. This provides important resources to people who are otherwise disadvantaged, as Rumbaut 1989 shows in his classic work on refuge.

34. Brekke and Brochmann 2015

35. United States Department of State, Department of Homeland Security and Department of Health and Human Services 2017.

36. Gulliver 2018

37. Lennox 1993; Orrenius and Zavodny 2015

38. Brown 2011, 2013

39. Gowayed 2020a

40. Omi and Winant 2014. Importantly, in this book, I use the terms "racialization" and "racism" rather than Islamophobia or xenophobia. Observing anti-Muslim or anti-Arab sentiment through the lens of "phobia"—Islamophobia or xenophobia—would paint them as individual dispositions, rather than systemically reinforced and historically based racism. In this chapter I document how Syrians are perceived within the broader racial orders in each of these three countries.

41. Gowayed 2019; Maghbouleh 2017; Selod 2015

42. Joppke 1999

43. Faist 1995; Jurgens 2017

44. Ramm 2010

45. Gowayed 2020a

46. I have chosen to capitalize White in this book because I believe that Whiteness is a socially constructed category and a political project that speaks to more than a person's skin tone. Who is included and excluded from Whiteness legally, politically, and socially is a topic of meaningful historical consequence. To me, capitalizing Black and not White runs the risk of leaving White as an unmarked category, the "default" to the Black other. That said, I am also supportive of my colleagues who choose not to capitalize White as a demonstration of Black pride, to attempt to recast the imbalance between Black and W/white, and to reject the capitalization of the word by supremacists and zealots. Here is one place where I sincerely believe reasonable people can disagree; and where maybe sometime in the future we can come to a consensus. In my decision to capitalize, I was strongly influenced by Eve Ewing's 2020 piece published in *Zora* for Medium (full citation in Works Cited).

47. In my article "Resettled & Unsettled" (2020a), I explain this issue of racialization further:

> Syrians were historically racialized as "Arab" though they include many ethnic groups such as Arabs, Kurds, Druze, and Assyrians. This categorization has long been complicated by its intersection with religion (Naber 2000). The vast majority of Syrian immigrants who arrived in the United States prior to 1924, after the passing of the National Origins Act that set quotas on immigrant arrival by country of origin, were Christians (Kayal 1973). Like other immigrants, they advocated in court for legal recognition as "White," then a prerequisite for naturalization, arguing that they were Semites *and* that they had religious affinity with Whites (Beydoun 2013; Gualtieri 2001). Over the course of the 20th century, through these court cases, Middle Easterners were legally classified as "White" (Tehranian 2009). This legal classification continues to be reinforced through the United States census, which makes them invisible as a distinct group. Meanwhile, Arabs, including Arab Christians, have not escaped discrimination and racism: they were lynched in the Jim Crow South, stereotyped via orientalist tropes in films post-WWII, and as terrorists post 9–11. (Jamal and Naber 2008)

48. Bannerji 2000, Mahtani 2002
49. Abdulhadi, Alsultany, and Naber 2011; Abu-Lughod 2013
50. Gowayed 2019
51. Patricia Collins 2019; Crenshaw 1990
52. Manuelli and Seshadri 2014; Smith 1776
53. Pager 2003
54. Portes and Rumbaut 2014; Sanders and Nee 1996. A notable study that has recently questioned whether this is the right approach to human capital is Hagan et al. 2015. In their book they show that immigrants are never really "unskilled" and that destination contexts create a space for their reskilling. I agree with these premises, but ask a different question—what is the role of the state in the "deskilling" and "reskilling"?
55. Occhiuto 2017; Xu 2012
56. Basilio, Bauer, and Kramer 2017
57. Friedberg 2000
58. Lancee and Bol 2017; Bol Van de Werfhorst 2011
59. Singer 2012
60. Gowayed 2019
61. Orloff 2002
62. This is a federally funded eight-month program, intended for single adults or couples without children, that offers USD 460 for one person or USD 647 for two people. This is the amount allocated to couples without children under the age of eighteen, because they would not qualify for TANF. If a family with children under the age of eighteen arrives in a state where TANF is available and they are eligible for it, but where the amount of TANF is substantially lower than RCA, then they receive RCA instead.
63. In the spring of 2018, I also participated in conducting focus group discussions run by a team at York University. This data does not appear in the book. However, because the focus group discussions included Syrians from all different backgrounds, attending these allowed me to position the experiences of the families in my study within a broader national context. I am grateful to the team at York University for allowing me to attend.

Chapter 2. Becoming a Refugee

1. Le Strange 1890
2. Horree 2011
3. BBC 2015

4. BCC 2015

5. Fitzgerald and Arar 2018

6. Zerubavel 1996

7. Berti and Paris 2014

8. Makki 2018

9. World Bank 2020

10. Shackle 2017

11. Crossette 2011

12. Conduit 2016, 2017

13. Doucet 2012

14. Cumming-Bruce and Gladstone 2013; Meyer 2015

15. Syria is a country with conscription, which requires "able-bodied" men over the age of eighteen who have at least one other brother (to preserve a male to take care of the family) to serve in the military. In a time of war, this reserve of trained soldiers can be drafted (while technically drafting only includes men under thirty, during the war, I was told by respondents, they attempted to draft much older men). What's more, given the brutality of the war, others had to take up arms against this drafted army. So when the UNHCR has to assess whether Syrians have been involved in human rights abuses either as part of this conscription, or as wartime combatants, this can be a complicated process as the majority of men will have weapons training.

16. UNHCR 2014

17. Rannard and Yalcin 2019

18. In this paragraph, I choose to omit the pseudonyms, because in the event that my respondents are identifiable to each other, I want to be careful to protect their privacy.

19. Importantly, *who* constituted "family" was important in this vetting process. Though Syrians often lived in extended family units, with grandparents and sometimes with siblings and nieces and nephews, the UNHCR, and other international agencies take a view of family as a nuclear unit including a monogamous spouse and all unmarried children who are under the age of twenty-one. What's more, in Syria, bigamy, while not a widespread practice, is legally permissible. In cases of bigamous unions, these laws make it so that one wife is not recognized by asylum or resettlement policy and is thus left unprotected. For more see Cvejić Jančić 2010.

20. Griswold 2016

21. My translation.

22. Fee 2021

23. In addition to doing research in the United States, Canada, and Germany, I also did two years of research in Italy that does not feature in this book. I wrote about this in the On Methods section of this book. Walaa's quote was hugely impactful to me, which is why I included it in this book despite the fact that she is in Italy. Like the Syrians who made their way to Germany, however, her family also took the boat journey from Izmir to Greece. There, in Greece, they were chosen for refuge by Pope Francis, who was making a statement that European nations should be doing more to resettle and offer asylum to refugees. She was one of three families flown to Rome by the Pope. Her family has multiple photos with him at the Vatican, and she has a deep love for him despite resenting how she was treated in Italy overall.

24. UNHCR 2020

Chapter 3. American Self-Sufficiency

1. I was the interpreter for their arrival, and the resettlement agency caseworker and executive director asked me to explain to them what had happened during the drive to their home.

2. State of Indiana 2015

3. United States Congress 1980

4. Darrow 2015 writes about the role of resettlement workers who, as street-level bureaucrats, are tasked with getting refugees to work despite all of the obstacles that surround that pursuit.

5. He would demonstrate these skills a few months later when the resettlement agency hired him to manage their coat drive. Ahmed turned a room filled with piles of used coats into an organized display sorted by size and color. When people came in, he directed them to the right area. However, after hiring him for this seasonal task, the agency did not have additional use for him. He would end up working in housekeeping at a hotel.

6. Ajrouch and Jamal 2007; Gowayed 2020a; Jamal and Naber 2008; Maghbouleh 2017

7. Gowayed 2019

8. United States Department of State, Department of Homeland Security and Department of Health and Human Services 2017.

9. As Whiteness was a criterion for naturalization in the United States, immigrants petitioned to be recognized as White in the courts. Arabs, and particularly Syrian immigrants, petitioned, citing their Christianity as evidence of their cultural similarity. For this reason, North Africans, people from the Levant, and people from the Arab Gulf are all categorized as "White" for legal purposes (explained further in the endnotes to chapter 1, "Finding Refuge").

10. Jamal and Naber 2008; Love 2017; Maghbouleh 2017

11. American Immigration Council 2021

12. Time Magazine 1955

13. Meyer 2015

14. Esping-Andersen 1990

15. Breitkreuz and Williamson 2012

16. Fox 2012; Katz 2013

17. In other words, agencies in expensive areas avoid large families because they necessitate more housing. Or an agency that is rural and far from a hospital might avoid taking a case that requires constant medical attention. Some agencies also have a higher capacity to do extended case management of families with higher chronic burdens.

18. While this is outside of the purview of the book, as it currently stands it is important to report that there was little support for Sarah's husband, Atef, as he experienced his mental health crisis. The lack of robust mental health support was a fact across all three countries. However, in the United States, mental healthcare was particularly problematic due to its link to police. Early in 2017, Atef skipped a scheduled therapy appointment to have friends over. "We thought it would raise his spirits," Sarah explained. Unbeknownst to them, skipping the appointment set off a "wellness check," which, due to a lack of clinical personnel available that night, resulted in the New Haven Police Department (NHPD) responding to the call. When they arrived at the house, the NHPD shined their high beams into the couple's apartment, banged on the front door, and barged into the apartment with dogs (an animal that is seen as dirty by Muslim faithful). No interpreter was present for the check. The violence with which the police entered triggered Sarah's trauma. Without thinking, she recounted, she dragged her three children down the fire escape, as the officers chased her down the stairs. Sarah called it one of the most traumatic moments of her already traumatic life. "It took me back to the fear we felt in the war," she said. "I didn't think something like this could happen here." After this event, others in the community were also hesitant to seek out mental health care.

19. Waters 2009

20. Kalleberg 2011

21. In *Family Tightrope* (1995), Nazli Kibria describes the ways in which this process of managing is deeply gendered and shaped by these variations in social assistance.

22. Halpern-Meekin et al. 2015

23. Edin and Shafer 2015

24. Another person to whom the email was forwarded, who was annoyed with their co-workers' position, shared this email with me. It is important to note that while the federal

restrictions on the agency impose constraints on their work, the vast majority of workers at the agency were sympathetic, to the extent that they could be, to refugee needs. However, this form of work also often involves predominantly White providers and non-White recipients, which results in a power imbalance and comes with racial scripts around development/saviorism/morality and expectations for behavior and showing of gratitude.

25. After their Arabic exam had been leaked several years prior, the Department of Motor Vehicles did not provide the driving exam in Arabic at the time when the men and women in this study first arrived, though the State of Connecticut claimed that it did offer the exam in that language. After lobbying and multiple phone calls (including on the part of the author), this was rectified. However, for their first year or longer, those who drove in this book (predominantly men) did so with an international driver's license that cost USD 200 to get printed and shipped from Syria. This was not a legitimate document to use for driving and exposed those who used it to possible arrest for driving without a license.

Chapter 4. Canadian Integration

1. Government of Canada 2016, 2019
2. Government of Canada 2020
3. Government of Canada 2018
4. This includes 2,405 people who came through the Blended Visa Program (BVOR) and 11,055 privately sponsored refugees (Houle 2019).
5. Esping-Andersen 1990
6. Zuberi 2006
7. Trudeau 1971
8. Banting 2010
9. Day 2000; Thobani 2007; Lee 2013
10. MacDonald 2014. Sunera Thobani 2007 suggests that it makes immigrants—who are pulled into the "multiculutural" fold by entering these institutions and languages—complicit in the long-time colonial violence propagated against indigenous Canadians by the Canadian state.
11. Gulliver 2018
12. Bannerji 2000
13. CBC Radio 2017a
14. Banting 2010
15. Gest 2018
16. Banting 2010
17. Sanders 2020
18. Mas 2016
19. Lu and Hou 2020
20. Bauder 2003
21. Reitz 2013; Reitz and Verma 2004
22. Hopkins 2015
23. Harris 2017
24. Valdez-Symonds 2017
25. Guff 2015
26. Lynch 2016
27. Angus Reid Institute 2016
28. Samuel 2018
29. Johnston 2019
30. Government of Canada 2017
31. Houle 2019

32. IRIS, in Connecticut, attempts to involve local groups, including church groups and NGOs, in the work of resettlement. This provides new arrivals with the extra support of locals who are well-resourced, both financially and in terms of their social networks. However, it also in effect outsources the work of resettlement to private actors, who because they tend to be wealthy (and White) have no experience with the highly complicated United States social welfare system. The relationship of sponsors to refugees, and the use of sponsors' private money to support the resettlement of new arrivals, can sometimes cause the process of resettlement to feel like a gift, rather than a state-sponsored benefit. While the Canadian system offers a social safety net in the form of the Child Benefit or welfare to those transitioning from private sponsorship, in the United States, there's no such safety net—leaving those seeking refuge in greater need of private support.

33. Pfrimmer 2019

34. CBC Radio 2017b; Pfrimmer 2019

35. Evaluation Division 2016

36. Hyndman, Payne, and Jimenez 2016

37. Hoodfar 1997; I also found this in my work (Gowayed 2018) on Conditional Cash Transfers in Cairo, where women, within the context of family poverty, drew on Islamic jurisprudence and notions of men as breadwinners to demand that they and their children be economically supported in a situation of dire economic scarcity.

38. I found it interesting that she had disassociated herself from the financial responsibility of that debt. This is something I found in earlier fieldwork in Cairo as well, where women were careful to distinguish between their own debt (incurred typically for clothing they wore, or trousseau items for their daughters) and their spouses' debt (incurred for larger items such as paying rent or household appliances).

39. There is a similarity between this story and Narjis' experience of telling her mother she was considering trying to become a doctor in the United States.

40. Government of Canada 2019.

41. The numbers were much lower for French speakers. Only sixty percent felt they could visit their doctor, seventy percent could speak in social situations, seventy percent felt that they could go shopping, and seventy percent felt that they could do their job entirely in French.

42. Occhiuto 2017

43. Picot, Zhang, and Hou 2019

44. Mas 2016

45. Kantor and Einhorn 2017

46. Immigration, Refugees and Citizenship Canada 2020

47. Rinne and Schneider 2017

Chapter 5. German Credentialization

1. BMBF 2020

2. This was a job ad copied from a page entitled "Apprenticeship Jobs in Germany." The website regularly has job postings of this sort. The site was accessed in 2018, and the job is no longer available. https://en.life-in-germany.de/bus-driver-work-schmalkalden-meiningen-germany-vacancy-81/.

3. Copley et al. 2015

4. BQ Portal 2018

5. OECD 2021

6. Esping-Andersen 1990

7. Caitlyn Collins 2019

8. Faist 1995

9. Joppke 1999

10. Jurgens 2017

11. El Tayeb 1999

12. Mandel 2008

13. Ramm 2010

14. Staudenmaier 2018

15. de Maizière 2017

16. Delker 2015

17. Barry 2019

18. Bartl 2019

19. Reimann 2016

20. Kumar, Seay, and Karabenick 2015; Wilson and Portes 1980

21. Taube 2020

22. EuroStat Database 2021

23. Heinemann 2018

24. The amounts provided were EUR 389 per month for spouses, life partners and other partners who live together, EUR 345 per month for adult persons in an inpatient facility, EUR 328 per month for children aged fifteen and over, EUR 308 per month for children between seven and fourteen years, and EUR 250 per month for children under six. (European Commission for Social Affairs, 2021)

25. For families like Imad's, comprised of five people, cash assistance, without rent or other in-kind support, was EUR 1500 a month.

26. Heinemann 2018

27. Their exchange made me wonder whether there's something gendered about being willing to be vulnerable and sit in a classroom where one is an adult learner; a situation that requires humility.

28. The word for abortion is actually *Abtreibung*.

29. C. Collins 2019

30. This number is spelled out in OECD 2014, though recent data indicates that the gap may be even less for new generations and that unemployment is experienced more harshly for those who lack an education (and among whom immigrants are disproportionately represented). See Statistisches Bundesamt 2019.

31. Speckesser 2013

32. Der Spiegel 2017

33. Human Rights Watch 2009

34. Anderson 2017

35. Weichselbaumer 2016

36. Trines 2019

37. Schuster 2021

Chapter 6. Here and There

1. Dreby 2006; Zelizer 2014. Also Shams 2020, whose book title *Here, There & Elsewhere* was the inspiration for the title of this chapter, describes how an immigrant's sense of self, in addition to their relationships, is shaped by politics in the homeland and host-land and by various global hierarchies.

2. Lindley 2009; Portes, Guarnizo, and Haller 2002; Singh, Robertson, and Cabraal 2012; Zelizer 2014

3. Garip 2016 and Carillo 2018 show that this is one of many ways that people move from one place to the other—but it is by no means the only motivator.

4. See note 18 in chapter 3, "American Self-Sufficiency," on his mental health crisis.

5. Singh, Robertson, and Cabraal 2012

6. Zelizer 1994

7. Gamal Moursi Badr's research explains that the ancient system of *hawala* is the origin of the notion of "agency" in civil law, or the idea that one person can act on behalf of another person. He writes,

> In fact many French and Italian writers mention among other things the case of the transfer of debt which was not permissible under Roman law but became widely practiced in medieval Europe, especially in commercial transactions. The *aval* of medieval French law is said to be derived from the hawala of Islamic law [. . .] In fact the word *aval* in French is admittedly a loan word from the Italian *avallo*, and we all know the extent of the trade conducted by the Italian cities with the Muslim world in the Middle Ages.

8. Gozde Guran's 2020 dissertation, entitled "Brokers of Order," a study of how money moves in wartime Syria, explores this process specifically.

9. Blumenstock et al. 2019

10. Wilson and Portes 1980

11. Tichenor 2016; Wolgin 2018

12. In October 2020, I started a citizenship clinic with the help of student volunteers, and namely Kelley Gourley, a graduate student of anthropology at Boston University, to help families in New Haven demystify and study for the citizenship exam. This activism revealed the gap with the citizenship exam.

13. Gonzalez-Barrera and Krogstad, 2018

14. Gonzalez-Barrera 2017; Gowayed 2020b

15. It is important to note, as Hou and Picot 2020 show, that Canadian naturalization rates have declined with modifications to the citizenship exam that have made it more complicated for new arrivals to pass it.

16. Government of Canada 2018; Daniel 2005; Reitz 1998

17. To remind the reader, in this program the Canadian government selects refugees through the government sponsorship system, but the new arrivals also receive resettlement support from private sponsors. See chapter 4 for more information on this mixed status case.

18. O'Brien 2012

Chapter 7. Refuge

1. This is insight that derives from political sociologist William Sewell (1996), who says that events are not "events" until they're over and can be identified as such.

2. Alba and Nee 2003

3. Portes and Rumbaut 2014; Portes and Zhou 1993

4. Alba and Foner 2015; Alba and Nee 2003; Alba 2020

5. Maghbouleh 2017

6. Garcia 2019

7. Dreby 2006

8. Diehl et al. 2016

9. Not only does this human-centric approach to human capital contribute to scholarship on immigration, but it also adds to our understanding of human capital in economic sociology. Economic capital has long been understood as an outcome of unequal relationships, starting with Karl Marx (Emirbayer 1997). Viviana Zelizer adds that the value of economic transactions is constituted by the relationships between actors and the meanings they hold about a given transaction—for example, cash is only valuable if it is appropriate and seen as valuable by those transacting (Zelizer 1997, 2012). This is also true of human capital. One's skills and abilities derive

their economic value from social relationships (Coleman 1988), including within families where men and women have different expectations for their labor (Gowayed 2019; Read and Oselin 2008), within labor markets that look for distinct sets of signaled skills (Bol and Van De Werfhorst 2011), and, as I argue centrally in this book, with states that determine who is worth investing in and who is seen to have skills that matter (Bandelj 2012).

10. Fox 2012

11. Bloemraad 2006; Reitz 2012

12. Heinemann 2018

13. Bloemraad 2006

14. Reitz 2007, 2013

15. Çelik 2015; Mandel 2008; Ramm 2010

16. Hirschfeld et al. 2017

17. Gowayed 2018

18. Small, Harding, and Lamont 2010; Ridzi 2009; Edin and Lein 1997; Katz 2013; Stack 1975

19. Credit Suisse 2020

20. Harsha Walia, in the conclusion of her book, puts it as follows: "anti-migrant xenophobia, immigration enforcement, detention centers, migration controls, and border securitization are ultimately the tentacles of a much-larger ideological monster: the rule of racist, nationalist borders. [. . .] Like the regime of private property, borders are not simply lines marking territory; they are the product of, and produce, social relations from which we must emancipate ourselves. [. . .] A no borders politics is more expansive than an open borders one; it calls on us to transform the underlying social, political, and economic conditions giving rise to what we know as 'the migration crisis.'"

21. Mendoza 2021; McHarris and McHarris 2020; Kaba 2020

22. American Immigration Council 2021

23. Andersson and Keen 2019; European Commission 2020

24. Amnesty International 2019

25. Keller 2018

26. Loreto 2019, Sharp 2019

27. Chapter 2, "Becoming a Refugee," describes the difficult routes that the men and women in this book were required to take as a result of these systems. Chapter 6, "Here & There," describes the difficult lives of those still excluded by these same borders.

28. Andersson and Keen 2019

29. Behrman and Kent 2018

30. Mbebe 2019

31. Katie Jensen (2021) further emphasizes that the same legal status can offer different feelings of belonging and wellbeing, depending on the context.

Afterword

1. Najlaa's family went to Maine where they say that government support is more generous, while her husband undergoes chemotherapy. Afaf and Sarah's families went to Erie, Pennsylvania where there is availability in section 8 housing. Najlaa's sister, who was not in the primary sample, went to Dearborn, Michigan, which has a large Arab population.

2. It was a Trump administration decision to make the exam harder, later reversed by the Biden administration.

Appendix A. On Methods

1. Coleman 1988

2. Geertz 1972

3. Murphy and Dingwall 2007

4. Burawoy 1998

5. Swanson 1971

6. Like those who ended up in Germany, the Syrians in Italy I met had taken an inflatable dinghy from Izmir to Greece, fearing for their lives. However, because they arrived in early 2016, the pathway to Germany was closed. They were stuck in a refugee camp in Greece, waiting to see if another country would admit them. While on Lesbos, Pope Francis visited their camp. And, in a bid to show the rest of Europe that they should be admitting these refugees, the Pope chose three families to take with him back to Rome. They were resettled by the Community of Sant'Egidio, which started a program called the Humanitarian Corridor to bring Syrians from Lebanon to Italy in a bid to stop people from drowning in the Aegean. Through the Humanitarian Corridor, I met three additional families, one resettled in Umbria, one in Bologna, and a third also in Rome.

7. Small 2009

8. Braun and Clarke 2006

WORKS CITED

Abdulhadi, R., E. Alsultany, and N. Naber. 2011. *Arab and Arab American Feminisms: Gender, Violence, and Belonging.* Syracuse, NY: Syracuse University Press.

Abouzeid, Rana. 2011. "Tunisia: How Mohammed Bouazizi Sparked a Revolution." *Time Magazine.*

Abu-Lughod, Lila. 2002. "Do Muslim Women Really Need Saving? Anthropological Reflections on Cultural Relativism and Its Others." *American Anthropologist* 104(3): 783–90.

———. 2013. *Do Muslim Women Need Saving?* Cambridge, MA: Harvard University Press.

Ajrouch, Kristine J., and Amaney Jamal. 2007. "Assimilating to a White Identity: The Case of Arab Americans." *International Migration Review* 41(4): 860–79.

Alba, Richard, and Nancy Foner. 2015. *Strangers No More: Immigration and the Challenges of Integration in North America and Western Europe.* Princeton, NJ: Princeton University Press.

Alba, Richard, and Victor Nee. 1997. "Rethinking Assimilation Theory for a New Era of Immigration." *International Migration Review.* 31(4): 826–74.

———. 2003. *Remaking the American Mainstream: Assimilation and Contemporary Immigration.* Cambridge, MA: Harvard University Press.

Alba, Richard. 2020. *The Great Demographic Illusion.* Princeton, NJ: Princeton University Press.

American Immigration Council. 2021. *The Cost of Immigration Enforcement and Border Security.* January 20. *Washington DC: American Immigration Council. Accessed August 30.* https://www .americanimmigrationcouncil.org/research/the-cost-of-immigration-enforcement-and-border -security?__cf_chl_jschl_tk__=pmd_evBHvHP5icmt7B0gyYUQiqKj.ZhdfvooRISbn2dBiek -1630342955-0-gqNtZGzNAmWjcnBszQjR.

Amnesty International. 2019. "Greece Fire in Moria camp highlights abject failure of government and EU to protect refugees." September 30, 2019. Accessed September 7, 2021. https://www .amnesty.org/en/latest/press-release/2019/09/greece-fire-in-moria-camp-highlights-abject -failure-of-government-and-eu-to-protect-refugees/.

Anderson, Emma. 2017. "When Muslim Women Are Allowed to Wear Headscarves in Germany, and When Not." *Local Germany.* Accessed May 25, 2021. https://www.thelocal.de/20170704 /when-muslim-women-may-wear-headscarves-in-germany-an-ongoing-debate/.

Andersson, Ruben, and David Keen. 2019. "The West's Obsession with Border Security Is Breeding Instability." *Foreign Policy.* Accessed May 25, 2021. https://foreignpolicy.com/2019/11/16 /border-security-european-union-instability-illegal-immigration/.

Angus Reid Institute. 2016. "What Makes Us Canadian? A Study of Values, Beliefs, Priorities and Identity." Angus Reid Institute. Accessed October 18, 2020. http://angusreid.org/canada -values/.

Bandelj, Nina. 2012. "Relational work and economic sociology." *Politics & Society* 40(2): 175–201.

Bannerji, Himani. 2000. *The Dark Side of the Nation: Essays on Multiculturalism, Nationalism, and Gender.* Toronto: Canadian Scholars Press.

Banting, Keith G. 2010. "Is There a Progressive's Dilemma in Canada? Immigration, Multiculturalism and the Welfare State, Presidential Address to the Canadian Political Science Association,

Montreal, June 2, 2010." *Canadian Journal of Political Science / Revue Canadienne de Science Politique* 43(4): 797–820.

Barry, Orla. 2019. "In Orban's Hungary, Refugees Are Unwelcome and So Are Those Who Help." *World*, February 11, 2019.

Bartl, Walter. 2019. "Institutionalization of a Formalized Intergovernmental Transfer Scheme for Asylum Seekers in Germany: The *Königstein Key* as an Indicator of Federal Justice." *Journal of Refugee Studies.* http://doi.org/10.1093/jrs/fez081.

Basilio, Leilanie, Thomas K. Bauer, and Anica Kramer. 2017. "Transferability of Human Capital and Immigrant Assimilation: An Analysis for Germany." *LABOUR* 31(3): 245–64. https://doi .org/10.1111/labr.12096.

Bauder, Harald. 2003. "'Brain Abuse' or the Devaluation of Immigrant Labour in Canada." *Antipode* 35(4): 699–717. https://doi.org/10.1046/j.1467-8330.2003.00346.x.

BBC. 2015. "Homs: Syrian Revolution's Fallen 'Capital.'" BBC. Accessed October 18, 2020. https://www.bbc.com/news/world-middle-east-15625642.

Beaubien, Jason. 2017. "More People Living as Refugees Now Than Anytime Since WWII, New U.N. Reports Says." NPR, June 20, 2017.

Becker, Gary. 1964. *Human Capital.* 2nd ed. New York: Columbia University Press.

Behrman, Simon and Avidan Kent. 2018. *Climate Refugees: Beyond the Legal Impasse?* Routledge Press.

Berti, Benedetta, and Jonathan Paris. 2014. "Beyond Sectarianism: Geopolitics, Fragmentation, and the Syrian Civil War." *Strategic Assessment* 16(4): 21–34.

Betthäuser, Bastian. 2017. "Protecting Outsiders? Corporatism and the Dualisation of Unemployment Protection in Germany and Austria." *European Journal of Social Security.* 19(3): 209–24. https://doi.org/10.1177/1388262717724892.

Beydoun, Khaled A. 2013. "Between Muslim and White: The Legal Construction of Arab American Identity." *NYU Annual Survey of American Law* 69(1): 29–76

Bloemraad, Irene. 2006. *Becoming a Citizen: Incorporating Immigrants and Refugees in the United States and Canada.* University of California Press.

Blumenstock, Joshua Evan, Guanghua Chi, and Xu Tan. 2019. "Migration and the value of social networks." CEPR Discussion Paper No. DP13611. March 27, 2019. https://papers.ssrn.com /sol3/papers.cfm?abstract_id=3360078.

BMBF. 2020. "Recognition of Foreign Professional Qualifications." *Federal Ministry of Education and Research.* Accessed October 1, 2020. https://www.bmbf.de/en/recognition-of-foreign -professional-qualifications-1413.html.

Bol, Thijs, and Herman G. Van de Werfhorst. 2011. "Signals and closure by degrees: The education effect across 15 European countries." *Research in Social Stratification and Mobility* 29(1): 119–32.

Borjas, George J. 1985. "Assimilation, Changes in Cohort Quality, and the Earnings of Immigrants." *Journal of Labor Economics.* 3: 463–89.

BQ Portal. 2018. "Recognition by Country 2018." *BQ Portal.* Accessed October 1, 2020. https://www.bq-portal.de/en/Companies-and-recognition/Recognition-statistics/Archive /Recognition-Statistics-2018/Recognition-country-2018.

Braun, Virginia, and Victoria Clarke. 2006. "Using Thematic Analysis in Psychology." *Qualitative Research in Psychology* 3(2): 77–101. https://doi.org/10.1191/1478088706qp063oa.

Breitkreuz, Rhonda S., and Deanna L. Williamson. 2012. "The Self-Sufficiency Trap: A Critical Examination of Welfare-to-Work." *Social Service Review* 86(4): 660–89. https://doi.org/10 .1086/668815.

Brekke, Jan Paul, and Grete Brochmann. 2015. "Stuck in Transit: Secondary Migration of Asylum Seekers in Europe, National Differences, and the Dublin Regulation." *Journal of Refugee Studies* 28(2): 145–62. https://doi.org/10.1093/jrs/feu028.

Brown, Hana E. 2011. "Refugees, Rights, and Race: How Legal Status Shapes Liberian Immigrants' Relationship with the State." *Social Problems* 58(1): 144–63. https://doi.org10.1525/sp.2011 .58.1.144.

———. 2013. "Race, Legality, and the Social Policy Consequences of Anti-Immigration Mobilization." *American Sociological Review* 78(2): 290–314.

Burawoy, Michael. 1998. "The Extended Case Method." *Sociological Theory* 16(1). https://doi.org /10.1111/0735-2751.00040.

Capps, Randy, Kathleen Newland, Susan Fratzke, Susannah Groves, Greg Auclair, Michael Fix, and Margie Mchugh. 2015. "Integrating Refugees in the United States: The Success and Challenges of Resettlement in a Global Context." *Statistical Journal of the IAOS* 31(3): 341–67. https://doi.org/10.3233/SJI-150918.

Carrillo, H. 2018. *Pathways of Desire: The Sexual Migration of Mexican Gay Men*. Chicago, IL: University of Chicago Press.

Castles, Stephen. 2003. "Towards a Sociology of Forced Migration and Social Transformation." *Sociology* 37(1): 13–34.

CBC Radio. 2017a. "Expecting Gratitude from Refugees Can Be Toxic, Says Author." CBC Radio. May 3, 2017. Accessed May 18, 2021. https://www.cbc.ca/radio/thecurrent/the-current -for-may-3-2017-1.4095703/expecting-gratitude-from-refugees-can-be-toxic-says-author-1 .4095737.

———. 2017b. "When Canadians Came Together to Help Vietnamese Refugees." CBC Radio. Accessed October 18, 2020. https://www.cbc.ca/2017/canadathestoryofus/when-canadians -came-together-to-help-vietnamese-refugees-1.4110755.

Çelik, Çetin. 2015. "'Having a German Passport Will Not Make Me German': Reactive Ethnicity and Oppositional Identity among Disadvantaged Male Turkish Second-Generation Youth in Germany." *Ethnic and Racial Studies* 38. https://doi.org10.1080/01419870.2015.1018298.

Coleman, James. 1988. "Social Capital in the Creation of Human Capital." *American Journal of Sociology* 94: 94–120. https://doi.org/10.1086/228943.

Collins, Caitlyn. 2019. *Making Motherhood Work: How Women Manage Careers and Caregiving*. Princeton, NJ: Princeton University Press.

Collins, Patricia Hill. 2019. *Intersectionality as Critical Social Theory*. Duke University Press.

Copley, Caroline, Paul Carrel, Holger Hansen, and Georgina Prodhan. 2015. "Refugees Could Help Ease Skills Shortage in Germany: Merkel's Deputy." *Reuters*, September 10, 2015. Accessed May 12, 2021. https://www.reuters.com/article/us-europe-migrants-germany-economy -idUSKCN0RA1Z220150910.

Conduit, Dara. 2016. "The Syrian Muslim Brotherhood and the Spectacle of Hama." *Middle East Journal* 70(2): 211–26. https://doi.org/10.3751/70.2.12.

———. 2017. "The Patterns of Syrian Uprising: Comparing Hama in 1980–1982 and Homs in 2011." *British Journal of Middle Eastern Studies* 44(1): 73–87. http://doi.org/10.1080/13530194 .2016.1182421.

Credit Suisse. 2020. "Global Wealth Report." Accessed May 25, 2021. https://www.credit-suisse .com/media/assets/corporate/docs/about-us/research/publications/global-wealth-report -2020-en.pdf.

Crenshaw, Kimberlé. 1990. "Mapping the Margins: Intersectionality, Identity Politics, and Violence against Women of Color." *Stanford Law Review* 43: 1241.

Crossette, Barbara. 2011. *State of the World Population 2011*. United Nations Population Fund. Accessed Aug 30, 2021. https://www.unfpa.org/sites/default/files/pub-pdf/EN-SWOP2011 -FINAL.pdf.

Cumming-Bruce, Nick, and Rick Gladstone. 2013. "U.N. Says 5,000 People a Day Are Now Fleeing War in Syria." *New York Times*, February 8, 2013.

Cvejić Jančić, Olga. 2010. "The Definition of Family in Modern Law and Its Legal Protection." *International Journal of the Jurisprudence of the Family* 1: 77–100.

Daniel, Dominique. 2005. "The Debate on Family Reunification and Canada's Immigration Act of 1976." *American Review of Canadian Studies* 35(4): 683–703. https://doi.org/10.1080/02722010509481388.

Darrow, Jessica. 2015. "Getting refugees to work: A street-level perspective of refugee resettlement policy." *Refugee Survey Quarterly*, 34(2).

Day, Richard J. F. 2000. *Multiculturalism and the History of Canadian Diversity.* University of Toronto Press.

De Maizière, Thomas. 2017. "Leading Culture for Germany, What Is It Actually?" *Bild Am Sonntag*, April 29, 2017.

Delker, Janosch. 2015. "Merkel's Migrant Problem." *Politico*, August 26, 2015.

Der Spiegel. 2017. "Studium Und Ausbildung Im Einkommensvergleich." *Der Speigel*, March 9, 2017.

Devictor, Xavier. 2019. "2019 Update: How Long Do Refugees Stay in Exile? To Find Out, Beware of Averages." *World Bank Blogs.* Accessed October 18, 2020. https://blogs.worldbank.org/dev4peace/2019-update-how-long-do-refugees-stay-exile-find-out-beware-averages.

Diehl, Claudia, Marcel Lubbers, Peter Muhlau, and Lucinda Platt. 2016. "Starting Out: New Migrants' Socio-Cultural Integration Trajectories in Four European Destinations." *Ethnicities* 16(2):157–79.

Doucet, Lyse. 2012. "Homs: A scarred and divided city." BBC News. May 9, 2012. Accessed September 7, 2021. https://www.bbc.com/news/world-middle-east-18007945.

Dreby, Joanna. 2006. "Honor and Virtue: Mexican Parenting in the Transnational Context." 20(1): 32–59. https://doi.org/10.1177/0891243205282660.

Edin, Kathryn J., and H. Luke Shaefer. 2015. *$2.00 a Day: Living on Almost Nothing in America.* Houghton Mifflin Harcourt.

Edin, Kathryn, and Laura Lein. 1997. *Making Ends Meet: How Single Mothers Survive Welfare and Low-Wage Work.* Russell Sage Foundation.

El Tayeb, Fatima. 1999. "'Blood Is a Very Special Juice': Racialized Bodies and Citizenship in Twentieth-Century Germany." *International Review of Social History* 44(7): 149–69. https://doi.org/10.1017/S0020859000115238.

Emirbayer, Mustafa. 1997. "Manifesto for a Relational Sociology." *American Journal of Sociology* 103(2): 281–317. https://doi.org/10.1086/231209.

Esping-Andersen, Gosta. 1990. *The Three Worlds of Welfare Capitalism.* Princeton, NJ. Princeton University Press.

European Commission. 2020. "European Agenda on Migration: Securing Europe's External Borders." *European Commission.* Accessed May 25, 2021. https://ec.europa.eu/commission/presscorner/detail/en/MEMO_15_6332.

European Commission for Social Affairs. 2021. "Germany—Employment, Social Affairs & Inclusion." Accessed May 25, 2021. https://ec.europa.eu/social/main.jsp?catId=1111&langId=en&intPageId=4557.

Eurostat Database. 2021. First instance decisions on applications by citizenship, age and sex—annual aggregated data (rounded). Accessed May 24, 2021. https://appsso.eurostat.ec.europa.eu/nui/show.do?dataset=migr_asydcfsta&lang=en.

Evaluation Division. 2016. *Rapid Impact Evaluation of the Syrian Refugee Initiative.* Statistics Canada. December 21, 2016. Accessed September 7, 2021. https://www.canada.ca/en/immigration-refugees-citizenship/corporate/reports-statistics/evaluations/rapid-impact-evaluation-syrian-refugee-initiative.html.

Ewing, Eve L. 2020. "I'm a Black Scholar Who Studies Race. Here's Why I Capitalize 'White.'" *Zora* for Medium. Retrieved May 24, 2021. https://zora.medium.com/im-a-black-scholar -who-studies-race-here-s-why-i-capitalize-white-f94883aa2dd3.

Faist, Thomas. 1995. "Ethnicization and Racialization of Welfare-State Politics in Germany and the USA." *Ethnic and Racial Studies* 18(2): 219.

Fee, Molly. 2021. "Lives Stalled: The Costs of Waiting for Refugee Resettlement." *Journal of Ethnic & Migration Studies*. https://doi.org/10.1080/1369183X.2021.1876554.

Fildis, Ayse Tekdal. 2017. "The Troubles in Syria: Spawned by French Divide and Rule." *Middle East Policy Council* 17(4).

Fisher, Max. 2012. "The Only Remaining Online Copy of Vogue's Asma al-Assad Profile." *Atlantic*, January 3, 2012.

FitzGerald, David Scott, and Rawan Arar. 2018. "The Sociology of Refugee Migration." *Annual Review of Sociology* 44(1): 387–406. https://doi.org/10.1146/annurev-soc-073117-041204.

Fox, Cybelle. 2012. *Three Worlds of Relief*. Princeton, NJ: Princeton University Press.

Friedberg, Rachel M. 2000. "You Can't Take It with You? Immigrant Assimilation and the Porta-bility of Human Capital." *Journal of Labor Economics* 18(2): 221–51. https://doi.org/10.1086 /209957.

Gans, Herbert. 1992. "Second-Generation Decline: Scenarios for the Economic and Ethnic Futures of the Post-1965 American Immigrants." *Ethnic and Racial Studies* 15(2): 173–92.

García, Angela S. 2019. *Legal Passing: Navigating Undocumented Life and Local Immigration Law*. University of California Press.

Garip, Filiz. 2016. *On the Move: Changing Mechanisms of Mexico-US Migration*. Princeton, NJ: Princeton University Press.

Geertz, Clifford. 1972. "Deep Play: Notes on the Balinese Cockfight." *Daedalus: Myth, Symbol, and Culture* (101)1: 1–37.

Gest, Justin. 2018. "Points-Based Immigration Was Meant to Reduce Racial Bias. It Doesn't." *Guardian*. Accessed May 14, 2021. http://www.theguardian.com/commentisfree/2018/jan /19/points-based-immigration-racism.

Gonzalez-Barrera, Ana. 2017. "Mexicans Among Least Likely Immigrants to Become Ameri-can Citizens." *Pew Research Center*. Accessed January 28, 2021. https://www.pewresearch .org/hispanic/2017/06/29/mexican-lawful-immigrants-among-least-likely-to-become-u-s -citizens/.

Gonzalez-Barrera, Ana, and Jens Manuel Krogstad. 2018. "US Naturalization Rates Increase Most for Those from India, Ecuador." *Pew Research Center*. Accessed January 28, 2021. https://www .pewresearch.org/fact-tank/2018/01/18/naturalization-rate-among-u-s-immigrants-up-since -2005-with-india-among-the-biggest-gainers/.

Government of Canada. 2016. Government-Assisted Refugee Program. *Government of Canada*.

———. 2017. Syrian Refugee Integration—One Year after Arrival. *Government of Canada*. Accessed May 25, 2021. https://www.canada.ca/en/immigration-refugees-citizenship/services /refugees/welcome-syrian-refugees/integration.html.

———. 2018. Sponsor Your Relatives: About the Process. *Government of Canada*. Accessed October 17, 2020. https://www.canada.ca/en/immigration-refugees-citizenship/services /immigrate-canada/family-sponsorship/other-relatives.html.

———. 2019. How Canada's Refugee System Works. *Government of Canada*. Accessed July 23, 2020. https://www.canada.ca/en/immigration-refugees-citizenship/services/refugees /canada-role.html.

———. 2020. Groups of Five: About the Process. *Government of Canada*. Accessed August 10, 2021. https://www.canada.ca/en/immigration-refugees-citizenship/services/refugees/help-outside -canada/private-sponsorship-program/groups-five.html.

Gowayed, Heba. 2018. "The Unnecessary Nudge: Education and Poverty Policy in a Cairo Slum." *Sociological Forum* 33(2). https://doi.org/10.1111/socf.12421.

———. 2019. "Diverging by Gender: Syrian Refugees' Divisions of Labor and Formation of Human Capital in the United States." *Gender & Society* 33(2): 251–72. https://doi.org/10.1177/0891243218819753.

———. 2020a. "Resettled and Unsettled: Syrian Refugees and the Intersection of Race and Legal Status in the United States." *Ethnic and Racial Studies.* 43(2): 275–293. https://doi: 10.1080/01419870.2019.1583350.

———. 2020b. "Trump, Biden, and the Citizenship Exam Changes: The Case for Abolishing the Exam Altogether." *Slate.* Accessed January 28, 2021. https://slate.com/news-and-politics/2020/11/abolish-citizenship-exam-discriminatory.html.

Griswold, Eliza. 2016. "Why Is It So Difficult for Syrian Refugees to Get into the U.S.?" *New York Times.* Jan 24. Accessed August 30, 2021. https://www.nytimes.com/2016/01/24/magazine/why-is-it-so-difficult-for-syrian-refugees-to-get-into-the-us.html.

Grundy, Saida. 2021. "Lifting the Veil on Campus Sexual Assault: Morehouse College, Hegemonic Masculinity, and Revealing Racialized Rape Culture through the Du Boisian Lens." *Social Problems* 68(2): 226–49. https://doi.org/10.1093/socpro/spab001.

Gualtieri, Sarah. 2001. "Becoming 'White': Race, Religion and the Foundations of Syrian/Lebanese Ethnicity in the United States." *Journal of American Ethnic History* 20(4): 29–58.

Guff, Samantha. 2015. "Canadian Children's Choir Welcomes Refugees with Traditional Arabic Song." *Huffington Post.* Dec 14, 2015. Accessed Aug 30, 2021. https://www.huffpost.com/entry/canadian-childrens-choir-arabic-song_n_566ed792e4b011b83a6bcd58.

Gulliver, Trevor. 2018. "Canada the Redeemer and Denials of Racism." *Critical Discourse Studies* 15(1): 68–86. https://doi.org/10.1080/17405904.2017.1360192.

Guran, Gozde. 2020. "Brokers of Order: How Money Moves in Wartime Syria." Dissertation, Princeton University.

Hagan, Jacqueline, Ruben Hernandez-Leon, and Jean-Luc Demonsant. 2015. *Skills of the Unskilled: Work and Mobility Among Mexican Migrants.* Oakland, CA: University of California Press.

Halpern-Meekin, Sarah, Kathryn Edin, Laura Tach, and Jennifer Sykes. 2015. *It's Not Like I'm Poor: How Working Families Make Ends Meet in a Post-Welfare World.* University of California Press.

Harris, Kathleen. 2017. "Hate Crimes against Muslims in Canada up 60%, StatsCan Reports." *CBC.* June 13, 2017. Accessed Aug 30, 2021. https://www.cbc.ca/news/politics/hate-crimes-muslims-statscan-1.4158042.

Heinemann, Alisha M. B. 2018. "The Making of 'Good Citizens': German Courses for Migrants and Refugees." *Studies in the Education of Adults* 49(2). https://doi.org/10.1080/02660830.2018.1453115.

Hirschfeld, Julie, and Davis Somini Sengupta. 2017. "Trump Administration Rejects Study Showing Positive Impact of Refugees." *New York Times.* Sept 18, 2017. Accessed Aug 30, 2021. https://www.nytimes.com/2017/09/18/us/politics/refugees-revenue-cost-report-trump.html.

Hoodfar, Homa. 1997. *Between Marriage and the Market: Intimate Politics and Survival in Cairo.* Cairo: American University in Cairo Press.

Hopkins, Andrea. 2015. "Canada's Harper Shifts to Politics of Fear amid Refugee Crisis -Analysts." *Reuters,* September 11, 2015.

Horree, Peter. 2011. *Homs Syria Syrian Souq Market Shop Trade Town City.* Alamy Stock Photo. March 24, 2011. Accessed September 7, 2021. https://www.alamy.com/stock-photo-homs-syria-syrian-souq-market-shop-trade-town-city-36026855.html.

Hou, Feng, and Garnett Picot. 2020. "The Decline in the Naturalization Rate among Recent Immigrants in Canada: Policy Changes and Other Possible Explanations." *Migration Studies.* https://doi.org/10.1093/migration/mnaa010.

Houle, René. 2019. "Results from the 2016 Census: Syrian Refugees Who Resettled in Canada in 2015 and 2016." Statistics Canada. Accessed May 25, 2021. https://www150.statcan.gc.ca/nl /pub/75-006-x/2019001/article/00001-eng.htm.

Human Rights Watch. 1996. "Syria: The Silenced Kurds." *Human Rights Watch* 8(4).

———. 2009. "Discrimination in the Name of Neutrality." Accessed May 23, 2021. https://www .hrw.org/report/2009/02/26/discrimination-name-neutrality/headscarf-bans-teachers-and -civil-servants-germany.

———. 2019. "World Report 2019: Syria. Human Rights Watch." *Human Rights Watch*. Accessed October 18, 2020. https://www.hrw.org/world-report/2019/country-chapters/syria#.

Hyndman, Jennifer, William Payne, and Shauna Jimenez. 2016. *The State of Private Refugee Sponsorship in Canada: Trends, Issues, and Impacts.* RRN/CRS Policy Brief Submitted to the Government of Canada. December 2, 2016.

Immigration, Refugees and Citizenship Canada. 2020. "Syrian Outcomes Report." Accessed February 27, 2021. https://www.canada.ca/en/immigration-refugees-citizenship/corporate /reports-statistics/evaluations/syrian-outcomes-report-2019.html#s53.

Jamal, Amaney, and Nadine Christine Naber. 2008. *Race and Arab Americans Before and After 9/11: From Invisible Citizens to Visible Subjects.* Syracuse, NY: Syracuse University Press.

Jensen, Katherine. 2021. "Contexts of Reception Seen and Constituted from Below: The Production of Refugee Status Apathy." *Qualitative Sociology* 17.

Johnston, Angela. 2019. "Majority of Canadians against Accepting More Refugees." Accessed October 18, 2020. https://www.cbc.ca/news/canada/manitoba/refugees-tolerance-1.5192769.

Jones, James R. 2019. "Congress as a Racialized Social System. In *Race, Organizations, and the Organizing Process (Research in the Sociology of Organizations*, edited by Melissa Wooten, 171–91. Emerald Insight Limited.

Joppke, Christian. 1999. *Immigration and the Nation-State: The United States, Germany, and Great Britain.* Oxford University Press.

Jurgens, Jeffrey. 2017. "The Legacies of Labor Recruitment: The Guest Worker and Green Card Programs in the Federal Republic of Germany." *Policy and Society* 29(4): 345–55. https://doi .org/10.1016/j.polsoc.2010.09.010.

Kaba, Mariame. 2020. "Opinion | Yes, We Mean Literally Abolish the Police." *New York Times,* June 12, 2020.

Kalleberg, Arne L. 2011. *Good Jobs, Bad Jobs: The Rise of Polarized and Precarious Employment Systems in the United States.* Russel Sage Foundation.

Kantor, Jodi, and Catrin Einhorn. 2017. "Canadians Adopted Refugee Families for a Year. Then Came 'Month 13.'" *New York Times,* March 25, 2017.

Katz, Michael. 2013. *The Undeserving Poor: America's Enduring Confrontation with Poverty: Fully Updated and Revised.* Oxford University Press.

Kayal, Philip M. 1973. "Religion and Assimilation: Catholic 'Syrians' in America. *International Migration Review* 7(4): 409–25.

Keller, Tony. 2018. "Canada Has Its Own Ways of Keeping Out Unwanted Immigrants." *Atlantic.* July 12, 2018. Accessed September 7, 2021. https://www.theatlantic.com/ideas/archive/2018 /07/canada-immigration-success/564944/.

Kibria, Nazli. 1995. *Family Tightrope.* Princeton, NJ: Princeton University Press.

Koning, Edward A., and Keith G. Banting. 2013. "Inequality below the Surface: Reviewing Immigrants' Access to and Utilization of Five Canadian Welfare Programs." *Canadian Public Policy / Analyse de Politiques* 39(4): 581–601.

Kumar, Revathy, Nancy Seay, and Stuart A. Karabenick. 2015. "Immigrant Arab Adolescents in Ethnic Enclaves: Physical and Phenomenological Contexts of Identity Negotiation." *Cultural Diversity and Ethnic Minority Psychology* 21(2): 201–12. https://dx.doi.org/10.1037/a0037748.

Lancee, Bram, and Thijs Bol. 2017. "The Transferability of Skills and Degrees: Why the Place of Education Affects Immigrant Earnings." *Social Forces* 96(2): 691–716. https://doi.org/10.1093/sf/sox058.

Le Strange, Guy. 1890. *Palestine Under the Moslems*. Alexander P. Watt for the Committee of the Palestine Exploration Fund.

Lee, Emerald. 2013. "A Critique of Canadian Multiculturalism as a State Policy and Its Effects on Canadian Subjects." Master of Arts Thesis, Graduate Department of Theory and Policy Studies in Education, Ontario Institute for Studies in Education, University of Toronto.

Lennox, Malissia. 1993. "Refugees, Racism, and Reparations: A Critique of the United States' Haitian Immigration." *Stanford Law Review* 45(3): 687–724.

Lindley, Anna. 2009. "The Early-Morning Phone Call: Remittances from a Refugee Diaspora Perspective." *Journal of Ethnic and Migration Studies* 35(8):1315–34. https://doi.org/10.1080/13691830903123112.

Loreto, Nora. 2019. "Opinion | Canada Claims It Stands with Refugees—but a New Budget Tells a Different Story." *Washington Post*. March 26, 2019. Accessed May 26, 2021. https://www.washingtonpost.com/opinions/2019/03/26/canada-claims-it-stands-with-refugees-new-budget-tells-different-story/.

Love, Erik Robert. 2017. *Islamophobia and Racism in America*. New York: New York University Press.

Lu, Yao, and Feng Hou. 2020. "Immigration System, Labor Market Structures, and Overeducation of High-Skilled Immigrants in the United States and Canada." *International Migration Review* 54(4): 1072–1103. https://doi.org/ 10.1177/0197918319901263.

Lynch, Laura. 2016. "Liberals' Waiving of Travel Costs for Syrian Refugees Created 2-Tier System." *CBC News*. Accessed October 18, 2020. https://www.cbc.ca/news/canada/refugee-travel-costs-loans-1.3406735.

MacDonald, David Bruce. 2014. "Reforming Multiculturalism in a Bi-National Society: Aboriginal Peoples and the Search for Truth and Reconciliation in Canada." *Canadian Journal of Sociology / Cahiers Canadiens de Sociologie* 39(1): 65–86.

Maghbouleh, Neda. 2017. *The Limits of Whiteness: Iranian Americans and the Everyday Politics of Race*. Stanford University Press.

Mahtani, Minelle. 2002. "Interrogating the Hyphen-Nation: Canadian Multicultural Policy and 'Mixed Race' Identities." *Social Identities* 8(1): 67–90. https://doi.org/10.1080/13504630220132026.

Makki, Danny. 2018. "Syria's War Economy Exacerbates Divide between Rich and Poor." *Middle East Institute*. Accessed October 18, 2020. https://www.mei.edu/publications/syrias-war-economy-exacerbates-divide-between-rich-and-poor.

Mandel, Ruth. 2008. *Cosmopolitan Anxieties: Turkish Challenges to Citizenship and Belonging in Germany*. Durham, NC: Duke University Press.

Manuelli, Rodolfo E., and Ananth Seshadri. 2014. "Human Capital and the Wealth of Nations." *American Economic Review* 104(9): 2736–62. https://doi.org/10.1257/aer.104.9.2736.

Mas, Susana. 2016. "Do Government-Assisted Refugees Receive More Money for Food than Canadians on Welfare?" *CBC*. Accessed October 17, 2020. https://www.cbc.ca/news/politics/do-government-assisted-refugees-receive-more-money-for-food-than-canadians-on-welfare-1.3230503.

Mbebe, Achille. 2019. *Necropolitics*. Durham: Duke University Press. https://www.dukeupress.edu/necropolitics.

McCoy, Terrence. 2014. "Camp Bucca: The US Prison That Became the Birthplace of Isis." *Independent*. November 4, 2014. Accessed September 8, 2021. https://www.independent.co.uk/news/world/middle-east/camp-bucca-us-prison-became-birthplace-isis-9838905.html.

McHarris, Philip V., and Thenjiwe McHarris. 2020. "Opinion | No More Money for the Police." *New York Times*, May 30, 2020.

Mendoza, Anabel. 2021. "Defund Hate: Humane Immigration Starts with Dramatically Defunding ICE and CBP. President Biden's Proposed Budget Fails to Do That." *United We Dream*. Accessed May 26, 2021. https://unitedwedream.org/2021/04/defund-hate-humane-immigration-starts-with-dramatically-defunding-ice-and-cbp-president-bidens-proposed-budget-fails-to-do-that/.

Menjívar, Cecilia. 2006. "Liminal Legality: Salvadoran and Guatemalan Immigrants' Lives in the United States." *American Journal of Sociology* 112(4): 999–1037. https://doi.org/10.1086/499509.

Meyer, Ken. 2015. "Two Former Homeland Security Secretaries Wrote President Obama on Safely Welcoming Syrian Refugees." *White House*.

MIT. 2018. "Living Wage Calculator." *MIT*. Retrieved October 18, 2020. https://livingwage.mit.edu/.

Murphy, Elizabeth, and Robert Dingwall. 2007. "Informed Consent, Anticipatory Regulation and Ethnographic Practice." *Social Science & Medicine* 65(11): 2223–34. https://doi.org/10.1016/j.socscimed.2007.08.008.

NASEM. 2015. *The Integration of Immigrants into American Society*. Washington, DC: NASEM.

New York Times. 2017. "Rejected Report Shows Revenue Brought in by Refugees." *New York Times*. Accessed January 28, 2021. https://www.nytimes.com/interactive/2017/09/19/us/politics/document-Refugee-Report.html?mtrref=www.nytimes.com.

O'Brien, Rourke L. 2012. "Depleting Capital? Race, Wealth and Informal Financial Assistance." *Social Forces* 91(2): 375–96. https://doi.org/10.1093/sf/sos132.

Occhiuto, Nicholas. 2017. "Investing in Independent Contract Work: The Significance of Schedule Control for Taxi Drivers." *Work and Occupations* 44(3): 268–95. https://doi.org/10.1177/0730888417697231.

OECD. 2014. *Germany Country Report*. Accessed August 30, 2021. https://www.oecd.org/berlin/publikationen/bildung-auf-einen-blick-2014-deutschland.pdf.

———. 2021. Social spending (indicator). Accessed May 25, 2021. https://doi.org/10.1787/7497563b-en.

Omar, Hussein. 2019. "The Arab Spring of 1919." *London Review of Books*. Accessed October 18, 2020. https://www.lrb.co.uk/blog/2019/april/the-arab-spring-of-1919.

Omi, Michael, and Howard Winant. 2014. *Racial Formation in the United States*. 3rd ed. Routledge.

Orloff, Ann. 2002. "Explaining US Welfare Reform: Power, Gender, Race and the US Policy Legacy." *Critical Social Policy* 22(1): 96–118.

———. 2009. "Gendering the Comparative Analysis of Welfare States: An Unfinished Agenda*." *Sociological Theory* 27(3): 317–43.

Orrenius, By Pia M., and Madeline Zavodny. 2015. "The Impact of Temporary Protected Status on Immigrants' Labor Market Outcomes." 105(5): 576–80. https://doi.org/10.1257/aer.p20151109.

Pager, Devah. 2003. "The Mark of a Criminal Record." *American Journal of Sociology* 108(5): 937–75. https://doi.org/10.1086/374403.

Pfrimmer, David. 2019. "The Story behind the World's First Private Refugee Sponsorship Program." *Conversation*. Accessed October 18, 2020. https://theconversation.com/the-story-behind-the-worlds-first-private-refugee-sponsorship-program-126257.

Picot, Garnett, Yan Zhang, and Feng Hou. 2019. "Labour Market Outcomes Among Refugees to Canada." Statistics Canada. Accessed August 18, 2020. https://www150.statcan.gc.ca/n1/pub/11f0019m/11f0019m2019007-eng.htm.

Portes, Alejandro, and Min Zhou. 1993. "The New Second Generation: Segmented Assimilation and Its Variants." *Annals, AAPSS* 530(1).

Portes, Alejandro, and Ruben G. Rumbaut. 2014. *Immigrant America: A Portrait*. University of California Press.

Portes, Alejandro, Luis Eduardo Guarnizo, and William J. Haller. 2002. "Transnational Entrepreneurs: An Alternative Form of Immigrant Economic Adaptation." *Source American Sociological Review* 67(2): 278–98.

Ramm, Christoph. 2010. "The Muslim Makers: How Germany Islamizes Turkish Immigrants." *Interventions* 12(2): 183–97. https://doi.org/10.1080/1369801X.2010.489692.

Rannard, Georgina, and Dilay Yalcin. 2019. "Syrians Highlight Racism after Boy Dies in Turkey." *BBC News*. Accessed October 18, 2020. https://www.bbc.com/news/blogs-trending-49959947.

Ray, Victor. 2019. "A Theory of Racialized Organizations." *American Sociological Review* 84(1): 26–53. https://doi.org/10.1177/0003122418822335.

Read, Jen'nan Ghazal, and Sharon Oselin. 2008. "Gender and the education-employment paradox in ethnic and religious contexts: The case of Arab Americans." *American Sociological Review* 73(2): 296–313.

Reimann, Anna. 2016. "Flüchtlingskrise: Die Wichtigsten Antworten Zur Wohnsitzauflage." *Der Spiegel*. Accessed October 18, 2020. https://www.spiegel.de/politik/deutschland/fluechtlinge-was-eine-wohnsitzauflage-bedeuten-wuerde-a-1072717.html.

Reitz, Jeffery G. 1998. *Warmth of the Welcome: The Social Causes of Economic Success in Different Nations and Cities*. West View Press.

———. 2007. "Immigrant Employment Success in Canada, Part I: Individual and Contextual Causes." *Journal of International Migration and Integration / Revue de l'integration et de La Migration Internationale* 8(1): 11–36. https://doi.org/10.1007/s12134-007-0001-4.

———. 2012. "The Distinctiveness of Canadian Immigration Experience." *Patterns of Prejudice* 46(5): 518–38. https://doi.org/10.1080/0031322X.2012.718168.

———. 2013. "Closing the Gaps between Skilled Immigration and Canadian Labor Markets: Emerging Policy Issues and Priorities." In *Wanted and Welcome?: Policies for Highly Skilled Immigrants in Comparative Perspective*, 147–63. New York: Springer.

Reitz, Jeffery G., and Anil Verma. 2004. "Immigration, Race, and Labor: Unionization and Wages in the Canadian Labor Market." *Industrial Relations* 43(4): 835–54.

Ridzi, Frank. 2009. *Selling Welfare Reform: Work-First and the New Common Sense of Employment*. New York: New York University Press.

Rinne, Ulf, and Hilmar Schneider. 2017. "The Labor Market in Germany, 2000–2016." *IZA World of Labor*. https://doi.org/10.15185/izawol.379.

Rumbaut, Ruben G. 1989. "The Structure of Refuge: Southeast Asian Refugees in the United States, 1975–1985." *International Review of Comparative Public Policy* 1: 97–129.

Samuel, Sigal. 2018. "'There's a Perception That Canada Is Being Invaded.'" *Atlantic*. Accessed October 18, 2020. https://www.theatlantic.com/international/archive/2018/05/theres-a-perception-that-canada-is-being-invaded/561032/.

Sanders, Jimy, and Victor Nee. 1996. "Immigrant Self-Employment: The Family as Social Capital and the Value of Human Capital." *American Sociological Review* 61(2): 231–49.

Sanders, Richard. 2020. *A Layered Look at Canadian and U.S. Immigration*. Wilson Center.

Schuster, Kathleen. 2021. "Germany Maps the Road to Integration in 100 Steps." *DW*, March 9, 2021.

Selod, Saher. 2015. "Citizenship Denied: The Racialization of Muslim American Men and Women Post-9/11." *Critical Sociology* 41(1): 77–95. https://doi.org/10.1177/0896920513516022.

Sewell, William H. 1996. "Historical Events as Transformations of Structures: Inventing Revolution at the Bastille." *Theory and Society* 25(6): 841–81. https://doi.org/10.1007/BF00159818.

Shackle, Samira. 2017. "Syrian Feminists: 'This Is the Chance the War Gave Us—to Empower Women'." *Guardian*, August 7, 2017.

Shams, Tahseen. 2020. *Here, There & Elsewhere*. Stanford: Stanford University Press.

Sharp, Morgan. 2019. "Morneau Budget Proposes $1 Billion for Borders as Immigration Rhetoric Heats Up." *Canada's National Observer*. March 19, 2019. Accessed September 7, 2021.

https://www.nationalobserver.com/2019/03/19/news/morneau-budget-proposes-1-billion
-borders-immigration-rhetoric-heats.

Simes, Jessica T. 2021. *Punishing Places: The Geography of Mass Imprisonment*. Oakland: University of California Press.

Singer, Audrey. 2012. *Investing in the Human Capital of Immigrants, Strengthening Regional Economies*. Washington, DC: Metropolitan Policy Program at Brookings.

Singh, Supriya, Shanthi Robertson, and Anuja Cabraal. 2012. "Transnational Family Money: Remittances, Gifts and Inheritance." *Journal of Intercultural Studies* 33(5): 475–92. https://doi.org/10.1080/07256868.2012.701606.

Small, Mario Luis. 2009. "'How Many Cases Do I Need?' On Science and the Logic of Case Selection in Field-Based Research." *Ethnography* 10(1): 5–38. https://doi.org/10.1177/1466138108099586.

Small, Mario Luis, David J. Harding, and Michele Lamont. 2010. "Reconsidering Culture and Poverty." *Annals of the American Academy* 629(May): 6–27.

Smith, Adam. 1776. *An Inquiry into the Wealth of Nations*. London: Strahan and Cadell.

Speckesser, Stefan. 2013. *The Immigrant Workforce in Germany: Formal and Informal Barriers to Addressing Skills Deficits*. Migration Policy Institute.

Stack, Carol B. 1975. *All Our Kin*. Basic Books.

State of Indiana. 2015. "Governor Pence Suspends Resettlement of Syrian Refugees in Indiana." *Indiana Governor Archives*.

Statistisches Bundesamt. 2019. "Education, Research, and Culture: Educational Level." *Statistisches Bundesamt*. Accessed May 25, 2021. https://www.destatis.de/EN/Themes/Society -Environment/Education-Research-Culture/Educational-Level/_node.html.

Staudenmaier, Rebecca. 2018. "German Interior Minister Horst Seehofer: 'Islam Doesn't Belong to Germany.'" *DW*, March 16, 2018. Accessed August 26, 2021. https://www.dw.com/en/german -interior-minister-horst-seehofer-islam-doesnt-belong-to-germany/a-42999726.

Swanson, Guy E. 1971. "Frameworks for Comparative Research: Structural Anthropology and the Theory of Action." In *Comparative Methods in Sociology*, edited by I. Vallier. Berkeley: University of California.

Taube, Friedel. 2020. "Migrants Face Housing Discrimination in Germany." *DW*, January 29, 2020.

Tehranian, John. 2009. *Whitewashed: America's Invisible Middle Eastern Minority*. New York: New York University Press.

Thobani, Sunera. 2007. *Exalted Subjects: Studies in the Making of Race and Nation in Canada*. University of Toronto Press.

Tichenor, Daniel J. 2016. "The Overwhelming Barriers to Successful Immigration Reform." *Atlantic*. Accessed February 4, 2021. https://www.theatlantic.com/politics/archive/2016 /05/replicating-lbjs-immigration-success/483908/.

Time Magazine. 1955. "NEW YORK: Change of Course." *Time Magazine*, May 2, 1955.

Trines, Stefan. 2019. "The State of Refugee Integration in Germany in 2019." *World Education News and Reviews*.

Trudeau, Pierre. 1971. "Statement to House of Commons: Multiculturalism." October 8, 1971. Library and Archives Canada. Parliament. House of Commons. Debates, 28th Parliament, 3rd Session, Volume 8 (October 8, 1971): 8545–48, Appendix, 8580–85.

UN General Assembly. 1967. "Protocol Relating to the Status of Refugees." *Treaty Series* 606(267) January 31, 1967.

UNHCR. 2014. "Resolve Conflicts or Face Surge in Life-Long Refugees Worldwide, Warns UNHCR Special Envoy." *UNHCR*. Accessed May 23, 2021. https://www.unhcr.org/news /press/2014/6/53a42f6d9/resolve-conflicts-face-surge-life-long-refugees-worldwide-warns -unhcr-special.html.

UNHCR. 2020. "Operational Portal: Mediterranean Situation." Accessed October 18, 2020. https://data2.unhcr.org/en/situations/mediterranean.

United States Congress. 1980. "The Refugee Act of 1980."

United States Department of State, Department of Homeland Security and Department of Health and Human Services. 2017. "Proposed Refugee Admissions for Fiscal Year 2018: Report to the Congress."

Valdez-Symonds, Steve. 2017. "It Has Been Two Years since Alan Kurdi's Death—and Things Have Only Got Worse for Syrian Refugees." *Independent.* September 2, 2017. Accessed September 7, 2021. https://www.independent.co.uk/voices/syrian-refugees-libya-two-years-alan-kurdis-death-a7925616.html.

Waters, Mary. 2009. *Black Identities: West Indian Immigrant Dreams and American Realities.* Cambridge, MA: Harvard University Press.

Weichselbaumer, Doris. 2016. *Discrimination Against Female Migrants Wearing Headscarves. IZN Discussion Paper No. 10217.* Rochester, NY: Social Science Research Network.

Wilson, Kenneth L., and Alejandro Portes. 1980. "Immigrant Enclaves: An Analysis of the Labor Market Experiences of Cubans in Miami." *American Journal of Sociology* 86(2): 295–319.

Wolgin, Philip E. 2018. "Family Reunification Is the Bedrock of U.S. Immigration Policy." *Center for American Progress.* Accessed February 4, 2021.

World Bank. 2020. "Personal Remittances, Received (Current US$)." *World Bank.*

Xu, Li. 2012. *Who Drives a Taxi in Canada?* Citizenship and Immigration Canada.

Zelizer, Viviana. 1997. *The Social Meaning of Money.* Princeton, NJ: Princeton University Press.

———. 2012. "How I Became a Relational Economic Sociologist and What Does That Mean?" *Politics & Society* 40(2): 145–74. https://doi.org/10.1177/0032329212441591.

———. 2014. "Remittance Circuits." Working Paper. Princeton University, Woodrow Wilson School of Public and International Affairs, Center for Migration and Development. Accessed September 7, 2021. https://EconPapers.repec.org/RePEc:pri:cmgdev:15-01a.

Zerubavel, Eviatar. 1996. "Social Memories: Steps to a Sociology of the Past." *Qualitative Sociology* 19(3): 283–99. https://doi.org/10.1007/bf02393273.

Zolberg, Aristide, Astri Suhrke, and Sergio Aguayo. 1989. *Escape from Violence: Conflict and the Refugee Crisis in the Developing World.* New York/Oxford: Oxford University Press.

Zuberi, D. 2006. *Differences That Matter: Social Policy and the Working Poor in the United States and Canada.* Cornell, NY: Cornell University ILR Press.

INDEX

Abdelhameed (research participant), 62,
79–82, 121–122

Abo Mahmoud (research participant):
departure from Syria, 26; in Jordan,
27–28; remittances and, 115–116; resettlement process and, 34–35; sampling and,
156; in Syria, 25–26; transnational social
network and, 111–112

Adelman, Howard, 71

Afaf (research participant), 54, 56, 119

Afghanistan, 67

African Americans, 3. *See also* anti-Black
racism

Ahmed (research participant), 41–43,
45–46, 57, 92

Alawites, 7, 17–18

Ali (research participant): employment and,
5–6, 105, 107; in German refugee camp,
97; on Jobcenter staff, 96; language learning and, 99–100

Altinözü camp, 27

Amina (research participant): anti-Muslim
racism and, 93; employment and, 85;
family reunification programs and, 121–122;
journey to Europe and, 35–40, 91; language
learning and, 99; sampling and, 85, 157; in
Syria, 24–25; in Turkey, 27

Amjad (research participant): departure
from Syria, 2, 24; employment and, 1, 50,
52–54; language barriers and, 1; resettlement process and, 2–4; in Syria, 1, 23–24

Amnesty International, 132

anti-Black racism, 44, 47, 67

anti-Muslim racism: in Canada, 10, 66,
67–68; employment and, 96–97; in Germany, 89–90, 93, 96–97, 103, 142–143;
hijab and, 45, 58, 59–60, 93, 101; in the
United States, 9–10, 41, 44, 45, 58, 59–60.
See also *hijab*

anti-Semitism, 39, 44

Arab Spring protests (2010–2012), 1–2, 12,
18, 151

Arabic (language), 158–159

Arar, Rawan, 19

Asad (research participant), 116–117

al-Assad, Asma, 2

al-Assad, Bashar, 2, 7, 18, 21–23

al-Assad, Hafez, 2, 7, 23

asylum and asylum seekers: concept of, 2;
journey to Europe and, 35–40. *See also*
Germany

Atef (research participant), 114, 169n18

Ausbildung (vocational training), 90, 103–109,
143–144

al-Azraq camp, 29, 52

Ba'ath party, 7

Badr, Gamal Moursi, 173n7

Bahrain, 2

BAMF (Bundesamt für Migration und
Flüchtlinge, Federal Office for Migration
and Refugees), 94–95

Banki, Mahmoud Reza, 117

Bannerji, Himani, 65

Banting, Keith, 65, 165n17

Bassam (research participant), 108–109

Bataclan terrorist attacks (Paris, 2015), 41

Berlin, Germany, 93, 119

Biden administration (2021–), 119

bigamy, 100, 168n19

Black Americans, 3. *See also* anti-Black racism

Blended Visa Office-Referred (BVOR) program, 14, 72–73, 79–83, 121–122

borders and border security, 131–133

Bouazizi, Mohamed, 1–2

boundaries, 152–154

Braun, Virginia, 158

British Empire, 8

Bulgaria, 39

Bundesamt für Migration und Flüchtlinge
(Federal Office for Migration and Refugees, BAMF), 94–95

Burawoy, Michael, 154

Bush, George W., 7

family reunification programs: in Canada, 121–122; in Germany, 84, 92, 94, 107, 122–124, 145; human capital and, 112–113; in the United States, 119–120
Faten (research participant), 41–42, 43, 45–46, 57, 59
Fawaz (research participant), 47
Federal Bureau of Investigation (FBI), 33, 44
feminist protests, 22
First Nations, 65
Fitzgerald, David, 19
food stamps, 47, 51
France, 7, 41
Francis, Pope, 155, 168n23
Fraud Detection Unit, 33
Free Syrian Army (FSA), 24, 25, 26, 111
French (language), 62, 171n41
Frontex (European Border and Coast Guard Agency), 132
functionalism, 87–88

Gabriel, Sigmar, 92
García, Angela, 127–128
Gastarbeiterprogramm (guest worker program), 88
gatekeepers, 152–153
Geertz, Clifford, 152
gender roles and inequalities: employment and, 43, 48–54, 55–60, 74–76, 78–79, 105–107; German welfare system and, 88; human capital and, 5, 6, 12; investment and, 128–129; language learning and, 4, 50–59, 75–76, 99–101; recognition, 128–129; remittances and, 115; in Syria, 21–22
Geneva Convention Status, 94–95, 123–124
geriatric nurses, 106–107
German (language): citizenship exams and, 89; credentialization system and, 86–87, 105, 108; family reunification programs and, 122; integration and, 96–102
Germany: anti-Muslim racism in, 89–90, 93, 96–97, 103, 142–143; border security and, 132–133; childcare services in, 88, 95, 100–101, 128; as comparative case, 155–159; credentialization system in, 5–6, 14, 86–87, 88, 103–109, 112, 128–129; EASY system in, 91–94; employment in, 85–87, 90, 96–97, 104–107; family reunification programs in, 92, 94, 107, 122–124, 145; immigration laws in, 8, 37–38, 39–40, 88–93; integration in, 5, 92–93, 96–102; investment in, 5, 112, 128–130; journey to, 35–40; labor market in, 87; mental healthcare in, 122; naturalization process

in, 9, 86–87, 88–89, 145; remittances and, 115, 116, 118; research in, 14; residency status in, 144–145; Turkish immigrants in, 9, 88–89, 93, 130; unemployment assistance in, 95–97; welfare system in, 5, 9, 87–88, 95–97, 129–130. *See also* dual-education system (Germany)
Ghada (research participant), 58, 61–62, 156
Gourley, Kelley, 173n12
gratitude, 65, 81–82, 138–139
Greece, 36–37, 91
grounded ethnography, 154–158
Group of Five. *See* Private Sponsorship of Refugees Program (PSR)
guilt, 118

Hagan, Jacqueline, 167n54
Hama, Syria, 7, 22
Hanaa (research participant), 93, 123–124
Hania (research participant), 77–79
Harper, Stephen, 10, 35, 61–62, 66
hate crimes. *See* anti-Muslim racism
hawala system, 116, 117
healthcare systems: in Canada, 64, 68, 69, 77; in countries of immediate refuge, 30; in the United States, 47
Heim (German refugee camps), 90, 93–94, 96, 97, 144
Heinemann, Alisha, 98
Hesham (research participant), 102, 108
Hezbollah, 7
hijab: anti-Muslim racism and, 45, 58, 59–60, 93, 101; discrimination in the workplace and, 105–106; as marker, 10, 32
home health aides, 106–107
Homs, Syria: Arab Spring protests in, 2; civil war and, 18–19, 23–26, 113–114; population and economy of, 17–18; refugees' life in, 1, 19–21, 61
Hoodfar, Homa, 74
Horowitz Foundation, 155
Hou, Feng, 173n15
human capital, 4–6, 10–12, 152. *See also* credentialization systems; language learning; state-structured human capital
Human Rights Watch (HRW), 105
human-centric approach to immigration, 12, 127–129
humane refuge, 131–133
Hungary, 38–39, 91

Idaho, 49
Imad (research participant): anti-Muslim racism and, 93; employment and, 85–87;

A NOTE ON THE TYPE

This book has been composed in Adobe Text and Gotham.
Adobe Text, designed by Robert Slimbach for Adobe,
bridges the gap between fifteenth- and sixteenth-century
calligraphic and eighteenth-century Modern styles.
Gotham, inspired by New York street signs, was designed
by Tobias Frere-Jones for Hoefler & Co.

CPSIA information can be obtained
at www.ICGtesting.com
Printed in the USA
JSHW040216211022
31906JS00002B/90